What Clients Want from Law Firms

EDITED BY ALEX DAVIES

Commissioning editor
Alex Davies

Managing director
Sian O'Neill

What Clients Want from Law Firms
is published by

Globe Law and Business Ltd
3 Mylor Close
Horsell
Woking
Surrey GU21 4DD
United Kingdom
Tel: +44 20 3745 4770
www.globelawandbusiness.com

What Clients Want from Law Firms

ISBN 978-1-83723-061-7
EPUB ISBN 978-1-83723-062-4
Adobe PDF ISBN 978-1-83723-063-1

Contents

Executive summary

Research shows that most lawyers think they know what their clients want – but their clients don't always agree. How can lawyers and their firms truly understand the client perspective? How can they know what their clients are really asking for? What do lawyers need to know in order to get – and stay – hired?

Our opening chapter by Ian White argues that many external firms do not really understand what in-house counsel expect from their legal panel and the relationship they need to build and maintain with their corporate client. As an external lawyer, building a successful relationship with the general counsel is clearly critical if you want to work effectively with your client. However, many external law firms trip up because they don't put enough energy (and enthusiasm) into the relationship, missing the need to focus on building and maintaining that connection. There are some simple steps, says Ian, that you can adopt to ensure that you do this and provide added value to your client's business (and your own!). Chapter one also considers how best to work with the Board.

It stands to reason that no two businesses are the same, yet in-house lawyers frequently find that their external partners believe that if they've seen one company in a particular industry, they've seen them all.

Companies differ in more than just the kind of industry they operate in, and understanding what makes your client tick is as important as your legal advice being right. Values and mission are important indicators of how your client operates and should clue you into how they present themselves. Understanding what drives the organization, beyond profit, can make the difference between a one-off engagement and repeat business. An external lawyer who demonstrates an understanding of their client's values in their advice and behavior is one who is more likely to be retained again and again.

Chapter two by Adrienne Gubbay explores the essential importance of understanding your client's business. No GC expects a new external firm to get their business from day one. What they do want is a partner who is curious about what matters to their team and their wider business. This chapter explores how important it is to understand the business – not just the industry – when advising in-house legal teams and organizations, and how this will drive repeat business and lasting relationships.

At first pass, we all look the same. We all went to college, then law school and undertook a variety of internships. Thereafter, we split – some to law firms and some to go in-house to work for companies. So, we should all know how to work well with each other. Fair, but somehow, over the years, there seems to have grown a larger disconnect between law firms and their counterparts in-house. There seems to have arisen a gap between the law firm and a GC, and with this gap distinct roles and responsibilities. Chapter three, by Terezka Zabka, explores how GCs and law firm lawyers differ, and how they can find common ground.

Chapter four looks at the business-critical skills that lawyers need in order to work successfully with their clients. Natasha Norton, an innovative C-suite leader who thinks outside the box and creates environments where others can thrive, looks at the essential softer skills that lawyers must cultivate in order to show their true value to the client.

Business development is about more than just winning work. Yes, that is a big part of it. However, underlying everything is a relationship. Work is often won or lost because of a connection. In chapter five, Claire Rason shares some of the psychology of relationships, combined with her business development professional knowledge to help lawyers think about how to stay front of mind and build stronger relationships with GCs.

Whether the term ESG will endure, the underlying elements of Environment, Societal, and Governance have become fundamentals of business and the investment and demand cycles that underpin it. Chapter six, by Jenifer Swallow, is about what clients want and need from their law firms and other legal suppliers as they tackle the vast and increasing pressures of sustainability regulation, societal responsibility, and governance dynamics. Spanning strategic framing, operational scope, and cultural commitment, this chapter is an insight into the home truths and span of opportunities for law firms in how they approach ESG in service offering and structure for the future.

Panel selections are a fact of corporate legal life and, whilst they may be painful (for the law firm and the client), there is no getting away from them. What is often not appreciated by the law firm is the amount of time, care, and thought that goes into the panel process way before the tender process has even started. That is when the head of the client's legal function defines the organization's needs and how these are going to be met whilst balancing the expectations of the procurement team, amongst other internal stakeholders.

For a variety of reasons, clients will always be focused on the size of the panel and will want to ensure that they have the right law firms with the right technical skills and sector knowledge to be able to meet their requirements. The client will also want flexibility and competitive fees, but importantly the right cultural fit for their organization. In the first of three chapters, Joanna Day brings to life the all-important factors that clients look for when selecting the right law firms for their panel, what they really regard as "added value", and how to prepare for a successful panel selection exercise.

Panel management is just as important as selecting the right firms to go on the client's panel; arguably even more so. Whatever the length of the panel appointment, effective panel management is crucial. The law firm should be regarded as an extension of the client's in-house legal function and a client that is serious about successful panel management will ensure that the law firms on their panel are kept plugged into the organization's strategy, vision, and key projects – not just when a piece of work is needed but on an ongoing basis. Often, the panel appointment comes with a requirement to provide ongoing data or key performance indicators. Whilst this may seem an administrative burden, that data, if properly used, can prove a really helpful tool and help both parties understand the true value of the relationship. There can be various types of panels, depending on the type of organization that is being supported by the law firms. In chapter eight, Joanna touches on a few and explains how a "one size fits all" approach doesn't necessarily work for either party. She also explains the subtle differences between panel management and relationship management and why the two shouldn't be confused.

Joanna returns in chapter nine to look at fees and billing. If your systems and processes for managing billing and fees is working well, there should be no surprises. If your bill doesn't match up to the purchase order or the amount the client has budgeted for, it not only means your invoice is going to be delayed but it also adds to the client's administration – all factors that could strain the relationship. The rigidity of payment and accounting systems means it is important to get this right first time, whatever the size of your client organization. We all know that client requirements (and expectations) often change as the work progresses, so it is all too easy to get swept up in delivery and overlook readjusting the agreed fee. Clients would always prefer to readjust the budget at the right time rather than face a nasty surprise when the work is complete. Transparency is just that – be upfront and clear about what you are charging for and get approval for any additional work from the client first. In this chapter, Joanna offers tips and guidance on providing transparency around costs and really delivering value to build a solid and successful client relationship.

In today's volatile, uncertain, complex, and ambiguous (VUCA) world, clients want external lawyers to collaborate, and effective matter management demands collaboration and communication. This needs to be done both internally, with the business and legal department, and with external parties, such as outside counsel. In chapter ten, Dr Heidi Gardner and Csilla Ilkei xplore the issues.

What is at the cutting edge of client listening? In chapter 11, Claire Rason argues that the time has come for many firms to think about how to implement a step change in their client listening programs. In this chapter she writes about the shift from passive to active client listening. Active listening is deliberate and conscious. It is human-centered and it enables the listener to empathize and go deeper. In the context of client listening, it enables conversations to be client-led rather than question-led.

Chapter 12 continues this theme, with Paul Roberts looking at the purpose of client listening and how to design a client program from the 'outside-in' – from the client's perspective rather than the firm's. Paul discusses the importance of broadening your sources of client voice (testimonials, complaints, conversations etc.) and how to ensure you are always listening.

In an era where the legal sector is increasingly driven by technology and efficiency, the human element remains indispensable. Personalized attention in client relationships isn't just a nice-to-have; it's a strategic imperative that can define a firm's reputation and success. At its core, personalized client care involves more than just meeting client needs – it's about creating meaningful, empathetic connections that resonate at an individual level. Chapter 13 by Helen Hamilton-Shaw explores how law firms can harness the power of personalized client care to build lasting trust, enhance client satisfaction, and ultimately, distinguish themselves in a competitive marketplace. By delving into strategies for empathy, transparent communication, and the balance between technology and personal touch, Helen considers the essential elements for a truly client-centric approach in modern legal practice.

Chapter 14 by Thomas Santram looks at how to build lasting, positive relationships with clients. Thomas first explores the concept of what should be the goal of external counsel – the "trusted advisor" (much more than simply being an external legal service provider), and indeed an extension of the in-house legal department. Core to the relationship is understanding why general counsel hire external counsel, and the fact that people hire lawyers, not law firms. Thomas suggests some strategies for starting, growing, and maintaining the relationship, from before you are even hired, right the way to the first and subsequent files.

Chapter 15's broad ambition is to review the evolution of the current law firm–corporate client relationship over the past 150 years and the conditions that animated it, then to re-imagine this dynamic in a constructive, hopeful sense, considering the conditions of today's world and how we expect it to develop in an age of AI ubiquity and data-centricity. Drawing from his collective law firm and in-house experience, Robert Dilworth reframes the relationship for today's world with suggestions to make it more client- and human-focused in the broadest sense. The goal of updating and improving this relationship is to make it fitter for purpose – from the dual perspective of law firms' clients and the clients' stakeholders in civil society.

About the authors

Joanna Day has over 35 years' experience as an in-house lawyer and started her career when she joined Abbey National Building Society in the wake of the 1987 "Black Monday Crash". Joanna soon became immersed in the transition of the organization from building society to bank, and its many acquisitions of big-name UK financial service providers such as Scottish Mutual, Alliance & Leicester, and Bradford and Bingley. As director of legal services, Joanna was responsible for the management of legal spend by or through Santander UK plc and its legal supply arrangements through the creation and management of effective legal panels. In recent years, Joanna has parachuted into a number of interim general counsel roles in the financial services sector, which has enabled her to build upon her expertise of dealing with the issues common to all financial services organizations, ranging from the regulatory aspects to managing internal and external resource.

Robert Dilworth is a legal innovation thought leader. He is managing director and associate general counsel at Bank of America. His legal career began with education in the US and France, followed by six years of Wall Street law practice at Cleary Gottlieb. This led to in-house roles at Deutsche Bank in New York and Frankfurt, then his current position at BofA in 1998. He is a founding co-chair of his legal department's AI steering committee. Robert's expertise spans derivatives, banking, and securities law. He participated in the evolution of the derivatives market from its bespoke beginnings to today's standardized and automated landscape. This experience underscores the urgent need for innovation in the legal sector, particularly in response to increasing workloads, regulatory complexity, and data-intensive processes. As the Liquid Legal Institute's ambassador to North America and the financial services sector, and as a Digital Legal Exchange faculty advisor, Robert is committed to sharing his insights and advocating for legal profession modernization. He recommends upgrading one's "human operating system" (hOS) and believes in the power of personal example to inspire change across generations of lawyers. His vision includes greater data literacy, more scalable solutions, and a shift towards client-centric practices that make law more accessible and humane.

Dr Heidi K. Gardner is a sought-after advisor, keynote speaker, and facilitator for organizations across a wide range of industries globally. Named by Thinkers50 as both a Next Generation Business Guru and one of the world's foremost leadership experts, she is a distinguished fellow at Harvard Law School and former professor at Harvard Business School. She is currently the faculty chair and instructor in multiple executive education programs at both institutions. Heidi works extensively with her team at Gardner & Co., partnering with boards, executive teams, and other senior leaders to boost performance by embedding the principles and practices of smarter, agile, cross-silo collaboration within those groups and across the broader organization and ecosystem. This results in concrete, quantifiable performance improvements. Altogether, Heidi has authored (or co-authored) more than 100 books, chapters, case studies, and articles. This includes bestselling books *Smarter Collaboration: A New Approach to Breaking Down Barriers and Transforming Work* (2022) and *Smart Collaboration: How Professionals and Their Firms Succeed by Breaking Down Silos* (2017). Her research received the Academy of Management's prize for Outstanding Practical Implications for Management, and has been selected five times for Harvard Business Review's "best of" collections.

Adrienne Gubbay is a senior commercial lawyer with experience advising across multiple jurisdictions in complex transactions. Adrienne is currently working with Heritage and People's Choice bank as a senior legal counsel. Adrienne holds degrees in business and law and has worked extensively in transactional matters over the course of 19 years in both London and Sydney. Adrienne has a deep interest in legal operations, creating effective working partnerships with business colleagues, and developing a commercial mindset in legal practitioners. In a culture of "more for less", Adrienne is keen to find pragmatic solutions that effectively address the risk priorities of her business colleagues, whilst ensuring the legal team can sleep at night. Adrienne has worked across multiple industries, including facilities management, building, construction, PFI/PPP projects, energy projects, film and distribution, and most recently, consumer banking.

Helen Hamilton-Shaw is the member engagement and strategy director for LawNet, a mutually-owned national network supporting SME law firms with collective purchasing, best practice, shared knowledge, and specialist expertise. With over 20 years of legal sector experience, an MBA from Aston Business School, and as a Fellow of the Chartered Management Institute, Helen brings deep insight into the strategic and business management challenges facing SME law firms. Known for her creative and strategic thinking, Helen continually enhances the experience and value for LawNet members, driving key developments to ensure the network's proposition remains relevant. A recognized thought leader in client experience and innovation, she led the creation of the network's award-winning Excellence Mark, which allows firms to differentiate through measurable client care and experience, now integrated into LawNet's ISO9001 standard. The Excellence Mark has been recognized for its sector impact, receiving a Modern Law Award in the Supporting the Industry category. Helen also leads on LawNet's annual flagship thought leadership conference, part of the network's extensive learning and development program, which was recognized for its contribution to the sector with an award in the same category.

Csilla Ilkei is an international thought leader, exceptionally skilled in translating science-backed research into pragmatic plans. During her more than 20 years as global manager and knowledge leader at McKinsey & Company, she was instrumental in unearthing global economic, business, and industry trends. With her experience living on three continents and working in 40 countries, Ilkei possesses an inspiring ability to partner with leaders to recognize potential challenges before they become obstacles to success. Her dedication to helping executives, and others, create an inclusive environment that sustains collaborative behaviors is incomparable. Ilkei has designed and delivered countless innovative products and programs that guide executives, across a wide variety of sectors and regions of the world. As insights director at Gardner and Co., she rigorously researches, meticulously designs, and skillfully leads programs for C-suite executives. Her perseverance in challenging status quo thinking and commitment to leaning forward into beneficial changes foster bold and dynamic learning environments that advance strategic goals. Ilkei holds an MBA from Corvinus University of Budapest.

Natasha Norton is a business leader and innovator, whose career covers APAC/North Asia, specializing in operations, partnerships, and growth strategies across the legal and tech consulting sectors. Currently working with KorumLegal, a Hong Kong headquartered ALSP, Natasha combines a strong background in stakeholder and people leadership to work with businesses that seek growth, change, and a desire to create impactful solutions. Natasha has also contributed significantly to the sports and LGBTQIA+ communities in business and advocacy, with a number of board roles that reflect her passion for women in sport and the importance of equity for both communities. Natasha continues to look for opportunities to innovate and push the boundaries in business as she encourages others to think of what is possible.

Claire Rason is a consultant, podcaster, and accredited individual and team coach. She founded Client Talk (a coaching-powered consultancy) to help firms enhance their relationships both inside the firm, as well as externally with clients. Claire is skilled at creating business and client development strategies for professional services companies alongside the provision of the training and coaching needed to bring these to life. However, what sets her apart is her understanding of the psychology that sits behind all of this. She works with professionals to help them communicate better, whilst embracing change and challenge. She is passionate about seeing more parity in professional services firms and works with firms to create systemic change.

Paul Roberts is the CEO and co-founder of MyCustomerLens, the AI-powered client listening platform for professional services firms. Before co-founding MyCustomerLens, Paul worked with financial and professional services firms including MBNA Europe and PwC Australia, helping businesses create customer insights that improved client acquisition, profitability, and retention.

Thomas Santram is the senior vice president, general counsel, and corporate secretary of Cineplex. Inc. Thomas joined Cineplex in 2008 and oversees all legal, corporate, governance, and securities matters for Cineplex and its subsidiaries. Prior to joining Cineplex, Thomas was in private practice and represented public and private companies, large financial institutions, crown corporations, and all levels of government. Thomas serves as the chair of the board of directors of the Academy of Canadian Cinema and Television. He is also a member of the board of directors of the Movie Theatre Association of Canada. Thomas has a BFA (Honours) from York University and an LLB from The University of Western Ontario. He was called to the Bar in 1995 and is a member of the Law Society of Ontario.

Jenifer Swallow advises and coaches tech founders, GCs, and policy makers on legal and strategy matters. With a background in high growth environments, she is formerly general counsel at the fintech unicorn Wise Plc, product and human rights lead at Yahoo! EMEA, and CEO of the government-backed organization LawtechUK. She has won multiple awards, including for her work in governance and ethics and is on the advisory board of the Post Office Project, is a member of the sub-committee of the civil justice body the OPRC, and contributes to a range of initiatives towards the advancement of legal services for society.

Ian White has been the chief legal officer and company secretary for both listed and major private companies. While he spent most of his previous career as a lawyer, he has spent some time working as a strategy consultant. He now works as a consultant, coach, trainer, and facilitator. His previous experience has led him to develop an expertise in corporate governance, working with boards on effectiveness and enhancement. He also works with directors and lawyers on development. Ian holds an MBA from Ashridge Business School, a coaching qualification – being both an APECS (Association of Professional Executive Coaching and Supervision) Certified professional executive coach and a CEDR (Centre for Dispute Resolution) accredited mediator. He is also the director for the Cranfield non-executive directors program.

Terezka Zabka is entering her fourth season with the San Diego Padres and second as vice president, general counsel. She originally joined the Padres in May 2021 as associate general counsel. In her current role, Terezka oversees all operations of the legal department, from advising ownership and handling baseball and player matters, to contracting partnership, event, sponsorship, and marketing opportunities, to managing litigation and overseeing general ballpark operations. Prior to joining the Padres, Terezka worked as an associate general counsel at Viasat, a global satellite and communications public company for six years in various departments such as mergers and acquisitions, aircraft wifi, strategic sourcing, satellite development, and telecommunication expansion worldwide. Before attending law school, she worked in Prague for a software engineering company as the marketing and public relations manager in charge of the EMEA regions, including the former Eastern Bloc.

Chapter 1:
What do clients want? Working effectively with the general counsel

By Ian White, consultant, executive coach, mediator, facilitator, and trainer

As an external lawyer, building a successful relationship with the general counsel is critical if you want to work effectively with your client. However, many external law firms trip up here because they don't put enough energy (and enthusiasm) into the relationship, missing the need to focus on building and maintaining that relationship. There are some simple steps you can adopt to ensure that you do this and provide added value to your client's business (and your own). This chapter looks at these steps, and considers how best to work with the Board.

In the course of my former career as a general counsel, I used lots of external law firms and lawyers. Like all relationships, some have been good and some not so good. And like all (good) relationships they go through ups and downs. The trick, of course, is to make sure the relationship is anchored mostly to the positive, although this is harder than it might first appear.

So how do you go about working effectively with the general counsel and their team? And – if you get the opportunity – how do you work effectively with the Board? I have outlined below some of my tips on how this might be best achieved.

Understand the business
Chapter two of the book goes into more detail on this, but I want to cover it here as it is a fundamental component of building a good relationship with the general counsel. If you are to be of maximum benefit to the in-house legal team then you have to understand the business of the client. Peripherally, this means knowing what the company does – its products, processes, and procedures. This can be more rewarding than it initially sounds. When I was the general counsel of a retailer, many of the external panel firm lawyers were only too happy to come and see our products and how they travelled along the supply chain in the distribution centers. If your client is a financial services firm, it may not be quite so exciting – you can't touch the product, after all. However, it remains necessary.

Understanding what the business does is not enough. If the client manufactures widgets, it is not really a useful end in itself. More fundamentally, you really need to understand the culture of the organization and the people who work there – not just the legal team but the other people you may come into contact with. You need to know who you can trust – which is important because you will be reliant on the instructions you are given from both the legal team and others within the organization. This means you must always be curious in your dealings with the in-house client and be prepared to challenge (constructively) what you are being told. Adopting an independent stance is crucial.

There are other things you need to understand about the client's business, such as its appetite for risk. This is important because one company in a particular sector is not the same as another. In financial services, a retail bank will have a very different risk appetite to a hedge fund; while in retail a food supermarket might consider risk in a different way to an online clothes retailer. Your approach to the client will need to reflect this. I once worked for two asset managements – one had a slightly aggressive operational stance while the other, which had been built gradually, was very conservative in its approach to building and developing its business. The external lawyers for these companies acted in a completely different way, knowing what approach was likely to work with the client. The latter company used a very conservative firm of lawyers that would not have suited the former.

Knowing the external market in which the client works is also very useful. You will have an advantage if you act for other companies within the sector, although you do need to watch out for potential conflicts. However, you will be of much more use to your client if you understand the market and sector in which they operate.

By understanding the business, the external counsel will be seen as an extension of the in-house legal team. This has to be as seamless as possible, so you must know and understand the client's business in order to be a trusted adviser. I recall using an external lawyer who had been involved in setting up the company I worked for and he really knew the business inside-out. He therefore was of great benefit when we had major legal issues to deal with. Principle one, therefore, is understand the business.

Like the business

This may be easier than it sounds! A client that manufactures drawing pins may not be sexy, but you still need to have some enthusiasm for the business, if not its products or services. This is more of a cultural thing – if you don't like working with the client, or they pay late or quibble over everything on the bill, it may not make for a happy relationship. Under these circumstances you should ask yourself whether you really want to work for them in the first place, although that may not be a practical approach. The more enthusiastic you can be for the client (remembering the need to be independent) the more likely you will make it a successful relationship. It is all about developing and maintaining good and effective relationships.

Independence is key (and becoming more important)

As a lawyer, you are subject to certain regulatory rules and guidance. These are matters you must never overlook or forget. When I work with Boards, I always advise non-executive directors that they must maintain their independence and (constructively) challenge the executives, as well as being curious in everything they do. This is guidance that should also apply to both external and internal counsel. Curiosity is an attribute you should apply in all you do with your clients – it will demonstrate that you are enthusiastic about them and what they do. However, it is also a very critical component for a lawyer. Lawyers – particularly those working in-house – are often told to offer a (more) commercial approach to what they do. This can be translated as finding a way around the rules or turning a blind eye to what is being proposed. You have to be objective and maintain your independence and not be pressured into doing something that is not right. To be fair, your role here is easier than that of your in-house counterpart who has only one client who they report to and are employed by. That can be a challenge at times. Nonetheless, I have come across many situations where external lawyers were pressured to take a more "commercial" stance – the legal press is full of corporate scandals whereby lawyers were forced to overlook the pertinent details of what was going on. However busy you are, you can't afford to act in this way, especially when regulators are (rightly) likely to be tougher on this type of behavior.

Providing difficult advice and messages to your client is not easy or enjoyable but in the longer term you will be serving both the interests of the client and society as a whole (which has to have confidence in lawyers). It is why building a good relationship with your client is essential if you, as an external lawyer, are to be effective. Lawyers who are tarred with the brush of being "uncommercial" are seen as difficult or abrasive. I recall once coaching a general counsel who used to say "no" to her clients in an aggressive and defensive way. That, of course, just got their backs up. There are far more effective ways to give advice that may not necessarily please your client, even if they have to adjust their plans or halt them altogether. I advised the general counsel to tell her internal clients gently and calmly why they might not be able to do something or at least not in exactly the way they envisaged. When you are dealing with clients, having a degree of empathy will help the message be more effective. More importantly, it is worth remembering the words we say are only a very small part of the message conveyed and that body language and tone are much more important. Trying to convey difficult messages is best done face-to-face where possible, or by phone; certainly not by email (other than to back up an already conveyed verbal message).

This might all sound a bit too challenging! However, it comes with the job. As an external (or internal) lawyer, you might not always be liked but you must maintain your independence and the respect with which others hold you if you are to be an effective, trusted adviser.

Likeability

As an external or internal lawyer, your main motivation should never be a people pleaser, not least because you'll get swamped with things to do. However, as an external lawyer, you should remember that the general counsel and their team are humans too. Their roles, like yours, can be stressful and lonely. If you're the most brilliant lawyer in the world, but arrogant and aggressive, it's not going to make for the best of relationships. We all prefer to work with people we can get on with to some degree. A little bit of charm helps, including a kind word or two when the general counsel has just been in a meeting with a disgruntled CEO. If you're the type of person who can go out with the legal team for a coffee or beer, even better. Again, it is all about building (good but objective) relationships with your client. And remember what I said about curiosity? That too comes into play here. If you can get to know the members of the legal team outside of a purely business relationship, that will help too. I have mentioned how Boards and non-executive members work effectively together. One of the things I often advise them to do is to get to know each other better to enhance their effectiveness. That may not be possible with all your clients but if you're able to talk about things other than work, that will help strengthen the relationship. Of course, not all GCs will want this, and you have to respect their wishes. But most – me included – benefit from getting to know our external lawyers better and to be able to talk about things other than business and law.

Live up to what you say

I still find it extraordinary that, as a general counsel, paying not insignificant sums for external legal advice, some firms still thought it reasonable to supply what they had promised late – or not at all! Or something that wasn't asked for in the first place. And yet, they were rarely late in billing me for the advice they provided! It is critical that you deliver what you have promised, and on time. Often the GC and their team will be commissioning the advice on behalf of someone else in the business, which could be the CEO or the Board. They won't be forgiven for providing advice to those parties late – and nor will you. By not delivering on time, you're making the GC look bad in the eyes of their client. That is not a good record to have when the next panel review comes up. So do what you say you will, when you say you will. If there is going to be a delay, let the client know well in advance and have a good reason. I once reported to a US GC who was both a great lawyer and business person. Unlike many of the people I have reported to who were control freaks he just said, "Ian, I ask just one thing: no surprises!". It's as good a mantra as any. You only get one chance at this. And on the panel review! In all your dealings with your client, be transparent. The matter speaks for itself.

Don't get it wrong – but if you do, own up

The best and most effective lawyers get it wrong from time to time. They are good lawyers because they own up to the fact they have got it wrong. It shows a degree of humility, which can be sadly lacking with lawyers. We all make mistakes and trying to cover them up will make the hole bigger. In line with your regulatory responsibilities, you must act in the best interests of the client – covering up mistakes is not part of this remit. If you do make a mistake, owning up early will make it easier to be remedied. Sooner rather than later is best. If it does happen, be open, transparent, and act ethically.

Listen

This sounds straightforward, right? Listening is a skill that few of us – including lawyers – do well. The relationship often goes wrong because external lawyers fail to listen actively to what their client is saying. We are all guilty of talking over others and focusing on other things without really listening to what the other person is saying. In my work with Boards, I often observe their meetings and it is clear to me that some members don't really listen or are engaged elsewhere. This makes the Board ineffective. The same will be true if you don't really listen to your client. The good manager listens first and speaks last. This applies equally to directors, lawyers, HR officers, accountants – everyone. Try and really listen to what your client – the GC – wants. It may not be what he or she says. That's the challenge.

Shadow the general counsel

One way of finding out some of the challenges (and benefits) of being a general counsel is to shadow them and see how the role really works. I used to let partners from law firms shadow me when I was a GC – firstly so that they could get to understand the business better; secondly in order that they meet other people who worked within the company and could soak up some of the culture; and finally to show how diverse the role was. Most external lawyers these days are reasonably specialized and so know a lot about a little. For the general counsel, this is an unaffordable luxury – you can't know everything and often your team will be small. You can't possibly hope to cover every area of the law, at least not with any degree of success. That is why, of course, general counsel call on people like you to help them. I remember explaining this to a law firm partner who spent two or three days working with me. She was amazed at the breadth of things I had to cover. I admitted it was a challenge – working in-house, you are expected to come up with an opinion even if you caveat it by saying, "This is my initial view but I will need to take external legal advice". It is probably most challenging in the Board Room where you can be asked absolutely anything and have to provide some type of answer. On the positive side, having built up a good panel of external lawyers, I was able to deal with the issues that were thrown my way, even if not immediately. So I would strongly encourage you to shadow the general counsel. You won't get paid (and don't even think about billing the client), but you will gain an understanding and appreciation of the in-house environment. You might even decide to become a general counsel yourself.

Better yet, go on secondment. If you can afford the time, it would be worthwhile going on secondment to an in-house position. This is easier to do when you an associate who has not yet built up your own bank of clients – if you leave it until you're a partner it may be very difficult to pick up your practice, even if you have only been out of a law firm for a relatively short time. The advantage of going on secondment is that it may help you strengthen links with a particular client (useful for when you return to your firm) as well as allow you to find out more about a specific sector. You may even end up joining the client – although your external law firm may restrict this. However, there are benefits to both the law firm and client having people go on secondment – again strengthening the relationship.

Read about and be interested in business

Read as much about business as you can. If you are interested in business generally, there are many good books that will deepen and widen your knowledge. Equally, if you are interested in a particular sector, try to read as much on that area of business as you can. Doing this will make you much more useful to both your client and your law firm. You might also want to look at areas of business outside your specialism to help you in your work. For example, I undertook a Masters of Business Administration (MBA) course because I was the company secretary but had little knowledge of strategy and finance. My objective was not to replace the chief financial officer but to gain a better understanding of the things being discussed at the boardroom table. You might think of other (non-law-based) courses that might help you enhance your role and the service you can provide to your clients. For example, doing a finance for non-financial managers short course is a valuable exercise.

Read the work of others. Peter Drucker began his life as a journalist, became a banker and finally a business academic. His vision was great, his insight vast. His essay *Managing Oneself*[1] is a classic treatise on career development and progression. Charles Handy sees business as being far more than simply profit – it has to lead to a better society. If corporate governance followed Handy rather than its numerous codes and standards, corporate scandals would be a thing of the past. Another book well worth reading is *Consiglieri: Leading from the Shadows* by Richard Hytner,[2] which is an excellent outline of working with leaders. Finally, a very recent book, *The Corporation of the 21st Century* by John Kay[3] provides a valuable perception of companies and "why (almost) everything we are told about business is wrong".

Giving back and the rise of ESG

In the last few years, ESG (Environmental, Social, and Governance) has come to the forefront of many companies and organizations. ESG is explored elsewhere in this book, so I am not going to discuss it here. Most companies are now keen to establish their ESG credentials and one thing that is encouraged is employee volunteering. This helps both the individual and organization concerned and is something that you might be asked about at a law firm panel interview – e.g. "What ESG programs do you have?" or "Are you involved in any type of EGS initiative?". As part of this, volunteering is a useful component and giving something back to society is something to aim for. Become a trustee of a charity – your business skills may be of real help to a small organization that is doing something great in the community but has no money. Or be a volunteer or support for an organization. The list of what you can do is endless.

Working with the Board

In your role as an external lawyer, you may have to present to the Board of an organization. Advice on this is worthy of a whole chapter or book,[4] but here are a few tips:

- Boards can be wary of lawyers – all lawyers – so be on top of your brief.
- Stick to the point – your time in the boardroom will be limited.
- Boards are generally interested in the practical application of the law rather than the law itself, so focus on practical answers and solutions.
- Wear your intellect lightly but your gravitas highly.
- If you have no experience of Boards, read up about how they work and operate. Patrick Dunne's book *Boards*[5] is a good start.

If there is one key takeaway from this chapter, it is all about developing and maintaining good relationships. The more senior you get, the more important your people skills become and the less apparent your technical ones should be.

References

1   Peter Drucker, *Management Challenges for the 21st Century*, Routledge, 1992.
2   Richard Hytner, *Consiglieri: Leading from the Shadows*, Profile Books, 2019.
3   John Kay, *The Corporation of the 21st Century*, Profile Books, 2024.
4   Ian White and Simon McCall, *Your Role as General Counsel: How to Survive and Thrive in your Role as GC*, Globe Law and Business, 2021.
5   Patrick Dunne, *Boards: A Practical Perspective*, Governance Publishing and Information, 2021.

Chapter 2:
Understanding your client's business

By Adrienne Gubbay, senior commercial lawyer

Introduction

It stands to reason that no two businesses are the same, yet all too frequently, those of us working in-house are left feeling that our external partners believe that if they've seen one company in our industry, they've seen them all. However, the reality is that whilst the legal issues may be similar, each company is as different as any individual private client would be. Therefore, it's crucial for our external partners to also understand the drivers for our corporate customer – including its values, mission, and internal culture – as this is critical to providing relevant, bespoke advice.

Companies differ in more than just the kind of industry they operate in, and understanding what makes your client tick is as important as your legal advice being right. Values and mission are important indicators of how your client operates and should clue you into how they present themselves. Understanding what drives the organization beyond profit can make the difference between a one-off engagement and repeat business. An external firm that demonstrates an understanding of our values in their advice and behavior is more likely to be retained repeatedly. An external firm that treats us – and the work we send them – as routine without showing an understanding of who we are as a business is less likely to get repeat work.

No general counsel expects a new external firm to understand the ins and outs of their business from day one. We want a partner who is curious (and not just when on the clock) about what matters to our team and our wider business. This chapter explores the importance of understanding the company – not just the industry – when advising in-house legal teams and organizations and how this will drive repeat business and lasting relationships.

What does it mean to understand a business?

Understanding a business is more than knowing about its industry and the laws that apply to that industry. It also goes beyond its current published accounts or its ESG statement. Understanding a business is really about all the little things that make a company different from the one next door – even if it produces substantially the same products or services.

Having worked in the UK for two different French-owned multinationals, as well as for a US-owned multinational, I can attest that even though the three businesses were very similar and operated in the same industry, what made them each unique was not the services they offered, or how they offered those services, but the leadership style and company values each sought to embody through the way they did business. Some of the differences can be attributed to the different legal regimes in the country of ownership versus the areas where I was mainly practicing (European employment laws, for example, confounded US-based executives). However, most of the differences tended to be about how the companies came to be formed and how they continued to be owned. A company that started as a small, family-owned enterprise before growing into the global name it is today had very different values and drivers to one that had been created as a "side-hustle" to the central business and was formed through multiple acquisitions, but never shed its "poor cousin" reputation internally.

To provide meaningful advice to help your corporate customer, understanding a little about their business – beyond what it says on the door – will be essential. This will mean more than just reading their website and regurgitating their values in your pitch. It will mean tailoring your advice to reflect both the stated objectives and what you understand their company culture to be and refining that with each subsequent instruction you receive.

If you're unsure what a company's main drivers are for the work you've been advising on, ask. With legal budgets always being under pressure, I'd much rather you called me up and said, "I want to understand what the business drivers are for this piece of work to make sure I pitch the advice correctly. Can you tell me more?" than go ahead and produce a piece of work that misses the mark and costs me both time and more money to fix.

Understanding a client's business is not a one-time task but an ongoing process. Now, you might be thinking that what I'm saying isn't rocket science – after all, everyone does this every time for a new client, don't they? Honestly? Not in the slightest. I've had firms pitching for business or a place on a panel that have assumed they know what we need or, even worse, presumed to tell me what I should want based on their extensive experience advising other companies from my industry in similar transactions. Those firms don't tend to get as far as those that aren't afraid to say, 'We've done this for similar companies, but to advise you properly, we'll need to work with you to learn what's important to you'.

What questions should you be asking about my business?

The following is a non-exhaustive list of questions that will assist in understanding an organization:

- What is the driver for this piece of work?
- Where can I find more information on the values of your organization?
- How do you like to put those values into practice when considering this type of work?
- What is the organization's risk appetite?
- Who should my advice be directed to?
- How do you want to receive my advice? Do you need written advice?
- Are there any matters you don't want me to advise you on concerning this matter?

How can you leverage your industry knowledge to benefit your in-house customers?

At a certain point in every lawyer's career, it's expected that you have solid legal skills, particularly a solid grasp of the law in the area in which you practice. But when a client engages you, they are coming to you for more than just your technical drafting skills or your knowledge of the law. They are engaging you typically because you have specific experience advising similar organizations with similar issues or transactions. Those clients are coming to you because you understand their industry and specific legal problems, and they want to leverage that knowledge for their particular situation. This responsibility and commitment to understanding their business is what sets you apart.

The trick, however, is showing that you can apply that deep industry and legal knowledge to the organization that has engaged you rather than taking a superficial approach of "one size fits all". Understanding the drivers and values of an organization will help you provide advice that better fits your client and is more likely to gain you repeat business. Yet those same customers want you because of your industry expertise, so you can't hide that.

In any transaction or dispute, you can demonstrate your understanding of the client's business and the industry in which they operate by tailoring your advice and referencing what you've seen be successful in similar situations. Particularly when you are advising an internal legal team, if you proactively offer up suggestions for how to move a matter forward that is based on your previous experience, or tell them when the position they are seeking is substantially off-market, then you are more likely to gain their business in the future. Why? When we see that you are looking to save us from heading down potentially costly paths rather than simply letting your costs increase, we can recognize a firm that is trying to be a true partner. This will also help us when presenting your invoice to the business or when we want to instruct you again on the next matter.

How else can you demonstrate your industry knowledge? In a quick poll of my current colleagues, providing some free value adds to the legal team and the broader business on industry-specific legal issues, which you have then tailored to the organization's needs, rated highly. Bonus points if you cross off some continuing legal education / continuing professional development points for the legal team in the process. This kind of value-added approach offers benefits in both directions – you get exposure to the broader business, and we get to know your expertise better. For an internal legal team, letting you demonstrate your expertise to non-legal colleagues allows you to build a connection with our business colleagues as a trusted partner, making it easier for us to obtain the budget to send you additional work. Offering different value-adds throughout the year also helps to keep you abreast of what is happening in our business, but also keeps you front of mind when it comes to outsourcing a piece of work.

Sharing industry-specific legal updates in bite-sized formats is another way to demonstrate your industry knowledge. What makes this particularly useful is when you take the extra time to relate that update to something you know we are grappling with in our organization. It doesn't need to be done that often to keep you and your firm front of mind. Suppose you are identifying legislative changes that we will need to implement. In that case, there is a good chance that we will look to you for assistance in altering our business practices to ensure compliance.

What steps can you take to deeply understand your in-house customer?

When developing a relationship with an in-house legal team (or even a new business), the best way to start is to listen more than you talk, at least at the start. You want to learn the organization's way of working, the legal team's preferred ways of communicating, how they present advice to the organization's executives, and the cadence of how work flows between the business, legal team, external counsel, and others. Listen to what is both said and unsaid. Then, when you've listened deeply, ask questions. What haven't you heard? Do you have a clear understanding of the organizational priorities for this work?

Becoming a trusted advisor is critical to deeply understanding your in-house customer. To do this, you will need to be clear about who your customers are, the different stakeholders in the organization, and their concerns in each matter. You will often have and need multiple entry points into the organization, and you need to develop an understanding of each business and its way of working. Many customers with an in-house legal team have a strict policy that only the in-house team can instruct external counsel. This isn't to say that the in-house team is your customer – they are just one part of the puzzle. The in-house team will be crafting your retainer's scope and keeping a close eye on your fees. They are also usually your conduit to the stakeholders for the relevant matter. Getting to know the legal team, the kinds of issues they brief, and when and why they do so will help you get to know the business. Hot tip: where an in-house legal team has any administrative support staff, take the time to get to know them as well. They are often best placed to organize urgent meetings or to get you the facetime you need with the right stakeholders in and out of the legal team.

Getting to know other key stakeholders, outside of networking and marketing events, is also crucial to becoming a trusted advisor and developing a deep understanding of the organization. Creating genuine connections – as humans – can also encourage the formation of relationships, which means the business will have you on their "to call when" list – the list of people we call when we just need to bounce an idea or problem off another trusted person. You may find that these calls – particularly when you don't invoice for them – are the ones that lead to more and more billable work as you become someone who multiple stakeholders in the organization lean on and trust when they need advice.

Suppose an in-house legal team repeatedly briefs you on a class of matters. In that case, identifying the underlying causes in conjunction with the relevant business stakeholders and working with those stakeholders and internal legal teams to develop proactive solutions are other excellent ways to integrate yourself into the organization as a trusted advisor. It's also a fantastic way to get to know the internal governance and decision-making process. All the advice in the world is wasted money if it isn't making its way to the decision-makers in a form they can easily digest.

Often, the most challenging transition for lawyers moving from private practice to an in-house role is changing how they provide business advice. Learning about house style – how a business prefers to communicate – can be an essential step in creating understanding. It is a skill that private practice lawyers can use to tailor their advice to the organization's needs. There are very few occasions where a piece of formal advice on a matter is required – and in those rare situations, the instructing legal team or executive will be clear that they need that advice and the form it is needed in. Most of the time, short, concise advice is more beneficial for the business, and the less time the legal team must spend translating "legalese" to plain English, the more valuable that advice will be. What is the best way to make sure you meet the client's needs on this front? Ask! There are few things more frustrating – for both parties – than external legal producing beautifully crafted advice if the internal legal team must either ask those external lawyers to rewrite it into something they can easily share with the business stakeholders or for the internal lawyers to have to rewrite it themselves.

If you are reviewing a contract for the first time for a particular client, asking for a guide for what is important to that client can help you focus on critical issues and further develop your deep understanding of the entity. We all know that some key issues arise in every contract – indemnities, warranties, liability caps, and insurance. However, finding out what else the customer is interested in before you start your review is crucial. If you advise on a contract in a highly regulated space, make sure you ask about any regulatory concerns the customer may have regarding the contract. Talking to your customers about their organizational requirements for the contract will ensure that you only raise those necessary issues and don't spend time advising on matters that are unimportant to the client. It's also essential to understand the format the business has agreed to provide their comments in, as some clients want a table of issues (and will have a format they need this in already), some want comments on the contract to discuss before you mark-up the document, and others want you to mark-up with comments as to why you've done so in-line with the text.

What is clear is that the best way to develop a deep understanding of your client is to talk to them. Ask questions. Don't be afraid to be curious. Why is data retention and storage important to this client when the industry is not usually that interested? Why are employee matters so crucial for that client – it's not usual in the market. You can only get to the bottom of these questions by being curious. Some of these concerns will directly result from how and where the organization was formed, and some will be peculiar to the deal at hand. What is certain, however, is that you will not win any friends by assuming you know the answers.

How does obtaining instructions from an internal legal team differ from receiving instructions from a non-legal customer?

Having an internal legal team as your customer can be both a blessing and a curse. It is a blessing as they are there to provide clear instructions, ensuring you focus on what is essential to their business. They are both legal experts and organizational experts. They know how to position information so that the relevant decision-makers get the information they need from your work. They can save you time – and their business costs – by working closely with you to help you identify the key issues at play. The internal legal team, however, can be a curse as well. Why? Because the internal legal team consists of both legal and organizational experts. They can act as gatekeepers – particularly if you haven't had an opportunity to develop a solid relationship with them yet – but you can also get push-back and challenges on your advice. As external counsel, this can be frustrating, but please remember that dialogue – push and pull – in the exchange of ideas ensures your advice is the best it can be for our organization.

One key difference between obtaining instruction from an internal legal team and a non-legal customer is that the internal counsel likely knows enough about the question of law being asked to know what they don't know. Your non-legal customers may know a bit – particularly if it relates to their core business – but they are not legal experts. Your duty of care to those parties is the same, but the product may look different. Your internal legal counsel doesn't want you to explain why the proposed documentation or deal structure isn't forming a valid contract. They want to know how to fix it. Your non-legal customer may need you to explain why a contract is not being formed and how to fix it.

How you craft your advice matters, and who your end audience is for that advice, will determine your output. You need to agree upfront on organizational expectations, be clear about your charging, and what is and isn't included in your quote. An internal legal counsel providing your instructions will likely ensure these are all set out at the beginning. A non-legal instructor may not know what they need, and this is where you have another opportunity to develop a trusted advisor relationship by being clear and transparent and asking lots of questions upfront to quote as accurately as possible to ensure there's no nasty bill shock. They will come to value your advice as being the right fit from both a cost and quality perspective.

Another critical difference between the two types of instructing parties is that in-house legal counsel knows when the work you've produced isn't worth the cost you invoice. We also recognize when the work product is precisely what was needed and asked for and when you've gone the extra mile without padding the invoice. We know when we're paying for you to train your staff at our expense – and we don't like it. We often know enough about the area of law you're advising on to question the advice, to push back, and when we want you to dig deeper. Your non-legal customers do not have our training or our legal knowledge. However, they have subject matter expertise that you often won't have, either in their organization or the industry itself, which you should leverage to produce meaningful advice to your customers.

Conclusion

This chapter has a critical theme – communication is crucial to developing a deep understanding of any business. Being open to learning about a customer rather than treating them as just another customer in a particular industry will help build a relationship, and spending time with multiple stakeholders outside of professional marketing and networking events will create deeper connections.

Chapter 3:
How do GCs and law firm lawyers differ? Finding common ground

By Terezka Zabka, general counsel, San Diego Padres

At first pass, we all look the same. We all went to college, then law school, then had a variety of internships, mostly went to law firms, and then some branched off to go in-house to work for companies. So we should all know how to work well with each other. Fair, but somehow, over the years, there seems to have grown a larger disconnect between law firms and their counterparts in-house. Over the years, law firms have invested in more and more marketing and business development, which used to be almost nonexistent, as business was brought in from the top, mainly through the rainmakers.

There seems to have arisen a gap between the law firm and a general counsel (GC). Law firms seem to have tried to fill that gap with marketing departments, who are tasked with getting a GC's attention. This may bridge the gap somewhat. I'll endeavor to say that this helps, but it doesn't get to the root of why the gap appeared in the first place. From my perspective – and I only speak from my own observations – is that the disconnect is caused by a law firm's limited understanding of what the client, the GC, and the company behind him, actually need. A GC still relies on outside law firms for a variety of reasons and a whole host of issues, and that business need won't go away. However, there is a sense of frustration that comes from misaligned expectations. A GC's frustration stems from a lack of client-centered, focused, and tailored attention, where the ultimate agenda is client-driven, not law firm-driven. Developing a better relationship with the GC can help realign those expectations. The silver lining is that fostering a deeper relationship is not only relatively easy, it actually benefits both parties in the long run, if they are looking to partner together and get repeat business.

As any half-decent attorney would, I have to caveat that this is only my opinion and one perspective, so take it with a grain of salt. But hopefully it sparks some ideas on how to refresh and deepen the relationships with your clients, and friends, in-house.

Law firm and GC distinct roles and responsibilities

Black and white versus gray

When a GC engages a law firm, the most typical scenario is that the law firm is tasked with a question and they research the applicable answer that they present to the GC. They look for the right answer to the question in terms of absolutes. Although they find the right answer, a GC may not simply be able to take that answer and implement it as-is because the GC doesn't live in a world of absolutes. The GC has to factor in competing business interests. Although the answer is technically correct, it hasn't always factored in outside constraints, such as a cost impact that the company hasn't budgeted for, the length of time needed to implement, lack of resources to oversee, the business impracticality or feasibility, given the circumstances. As time passes, the law firm may see that their recommendation never got implemented and may wonder how the business can carry on with such risk. The simple engagement results in the GC not getting what they need and the law firm not feeling heard. The relationship between the law firm and GC becomes strained because the law firm starts to think, I'll eventually tell the GC "I told you so".

Unlike in a black and white world, a GC lives in more of the gray, based on the culture of a company, including its budgetary constraints or its risk tolerance. It's not that they wouldn't want to implement the recommendation of the law firm. Many times, a GC has to take the advice of the law firm and translate it to make it applicable to their business in business language. So although the GC delegated this task to outside counsel, the GC becomes a little disgruntled because the finished product from the law firm was only a starting point for the GC who now still has to spend time on the matter.

Neither party is wanting to create inefficiencies, but the lack of understanding sometimes results in miscommunication or impractical advice. The more a law firm knows the ins and outs of the business and industry of each of its clients, the more practical and applicable their research and answers become and the synergy between the firm and the GC grows.

Time versus no time

GCs are constantly under time pressure. This is slightly different to being under the time pressure of deadlines, such as those of litigation, as those deadlines are known in advance. GCs find out about issues as they are happening, sometimes even after the fact, and their time crunch exists because they are hoping to avoid damage, mitigate as much of it as possible, or eventually do damage control. GCs don't have the luxury of overturning every stone to look for the best answer since the business has a plan that they are ready to execute on and having to wait for a legal analysis is not in their product road map (typically). In those instances, GCs have to make the best decision they have with the information currently available to them. Sometimes those decisions come with consequences, and that's often when the GC picks up the phone and involves outside counsel to help clean up the situation.

Law firms may struggle to see why GCs don't involve them sooner. The simple answer is because there may not always be time. The time it takes to explain a matter, let the law firm do research and come back with a thorough answer (that isn't always applicable, see point above), is simply time that the GC may not have when trying to navigate a crisis.

Practical advice

The more a law firm knows about the business, the industry, and the specific practices of the company, the more relevant advice they can provide. If a GC gets a canned legal memo, it's likely not the best guidance for the GC. It still puts the obligation on the GC to analyze all the options and figure out how to implement the best one for the company. The better course is for the firm to provide all the necessary options but lead with one that they would suggest based on their understanding of the GC's unique situation. This does take a little time to really understand the business, but it pays off as the advice is more tailored to the needs of the GC and the company.

The fact that a law firm has expertise in a certain subject matter will be evident. GCs know you're smart and qualified – after all, that's why they hired you. You don't have to send a 100-page memo with all the citations. As good a read as it may be, most GCs don't have the time to read it, let alone fully digest it. Give them the bottom line with all the relevant details needed to be able to make a decision.

Prioritizing billable hours and revenue vs focus on cost savings and efficiency

Ask more questions

It's a misconception that law firms are only focused on increasing billable hours and GCs are focused on cutting costs. There is definitely a sweet spot where billables and cost savings can live in harmony, but it does vary by matter. There are matters critical enough to a business that achieving the business goal can be more important while the cost of legal fees may be secondary. But it's probably true, that on average, keeping costs low and sticking to a budget are a GC's primary goal. It can be tricky understanding which scenario is in play. Law firms could add value and create greater synergies by asking more questions, both at the start of an engagement as well as the matter progresses since business goals tend to pivot.

Have you thought of asking:
- "What's the end goal?"
- "What are the other business factors?"
- "How big is this issue for the company?"
- "What other risks is the company currently facing?"
- "Is there an exponential impact of this decision?"
- "How and what do you want me to communicate with you?"

Although it's probably true that, most of the time, GCs are conscious of their budget, there are times when cost is less relevant. Sometimes we want to win at all costs and need the time, resources, and expertise that come with a large firm, and that typically comes with higher costs so that the GC has the confidence someone has their back at any hour of the day and the matter is being looked at closely. Other times, there are other cost-sharing agreements or insurance coverage that can help defray the costs of the total billable hours that make it easier for a GC to swallow a high bill.

Add value

That being said, cost savings and efficiency are typically top of mind for GCs. The high end of hourly rates has grown tremendously and, without a greater value add, these rates are hard to justify. Many law firms will not be considered for a matter simply because their rates are too high. At these law firms, special fee arrangements end up netting similarly, so they don't add as much value as the sales pitch tends to suggest. The fact that those law firms don't get chosen for some of the matters is also OK. If they can get business at those rates elsewhere, more power to them. However, GCs should be transparent with those firms and let them know that the reason they weren't selected is because their rates are not in the budget in order to maintain the longer term relationship.

And yet, there is a way to make the billables justifiable when you can incorporate good customer service and other value adds. Call me old fashioned, but customer service and respect are still important. Customer service these days, unfortunately, is how you stand out. The simple respectful gestures of following up, following through, and delivering excellent work product have gone by the wayside, putting more stress on the GC to remember to follow up, to carve out time to review the law firm's work, or shuffle tasks around to meet with a law firm that has procrastinated until the last day and needs input from the GC. Many times, any input needed from the GC requires input from their business people. Suddenly, the last minute request impacts a lot more people than just the GC. And although in that moment, that task may be the most important task at hand for the law firm, it's definitely not the most important task for the business people. The GC is now put in a position to ask his/her business people to prioritize something that is definitely not high on their agenda. Therefore, incorporating respect and awareness of the business into the standard practice of a law firm makes you stand out. These little things make it easier for a GC to be able to trust and rely on a law firm that they are in good hands. It will be one less thing to worry about when the law firm offers good customer service.

Another way to help justify billable rates is to add value in other areas. Here are two examples. Law firms have traditionally held their templates close. What's the result? In-house lawyers find bad templates online and cause more harm than good by using them. GCs tend to be more generous with their time (even though they don't have it) and talk to other GCs more openly about issues to bounce ideas off each other. They also share templates more freely. At the end of the day, it's about the specific scenario and the art of negotiating that will shape the final document. The template is just a starting place and not the holy grail of an agreement. However, more often than not, if you ask a law firm for a template, they posture that they need to draft it from scratch and need to know the details of the engagement. Meanwhile, the GC is probably rolling their eyes as it's a standard template that they know all the law firm clients have and the only real editing needed is the input from the GC of the business terms. If you share a template, it will go a long way.

The second example is to create connections. Law firms are in the best position to know about patterns of issues facing similar companies or industries. Without violating client confidentiality, the law firm could offer to introduce the GC of one company to another they know is facing a similar issue. The GCs can connect and discuss the legal and business issues and possible resolutions. Although, in the short-term, the law firm may not get business, both GCs will be grateful for that connection and knowledge sharing. Ultimately, if the issue is truly an issue, the law firm that made the connection will likely get the business anyway. Not making the introduction could cost the law firm the related business to another firm that does.

Specialization

GCs value access to highly specialized experts available at a law firm. As generalists, GCs are constantly torn between resolving an issue themselves versus outsourcing it to a specialist. Outsourcing work to a law firm typically happens for two reasons – lack of time or lack of knowledge. The first reason is fairly straightforward. The second, less so. First off, the GC has to recognize that they are dealing with an area that they don't know all too well. Sometimes an issue may seem straightforward enough, but it could be a nuanced area of the law that the GC is simply unaware has many thorns. Having the perspective to understand that the GC's knowledge has reached its limits is a skill that the GC has to develop. Second comes the analysis of whether the cost of the law firm to handle the issue justifies the risk at hand. It could either be an issue of high risk or high magnitude that ultimately makes the GC outsource the work. A GC's decision to use an outside law firm's expertise shows a great deal of trust and reliance on that specialist.

Once outsourced, the specialist can take over handling the matter and work in their niche area to provide the GC with the answer being sought, which, at first glance, may be a simple ask of the specialist. However, the perspective of a specialist may be only one piece of one issue. The specialist should be aware of that, so they can frame their answer accordingly. The specialist should consider formulating an answer that provides guidance that 1) under ideal conditions, this is the answer, but 2) given the constraints of the business, this answer is "good enough". Giving the GC this perspective will go a long way when the GC delivers the guidance to the business team. Failing to provide a "good enough" option may result in the business abandoning the specialist's advice entirely, which ultimately may be the worst scenario.

Expertise and ability to compel vs influence and persuasion at all levels

Another major difference between a GC and law firm is their role to the company. A law firm is tasked with a question and they deliver an answer. I'm simplifying, but a law firm is hired for their expertise in a niche area and they deliver a narrow, typically black and white answer. Conversely, the GC's role is to help strategize and advise. The more relationships the GC has across the organization, top to bottom, the more the GC can influence and advise the actions of the company in a very organic way. Typically, a GC can't tell their internal clients to do this or that. To do so comes off as an ultimatum or threat, which no one appreciates. These two different roles are important, but it's just as important to find commonality between the law firm and the GC so that the law firm can best support the GC in his goal to influence his internal clients. Most times, it's the GC that delivers the message from the law firm to the company management. After all, the GC is still a service provider to the individuals in a company, just as the law firm is a service provider to its clients. If the law firm can craft their answer in a way that positions the GC to best be able to influence company management to act a certain way, then synergies happen.

These synergies need to be continuously fostered, just like any relationship, and one way to do so is to ask the questions I mentioned above. The GC is managing 100 different things at any one time, and the task delegated to outside counsel may be one percent of the whole business picture. The more you know how that one percent impacts the rest, the better influence the outside counsel can have. Allow the answer to be tailored to and from the perspective of the greater goals and preferred outcome of the company.

Building a relationship and staying top of mind

At the end of the day, so much hinges on a good relationship. When in the high of a deal or in a turbulent time of litigation, the GC and law firm end up spending a lot of time working together. The better the relationship, the easier it is for the GC to give the law firm repeat business. Even when not working together on a daily basis, there are still cost efficient and not terribly time consuming ways a law firm can ensure it stays top of mind with the GC. The following are a few examples.

Passing along pertinent information such as articles they come across, interesting cases, or newly enacted laws can be extremely valuable to a GC. Not to mention that law firms have industry updates and alerts set up and daily digests coming to them that can be shared. Many GCs work solo or have very small legal departments. Unlike at a law firm, a GC can't get a quick legal update at the coffee machine on pertinent changes in several different industries or walk down the hall to pick someone's brain on a topic. A GC's coffee chat will be about a business proposal or sales dilemma. Forwarding an email, typing a quick text, or sending a screenshot of relevance can go a lot farther than the law firm may imagine. Even passing along information from a colleague in a different practice area can be very impactful for the GC and keep you top of mind.

As many GCs don't have a team they can bounce ideas off of, being open and willing to take a call from a GC to be a sounding board for a matter that does not merit engaging outside counsel is extremely valuable. Any interaction, conversation, and bouncing of ideas is truly appreciated, and even if not billable by the firm is valuable. It helps foster a strong relationship, building trust, engagement and understanding the business within which the GC navigates. When the GC has an issue, they are more likely to call the law firm with whom they have more frequent casual conversations, because through those casual conversations the law firm knows more details of how the GC's company operates.

Lastly, a critical piece to creating a long-term relationship is to bring in the associates early. All too often, the rainmaker closes the deal, handles the initial calls and analysis, then disappears after two months. The GC is then left with a team who were not hand picked by the GC and were not there in the initial conversations, and so much of the important information falls by the wayside. The associates may be very good at dealing with the task they were assigned, but they lack the overall picture, strategy, and goals that were provided to the partner when landing the business. The rainmaker heard all the rationale and backdrop, but all too often they don't convey the "why" behind the task being delegated to associates. Without that knowledge, the associate can't really know what is and isn't important to the GC while conducting the research or analysis. As time passes, the rainmaker becomes disconnected because they're not doing the actual work, but they're still the interfacing attorney for the GC. This leaves room for a lot of miscommunication as the GC, rainmaker, and associates are all talking past each with no one tracking the full picture. If the associate is brought in early or even at the beginning, there is more continuity in communication, more tailored work product, and better development for the associate.

There is still a place for the more traditional relationship builders, like lunches, networking events, and happy hours. Those are the cornerstones for business development and will continue to be so. But taking the relationship deeper, beyond those activities, through customer service, value add, and continuity of communication is critical for true relationship building. It shows the GC that the law firm is invested in the company and the GC's success in the long run, not just the short-term.

Chapter 4:
Beyond law – business-critical skills to navigate the intersection of law, business, and technology

By Natasha Norton, KorumLegal

The legal profession has evolved significantly in the last decade. The rapid pace of globalization, the integration of advanced technologies, and the complexity of regulatory environments have fundamentally shifted. As such, so has how lawyers work and how their roles are perceived. No longer confined to courtrooms or law firms, lawyers today are expected to serve as strategic partners in the broader business context.

The boundaries between legal and business advice have become increasingly blurred. Corporate counsel and private practice lawyers are now called upon not only to interpret the law but to understand business strategies, help mitigate risks, and add value outside of the field of "law" to their organizations. Legal expertise alone is no longer enough – lawyers must possess an array of skills to navigate the complexities of the modern business world, where their advice impacts everything from compliance and financial performance to reputation and sustainability.

Most recently, technology has been one of the most significant catalysts for change in the legal profession. Artificial intelligence (AI), machine learning, and automation are transforming tasks that were once time-consuming and labor-intensive, such as legal research, contract review, and discovery. These advancements have led to increased efficiency but have also raised the bar for lawyers, who must now be comfortable working alongside and utilizing these technologies to remain competitive.

Globalization has also added a layer of complexity to legal practice. International trade, cross-border transactions, and global supply chains require lawyers to be proficient in multiple legal systems and aware of international regulations. This trend has particularly affected areas such as intellectual property, international arbitration, and corporate compliance, where legal issues transcend national boundaries.

Lawyers are no longer peripheral figures in business. They are embedded within organizations, working closely with executives and managers to make strategic decisions. This new role requires a fundamental shift in how success is defined for lawyers. No longer is success solely measured by legal victories or technical prowess – it now includes the ability to understand and align with business objectives, navigate complex global regulatory frameworks, and integrate technology into legal workflows.

No more detached lawyers

For years, the image of the lawyer as a detached and specialized advisor has prevailed. This stereotype positioned lawyers as individuals who dealt with legal matters in isolation, offering advice when consulted but largely removed from the core business operations. They were specialists. This view is not only outdated but detrimental to the evolving role lawyers play in today's corporate environment.

The modern lawyer can no longer afford to be isolated from the business world. Lawyers are no longer confined to solving problems after they arise – they are essential contributors in preventing those problems in the first place. This shift from reactive to proactive legal practice is driven by the increasing need for businesses to navigate complex regulatory environments while maintaining agility in competitive markets. Whether it's advising on regulatory compliance, structuring deals, or managing risk, legal professionals are integral to shaping corporate strategy.

As businesses become more interconnected globally, and as laws become more intricate, lawyers are often at the table from the inception of major business decisions. They work closely with corporate executives, financiers, human resources teams, and marketing departments to ensure that the legal implications of decisions are fully understood and aligned with the company's objectives.

The idea of the detached lawyer also contributed to a perception that legal advice is inherently conservative, therefore stifling innovation and progress. However, lawyers who fully integrate into the business ecosystem offer not only legal expertise but also creative solutions that can drive business forward. By understanding the intricacies of the industries they serve, modern lawyers can identify opportunities and mitigate risks in ways that support growth and innovation.

A new definition of success

Traditional markers of success for lawyers – such as courtroom victories, securing high-profile clients, or mastering complex legal doctrines – remain important. However, they are no longer the sole indicators of a lawyer's effectiveness. Success now requires a broader, more dynamic approach that encompasses business acumen, technology capability, and leadership capabilities.

One critical element of success in today's legal environment is the ability to offer legal solutions that are not only technically correct but also commercially viable. Clients, whether internal or external, expect more than just legal advice – they seek counsel that are aligned with their strategic business goals. Lawyers who can provide legal frameworks that support innovation, market expansion, or cost reduction are far more valuable than those who merely focus on limiting liability or avoiding compliance pitfalls.

Success also means being proactive rather than reactive. The most successful lawyers are those who can anticipate legal risks and address them before they escalate into crises. This requires a keen understanding of not just the law, but the broader business context in which the company operates. Lawyers must stay ahead of trends in the market, keep up with emerging technologies, and remain vigilant about changes in regulations. By doing so, they can help their organizations avoid costly mistakes and seize new opportunities.

Finally, success in law today requires adaptability. The legal profession is in a state of constant change, and those who can quickly learn new tools, adapt to new processes, and pivot in response to changes in the legal landscape will thrive. This shift requires a mindset of continuous learning and professional development, as lawyers must be prepared to let go of outdated practices and embrace the new.

The business context – lawyers as business partners

The integration of lawyers into the broader business context is one of the most significant shifts in modern legal practice. In the past, legal departments were often viewed as obstacles to business goals, focusing primarily on risk mitigation and compliance. However, lawyers are now expected to act as business partners, contributing to strategy and decision-making from the outset.

For lawyers to be effective business partners, they must understand the goals and objectives of the companies and environment they operate within. This means gaining a deep understanding of the company's products, services, market position, and competitors. It also means being aware of broader economic trends, industry regulations, and technological developments that may impact the business.

Business acumen enables lawyers to provide legal advice that aligns with strategic objectives. For example, in a merger or acquisition, a lawyer who understands the financial and operational goals of the deal can craft legal agreements that not only protect the company from risk but also maximize value. In contract negotiations, a lawyer with business knowledge can help structure terms that promote long-term partnerships and growth.

Financial literacy

One aspect of business acumen that is often overlooked is financial literacy. Lawyers must be able to interpret financial statements, balance sheets, and key performance indicators (KPIs) to understand how legal decisions impact the financial health of the business. Without this understanding, lawyers may miss critical risks or opportunities when advising the business they operate in or their clients.

Financial literacy is especially important in areas such as mergers and acquisitions, corporate finance, and litigation. In these contexts, lawyers need to assess the financial implications of legal strategies and ensure that their advice supports the overall financial health of the business. For example, a lawyer advising a company on a merger must understand how the structure of the deal will affect the company's balance sheet, cash flow, and shareholder value.

In addition, lawyers who can speak the language of finance are better positioned to communicate with executives, investors, and board members. These stakeholders are often more concerned with financial outcomes than legal technicalities, so lawyers who can frame their advice in financial terms will be more effective in influencing business decisions.

Risk management and mitigation

Effective risk management is a critical skill for modern lawyers. However, the approach to risk management has evolved. Rather than focusing solely on avoiding risks, lawyers are now tasked with finding ways to balance risk with opportunity.

In today's competitive environment, companies cannot afford to be overly risk averse. Innovation often requires taking calculated risks, and lawyers must be able to guide their executives or clients in navigating these challenges. This involves understanding the company's risk appetite and helping to identify which risks are worth taking and which should be mitigated or avoided.

Risk management also extends to regulatory compliance, particularly in industries with complex regulatory frameworks. Lawyers must be able to help their clients navigate the ever-changing landscape of regulations while finding ways to innovate and compete. For example, in highly regulated industries such as healthcare, finance, or energy, lawyers must ensure that they comply with regulatory requirements without stifling innovation or growth.

Adaptability and resilience – legal work in an era of rapid change

The speed at which the legal and business landscapes are evolving requires lawyers to be highly adaptable. New regulations, technologies, and global events can disrupt established legal practices and force lawyers to rethink how they provide services.

The rise of legal technology in particular has had a profound impact on the profession. AI-powered tools for contract review, legal research, and predictive analytics have made legal processes faster and more efficient, but they have also increased the expectations placed on lawyers. Lawyers must now be proficient in using these technologies, not only to improve their own efficiency but also to provide better service.

In addition, globalization has introduced new legal challenges, as companies expand into international markets and engage in cross-border transactions. Lawyers must navigate a patchwork of international regulations, trade agreements, and jurisdictional complexities, often working with legal teams in multiple countries to resolve disputes or structure deals. This requires a global mindset and the ability to quickly adapt to unfamiliar legal systems.

Resilience under pressure

The demands of modern legal practice can be intense. Lawyers are often required to work long hours, handle multiple high-stakes cases, and manage complex legal and business challenges simultaneously. The pressure to deliver results in a fast-paced environment can lead to burnout if not managed properly.

Resilience is a key skill for lawyers who want to succeed in this environment. Resilience involves not only the ability to cope with stress but also the capacity to bounce back from setbacks and continue to perform at a high level. Lawyers must develop strategies for managing stress, maintaining focus, and staying motivated, even when faced with demanding workloads and tight deadlines.

Resilience also extends to dealing with failure in a profession where the stakes are high, not every case will result in a win, and not every deal will go smoothly. Lawyers must learn to handle these disappointments and use them as opportunities for growth and learning.

Learning and unlearning

One of the most important skills for lawyers is the ability to continuously learn and adapt. This involves staying up to date with the latest legal developments, technological advancements, and industry trends. However, learning also involves unlearning – letting go of outdated practices and embracing new ways of working.

For example, lawyers who have relied on traditional methods of legal research may need to adopt AI-powered tools that can perform these tasks faster and more accurately. Similarly, lawyers who have always operated within a single jurisdiction may need to develop an understanding of international law as their clients expand globally.

The ability to learn and unlearn is particularly important in a profession that is being transformed by technology. Lawyers who are willing to experiment with new tools and approaches will be better positioned to adapt to changes in the legal profession and provide more value to their clients.

Mindset of continuous improvement

A mindset of continuous improvement is essential for lawyers who want to thrive in a rapidly changing environment. This involves actively seeking out opportunities to improve skills, processes, and outcomes. Lawyers who embrace this mindset are constantly looking for ways to be more efficient, effective, and innovative in their work.

Continuous improvement also involves soliciting feedback from clients, colleagues, and mentors. Lawyers who are open to feedback and willing to make changes based on that feedback will be more successful in the long run. This approach fosters a culture of growth and development, where lawyers are always striving to enhance their performance and provide better service.

Business- / client-centric thinking and communication

One of the most critical skills for modern lawyers is the ability to understand the needs of both internal and external clients. Internal clients might include the company's executives, board members, or other departments, such as human resources or finance. External clients may be businesses or individuals seeking legal advice on a specific issue.

The key to providing effective legal advice is understanding the unique needs of each stakeholder. Internal clients may require guidance on how legal decisions align with broader business strategies, while external clients may need help navigating regulatory challenges or resolving disputes. Lawyers who can tailor their advice to each client's needs will be more successful in building trust and fostering long-term relationships.

Business-friendly communication

Clear and effective communication is essential for lawyers who work in a business environment. Legal jargon can be intimidating and confusing, especially for those who do not have a legal background. Lawyers must develop the ability to translate complex legal concepts into plain language so that stakeholders can understand.

Business-friendly communication also involves providing advice that is actionable and relevant to the client's specific needs. Clients do not want to hear about abstract legal theories – they want practical solutions that can be implemented to solve their problems. Lawyers who can offer clear, concise, and actionable advice will be more effective in helping their clients achieve their goals.

Building long-term stakeholder relationships

Building long-term relationships with stakeholders is one of the most valuable skills a lawyer can develop. In a competitive market, strong relationships can be a significant differentiator. Lawyers who take the time to understand the businesses, anticipate needs, and provide proactive advice will be more successful in fostering loyalty and trust.

Long-term relationships are built on trust, communication, and the ability to provide consistent value over time. Lawyers who can position themselves as trusted advisors / business partners - rather than just legal service providers – will be more successful in building lasting partnerships with their stakeholders.

The emphasis on EQ

Empathy and emotional intelligence are often overlooked in the legal profession, but they are essential for effective stakeholder management. Lawyers who understand the breadth of potential emotions, motivations, and concerns in the business context are better equipped to provide advice that aligns with both legal and personal priorities.

Empathy also plays a crucial role in managing difficult situations, such as litigation, disputes, or crises. Lawyers who can demonstrate understanding and compassion in these moments will be more successful in guiding their stakeholders through challenging legal and emotional landscapes.

Leadership and influence in the business world

As lawyers progress in their careers, leadership becomes an increasingly important skill. Leading a legal team requires more than just legal expertise – it involves managing people, delegating tasks, and providing mentorship to junior team members. Lawyers who can foster collaboration, inspire their teams, and manage resources effectively will be more successful in delivering results.

Leadership in the legal profession also involves building a positive work culture, where team members feel valued, supported, and motivated to perform at their best. Lawyers who can create an environment where their teams thrive will be more successful in achieving their goals.

Influencing business decisions

One of the most valuable contributions lawyers can make to a business is their ability to influence decisions. Lawyers who understand the broader business context can offer strategic insights that shape corporate policy, risk, and drive growth.

To influence business decisions effectively, lawyers must build strong relationships with key stakeholders, such as executives, board members, and department heads. By providing legal advice that aligns with the company's goals and helping decision-makers understand the legal implications of their choices, lawyers will become trusted advisors who play a key role in shaping the future of the business.

Cross-functional collaboration

Legal issues often intersect with other functions, such as finance, marketing, or human resources. Lawyers must be able to collaborate effectively with these departments to address legal challenges and ensure that the company's operations comply with regulatory requirements.

Cross-functional collaboration involves more than just providing legal advice – it requires lawyers to understand the priorities and concerns of other departments and work together to find solutions that benefit the entire organization. Lawyers who can navigate these cross-disciplinary relationships will be more effective in contributing to the overall success of the business.

Technological proficiency and legal tech expertise

On a daily basis, technology is reshaping the legal profession, and lawyers who fail to embrace it will find themselves at a disadvantage. AI-powered tools for legal research, contract review, and e-discovery are transforming how legal work is done, making processes faster, more efficient, and more accurate.

To remain competitive, lawyers must be proficient in using these technologies and understand how they can be integrated into their legal workflows. Lawyers who can leverage legal tech to streamline routine tasks will free up time for higher-value work, such as client advising, strategic planning, and business development.

Cybersecurity and data privacy knowledge

In today's digital world, cybersecurity and data privacy are critical concerns for businesses across all industries. Lawyers must understand the legal and regulatory frameworks governing data protection and cybersecurity to help their clients navigate these complex areas.

Advising clients on how to protect their data, comply with privacy regulations, and respond to data breaches is an essential part of modern legal practice. Lawyers who specialize in this area will be in high demand, as businesses increasingly prioritize data security and privacy compliance.

Efficiency through automation

Automation is one of the most significant trends in the legal profession. Lawyers can now automate routine tasks, such as contract drafting, compliance monitoring, and document review, allowing them to focus on more complex legal work.

By leveraging automation, lawyers can reduce the time and cost associated with legal services, providing more efficient and cost-effective solutions for their clients. Lawyers who embrace automation will be better positioned to provide value in a competitive market.

Ethical responsibility – ethical decision-making in business

As lawyers become more integrated into business operations, the line between aggressive business strategies and ethical considerations can become blurred. Lawyers must be able to balance the pursuit of business objectives with their ethical responsibilities, ensuring that their advice and actions uphold the integrity of the profession.

Ethical decision-making is particularly important in high-pressure environments, where business interests may conflict with legal or moral obligations. Lawyers who can navigate these challenges while maintaining their professional integrity will be seen as trusted and reliable advisors.

Sustainability and corporate social responsibility (CSR)

Sustainability and corporate social responsibility (CSR) are becoming increasingly important for businesses, and lawyers play a key role in helping clients navigate these evolving areas. From advising on environmental regulations to supporting CSR initiatives, lawyers must be able to guide clients in aligning their business practices with social and environmental expectations.

As governments and consumers place greater emphasis on sustainability, lawyers who specialize in this area will be in high demand. They will help businesses navigate complex regulatory environments and ensure that their operations align with broader societal goals.

Leveraging legal expertise in the boardroom – bringing strategic value to corporate leadership

Lawyers possess a unique set of skills that make them valuable contributors in the boardroom, allowing them to transcend traditional legal roles and provide strategic insight at the highest level of business decision-making. Their ability to analyze complex issues, identify risks, and navigate regulatory frameworks equips them to offer valuable guidance on governance, compliance, and risk management. Lawyers are trained to think critically, assess multifaceted scenarios, and communicate clearly – skills that are crucial when making high-stakes decisions that impact the entire organization. In the boardroom, lawyers can serve not just as legal advisors but as strategic partners, bringing their expertise in negotiation, ethical judgment, and corporate law to help shape long-term business strategies and ensure that the company operates within legal and regulatory boundaries while pursuing growth and innovation.

The lawyer of the future

The role of the lawyer has expanded beyond traditional legal expertise. Today's lawyers must be adept at balancing business strategy, technological proficiency, and ethical considerations while remaining resilient in the face of change. Those who can seamlessly integrate legal knowledge with business acumen, leadership, and adaptability will thrive.

Embracing these business-critical skillsets will not only protect their organizations from legal risks but also drive growth, foster innovation, and shape the future of the businesses they serve. The well-rounded lawyer of the future is a strategic partner, a problem solver, and a value creator – someone who can navigate the complexities of the modern world while staying true to the ethical responsibilities of the profession.

Chapter 5:
How to stay front of mind – business development and relationship building

By Claire Rason, Client Talk

Business development is more than just winning work. Yes, that is a big part of it. However, underlying everything is a relationship. Work is often won or lost because of a human connection. This chapter looks at the psychology of relationships to help lawyers think about how to stay front of mind and build stronger relationships.

When asked what they look for in an adviser, clients often respond in a similar way. Of course, they want the technical skill and for the advisor to be able to deliver the services they have been instructed for. They also want something else. They want someone who they can build a relationship with. They want an adviser who is easy to get on with. Who "gets them". Who they like!

Having conducted hundreds of client interviews, I can attest that this desire to connect on a human level is universal. It is why relationship building and business development go hand in hand. Indeed, building relationships and understanding how to do that is the best way to deliver what clients want. Building relationships takes time, but connecting on a human level is the best way to stay front of mind when instructions are up for grabs. It's the rapport that you have built that will help you succeed.

Let's explore what we mean by business development
In law firms, the terms "marketing" and "business development" are often used interchangeably. However, I refer to business development in terms of the traditional sales funnel. This model has stood the test of time, and whilst there are other models that adapt and change the funnel, such as the sales flywheel, the funnel remains a good way to understand what business development is and why relationship building is so fundamental.

At the top of the funnel, we find a large number of prospects, clients, and referrers. Here, firms need to raise awareness of who they are and what they do. It is here that firms employ a marketing strategy. Many firms will use a

AWARENESS
Generate interest in the brand

CONSIDERATION
Encourage prospects to think
about your market offering over
your competition

CONVERSION
Entice with a call to action

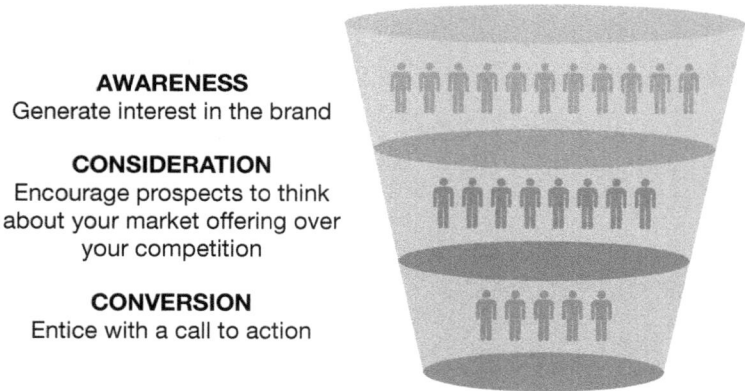

variety of tactics and often these sit with a dedicated marketing team to deliver. This is in reality what starts to tick the technical expectations box.

Let's take an example – such as writing an article for a website. This is something lawyers often have to do, usually at the bequest of the marketing team. Article writing has a myriad of benefits – but when used to raise awareness it is not business development, it is marketing. Marketing can be used to keep a firm front of mind. Personal branding and marketing can help keep individuals front of mind – but by itself, LinkedIn will likely not be enough.

The next stage of the funnel is where relationships start to form. Prospects or potential clients who have been made aware of the services you offer start to become more interested in what you do. The research has been done and they want to move to human connection. It is the job of business development to nurture these contacts and to move them from interest stage to desire or consideration stage. It is here where relationships count and human interaction takes center stage.

The bottom of the sales funnel is where firms convert these prospects into clients. This is about action – signing on the dotted line. It can be thought of as selling, and it is what many firms think of when they discuss business development. It is why firms put rainmakers on a pedestal. However, this level is better titled "sales". Once "sold to", this contact becomes a client and firms can turn to client development. The bottom of the funnel is about creating clients and nurturing existing ones. Relationship building is important here too. It is these relationships that will keep you front-of-mind for new projects and which, if they fall down, lose you business.

What does all this mean? It means that, at its heart, business development is relationship building. It is sophisticated relationship building – firms can be strategic in terms of who and how they build relationships – but fundamentally, if you overlook the human element, you are likely to fall short. Yes, marketing can help build awareness, but to truly stay front-of-mind you need to be remembered for the human connection that has been created. Anyone versed in sales will tell you that you buy on an emotional level, then rationalize on a thinking one.

Super skills

If I were to ask you, "What are the super skills needed to succeed at business development?", what comes to mind?

Often what we hear is "being able to navigate social media and build a brand", "negotiation", "public speaking", "writing articles", "networking", or simply "knowing how to be a rainmaker". These things are not without value, but a different set of skills is much more powerful. These are the super skills of relationship building.

The super skills are behaviors that build rapport, create a connection, and drive strong relationships. They are founded in psychology – not marketing or business development. As a result, these super skills are transferable outside of the sales funnel. However, the reason these are important is because business development is not just about building relationships with people like you – people you know – or people who already are in a relationship with you. There is an element of that. To excel at business development, you need to be able to build relationships with a broader range of people. The right people for your business.

The super skills are Curiosity, Empathy, Collaboration, and above all else, Self-awareness. There is a degree of overlap between these skills, as you will see below. As you read through the chapter, bring to mind some relationships that you are trying to develop at the moment. Consider how you might use these super skills to get closer to building rapport with those individuals.

Curiosity

All lawyers strive to be trusted advisors. In my opinion, the best resource when thinking about trust in the context of professional services is *The Trusted Advisor*, by David H. Maister, Robert Galford, and Charles Green. The book introduced the Trust Equation to the professional services sector – an equation providing the ingredients needed to create trust. In effect, it provides a formula for how to become a trusted advisor.

What is this formula and what does it have to do with curiosity?

$$\text{Trust} = \frac{\text{Credibility} + \text{Reliability} + \text{Intimacy}}{\text{Self-orientation}}$$

The C and the R in the equation – Credibility and Reliability – are two things that come easily to lawyers. They are the rational elements of trust. They relate to words and actions and they are objective variables that make sense to most advisers.

Firms tend to get the rationale right. Firms are well versed at setting out testimonials, qualifications, and experience. This is usually a given and indeed firms, or professionals, lacking credentials will fall at the first hurdle.

Clients will often say to us that they want their advisers to be responsive. Responsiveness is linked to reliability – and a lack of responsiveness is something that can erode trust and lose firms clients. However, this is an easy thing to solve and often comes later down the track, usually when clients are onboard and complacency kicks in. At the relationship building stage – when motivation to build a relationship is high – responsiveness tends to be a given. Indeed, some clients we speak to say this can be too high!

The I and the S – Intimacy and Self-orientation – are the emotional elements and they are the parts of the equation that we want to focus on here. Remember, people buy with emotion. Intimacy is a word that can seem out of place in the context of a professional relationship, but what this captures is whether someone feels safe to share. The more they feel able to share, the more the relationship is a trusted one.

Self-orientation is out on its own as the denominator. Those with a keen understanding of equations will recall that this bottom line is important. The higher it is, the less trust there is. What this denominator shows us is that where self-orientation is high – when the focus is on the advisor, rather than the client – trust will be low. Incidentally, understanding what clients want is key to being able to provide a solution and the best way to "sell" in any event.

However, at the relationship building stage, the emotional can be forgotten. Lawyers don't ask, "How willing is this contact to share with me and how do I increase this?", even though this question, and the answer to it, is crucial in the process of building a relationship. It can also happen much more quickly than many appreciate.[1]

Let's now combine intimacy with lack of self-orientation – shifting the focus of conversations onto the client and what they want, rather than on promoting what the lawyer does. Intimacy and lack of self-orientation, when combined, become the super skill of curiosity.

Curiosity occurs through a combination of active listening and the ability to be present without judgment. These behaviors are teachable. Being able to do these things enables you to be the adviser that clients want to speak to when they have a problem that they need to solve. They will want to open up. They will seek your guidance. You will be front of mind because they know they can trust you to act in their best interests. That might be saying that you are not the right person for the particular piece of work.

Empathy

The ability to create empathy with others helps build rapport and strengthens relationships – which is why it is our second super skill.

Empathy and legal are words that do not always go together. Often seen as something that you either have or you do not, empathy has historically not been discussed in the context of business development. However, some firms are starting to recognize its importance, not only to bring together employees and create cultures that foster teamwork and resilience, but also as the key to gathering insight and delivering what clients want.

Empathy is often described as the ability to put yourself into someone else's shoes. However, psychologists identify different levels of empathy – from understanding another's point of view, through to feeling along with another, to then sensing what they want from you. Empathy drives action and compassion and, as such, it has a huge part to play in the way we build relationships.

Empathy is central to Daniel Goleman's concepts of both emotional intelligence and social intelligence.[2] Interestingly, much like the trust equation, these concepts have been around for a long time, but their link to business development and clients has been underplayed and undertaught.

Research shows that we have more empathy with our "in-group" – people who are like us. However, that doesn't mean to say that we cannot have more empathy with "out-groups" and actually understanding how to do that will not only strengthen relationships, it will create more inclusive cultures inside firms too. As mentioned at the start of this chapter, business development is not just about gravitating to the people we like or are naturally drawn to. We have to be able to build rapport with a wide range of people.

The need for lawyers to be more empathetic is something I hear all too often from clients. Why? They want lawyers to see things from their point of view. They want them to understand the broader ramifications of the advice given, not only on the organization they are a part of, but on themselves as an individual.

Client challenges are increasingly complex, and they are faced with more and more choices of who to turn to for the answer. The result? Clients are calling the shots. "Good enough" just isn't enough. Advisors are expected to be commercial and understand their clients' businesses. However, more than that, they need to know how their advice impacts their client's strategy and how to help enable it. They need to understand this at a level that goes beyond the legal and beyond what is written on paper. It requires a deeper level of understanding of the web of relationships that the client themselves is dealing with. Empathy is key to unlocking this.

Firms have not traditionally been good at teaching soft skills. Even including the word "intelligence" next to emotion and social has not driven a widespread uptake in EQ learning and development programs for lawyers.

Collaboration

Collaboration is, on the face of it, an achievable super skill. As humans, we are wired to collaborate and it is something that should come easily. Historically, as a species, collaboration led to our survival.

In its truest form, collaboration is a co-creation of something that could not be achieved alone. It requires curiosity and it requires empathy. You will see later that it will also need self-awareness. The super skills work together! What is also needed is the ability to have hard conversations. Good collaboration doesn't always look conflict-free, and to provide clients with what they want, those hard conversations need to be had, right from the start.

Clients value advisers who are honest. A good example of why this honesty is needed early on? Often, clients will say that they have seen scope creep as a result of poor instructions, or parameters not having been set clearly at the outset. Usually this is because advisers at the start do not want to challenge, they do not want to push back, they do not want to have hard conversations. They do not want to collaborate.

Conflict is a word that can seem at odds with collaboration. However, being able to have healthy conflict is a powerful way to deliver what clients want, and at the stage of building relationships, make sure that you are front of mind when it comes to instructing an advisor. Knowing how to disagree, how to give feedback, and how to ask hard questions – all whilst maintaining respect and trust – is a subtle balance. However, if you get the balance right, you are well on your way to creating a lasting relationship.

Self-awareness

I've left self-awareness to the end, but it really is the super skill of super skills. It is what will fundamentally enable, or disable, all the other skills discussed in this chapter.

When asked, many will say that they have a good degree of self-awareness. Indeed, I have yet to meet a professional who would profess the contrary!

Learning how to increase your self-awareness and how to use the power of reflection is something that forms the foundation for success in relationship building, for business development, but actually more generally. We are, however, unaware of our own unawareness. The further you go on a journey of self-awareness, the more you realize you don't know what you don't know.

It is so easy to fall into the trap of thinking that everyone thinks, feels, evaluates, and experiences the world in the same way. Even when reminded of this truth, it is human nature to forget it when it counts. We overlook differences in the heat of an argument, or if someone has said something that has bruised our ego. It doesn't even have to be that extreme. Perhaps we are trying to influence someone in the way that we would look to be influenced, forgetting that we might not necessarily have any success with that approach at all.

Being self-aware helps us to think about differences and to think about how we can adapt our style when working with others. However, its power doesn't stop there. The next thing that self-awareness does is it helps us to understand our way of being. As we increase our self-awareness, we start to ask ourselves questions, like:

- How does who we are impact our role?
- How does who we are impact our relationships?
- How does who we are impact how we are seen by our clients?

One way to increase self-awareness is by coaching. Another is through mindful practice. However it is achieved, self-awareness is needed to be able to truly be curious, empathetic, and collaborative. Without it, we fall into the trap of judgment and risk only building relationships with people who are like us.

A model to practice – the Lawyer's Coach Business Development Matrix©

In order to build relationships and be successful in business development and in delivering what clients want, the super skills need to be understood, developed, and – crucially – practiced.

One way to increase both confidence in your ability to build relationships and "do business development" whilst putting into practice the super skills is the *Lawyer's Coach Business Development Matrix©*. The matrix sets out four areas where work can be won. At the top of the matrix are relationships where there is already trust and a high degree of connection between lawyer and individual prospect/client. On the right-hand side are clients/prospects, which are one step removed from the lawyer and connected to the firm's brand.

The matrix can be used to think about how you approach business development. It can also be used as a strategic tool – to identify relationships that you want to build and to think about which of the super skills you need to bring into play.

The matrix is over the page. As you explore each box, think about:

- Where you get most of your work from.
- How comfortable you feel inhabiting it – and what that tells you about you.
- The different activities you might do to win work.
- How the super skills might play a part.

Degree of personal connection →

Lawyer's personal contact	Firm's contact
Personal business development (work from personal connections) This box is often overlooked and often challenges a lawyer's perspective of what business development is all about. If you are able to provide a service that a connection needs, and you are creating value for them, this can be a source of work. Connections here might include those: • From school/university/law college. • Through social activity/sports clubs. • Through family/children. **What might you do to win work here?** Actively listen and understand what your personal contacts might need and make sure that they understand what you do. This should be all about them. Trust will soon be broken if you start to offer something that is for your benefit and not theirs.	**Existing clients (work as a result of doing a good job)** Clients want advisors who understand them. They want someone they can get on with. The best way to win new work is to do a good job for an existing client. This results in repeat business and also recommendations to others in your client's network. All lawyers will be doing business development to some extent this way, whether consciously or not. **What might you consciously do to win work here?** • Understand the client's context. • Be commercial. • Make sure that your clients are your promoters. Go the extra mile. • Think about using the work you have done for your client as a testimonial/case study.
Professional business development (work from people you have met professionally) This box is one that lawyers often feel comfortable inhabiting. However, depending on where the connections have been made, they might not feel comfortable seeing these connections as prospects. Understanding the value you bring and building trust is key. Connections here might include: • People from previous jobs. • Clients who have moved jobs. • Those made by networking. • People who work for referrers. **What might you do to win work here?** • Actively listen and understand what is coming up for these individuals. • Actively think about ways to meet and connect with prospects. • Make sure these connections know what you do – through newsletters, events, or social media.	**Internally through the firm (work as a result of the firm's marketing/brand)** Clients are often won as a result of a collective effort. Work is undertaken to position the brand of the firm with the right prospects, and the firm's business development team will create opportunities for lawyers to win work. Lawyers need to understand what is happening at each stage of the sales funnel and how they can support the wider firm effort. **What might you do to win work here?** • Doing great work, especially in a team, to increase your brand profile for a particular area. • Having a strong profile with colleagues in order to win referrals from them. • Taking part in firm pitches. • Living the firm's values.

Strength of contact/interaction — High ↑ / Low ↓

In summary

In reading this chapter, you hopefully have some clarity on a couple of truths. The first truth is that, in order to win work, clients need to remember you. The second is that how you achieve that is paradoxically not about telling them all about yourself, but about finding out more about them.

Finding out what clients want enables you to win work – it means that you can discover how you fit, and when you might not. The super skills that we have presented you with are all skills that are key for all human relationships. Business development might be more deliberate in the sense that you need to form a connection with someone who is a potential source of work, but that doesn't mean to say they need to be treated as a number. Deploying the super skills will enable you to build meaningful connections and be the person who they call when they need support.

References

1   See chapter eight for more on the Trust Equation.
2   Daniel Goleman, *Emotional Intelligence: Why it Can Matter More Than IQ.*

Chapter 6:
The client view on ESG

By Jenifer Swallow, strategic advisor and former general counsel

Introduction

This chapter is about what clients want and need from their law firms and other legal suppliers as they tackle the vast and increasing pressures of sustainability regulation, societal responsibility, and governance dynamics, wrapped up in the requirements of ESG. Environmental, social – or better said, societal – and governance considerations have become fundamentals of business, the investment and demand cycles that underpin it, and the wider decision-making landscape in which we all operate. A book about what clients want from law firms would be incomplete without addressing this now pervasive subject and its challenges and imperatives for clients, albeit re-framing how it is perceived, approached, and labeled, to meet the needs of where we are now and where we are heading.

Definitions

The term ESG started out in an investment context, as a way to evaluate a company's performance, risks, and opportunities beyond financial measures, as part of a movement towards socially responsible investing, and the acknowledgement of organizations having obligations beyond profit generation, which in reality they always had. It was a way for investors to influence organizations in the boardroom, and collectively, government and global affairs. ESG has become mainstream in investment decisions and baked into law, and corporate and state strategy as an internationally recognized framework.

At a basic level, ESG is about how an organization – or indeed the state – impacts the environment, how it impacts society, and how it holds itself accountable. To this end – and for grammatical consistency – the phrase would be more precisely Environment, Society, Governance. At a more holistic level, ESG is about the responsibility to take care of what is within our control to influence – our working and other environments, our world and shared resources, how we treat people and contribute to society, and how we govern our decisions, actions, and behavior in line with those responsibilities.

In many ways, without dogma and crazy regulatory overhead, ESG is simply sensible business strategy. Make money; take care of people and nature; leave things better than you find them. These things are not mutually exclusive.

What sits behind ESG is essentially the legal construct of "duty of care", rooted in the principle that people and organizations should act in ways that prevent harm to others. Lawyers will be familiar with the rotting snail in the ginger beer in *Donoghue v. Stephenson* and the responsibility Lord Atkin memorialized to take *"reasonable care to avoid acts or omissions which you can reasonably foresee would be likely to injure your neighbour"*. ESG is really this concept in action, where the scope of who is considered a "neighbour" and what are considered "acts or omissions" is what has evolved.

It is unlikely the term ESG itself will endure. It has become loaded and polarizing in many ways, attracting a backlash to how it has been used for partisan aims, greenwashing, and divisive ideologies. ESG has also become shorthand in many circles for climate related issues, which is but one of the many elements it encapsulates. With political shifts, it is also falling out of favor in different parts of the world. Alternative, less loaded terms include "Responsible Business" or "Sustainability and Responsibility", which are what they say on the tin, as a catch all for operating in a responsible manner that sustains and is healthy and productive over the long term.

There is a legal baseline to ESG in terms of compliance, but as is clear from the scope, it requires a wider-angle lens. It is this lens through which clients have to look in their decision-making and operations, and the one often missed in how law firms approach them.

The state of play

It has been painful watching law firms grapple with ESG. Repackaging existing service lines, making claims about purpose that are clearly not lived, and failing to spend time with clients on their challenges and service needs are pervasive mistakes. This has led to all sorts of false starts and missed opportunities, with few clients thinking of law firms as strategic partners in this space, and few law firms developing their businesses and culture or generating sustainable growth as a result of their ESG strategy. This has also added to cynicism in the market.

Meanwhile, clients across all industries have no choice but to be "getting on with it" across a range of ESG dimensions – struggling or otherwise and with no end in sight. It is simply not possible to operate successfully any other way. Most larger businesses must now report on environmental metrics like carbon emissions and energy efficiency, with many participating in emissions trading schemes and setting targets for reduction across supply chains. The many and growing requirements cascade downstream. The societal dimension requires increased transparency in workforce diversity, employee wellbeing, and community impact. Governance developments include a move to diverse boards and greater transparency in executive pay, risk methodologies, and anti-corruption practices. There are many challenges, with cultural and cost barriers, data inaccuracy, integration into core strategy, and global operational alignment. The trajectory of regulation and stakeholder pressure going only one way. Legal requirements drive the necessity, but it is behind-the-scenes pressure that is the driving force.

The reality is that a movement is happening, with or without law firms, and whatever the terminology or jurisdiction. People around the world are waking up to corruption in all forms. Social justice is no longer a niche issue. Purpose has power and the supply and demand cycle is shifting as a result. Two-thirds of consumers hold a company's purpose and values as important in their buying decisions, three-quarters have changed their own behavior around environmental issues, and many are prepared to pay a premium for ethical products and services. Younger generations vote with their values in work. Wellbeing has become a liability as well as a lifestyle issue. Corporate misconduct and institutional scandal has reached prime time TV, triggering national outrage. Activism and class actions are changing the landscape, including for those charged with regulating the regulators.

Policy makers have to make meaningful and manifest the contract organizations and their leadership have with society, and the greater expectations of society and all its stakeholders. The pace of expectation is rising alongside the scale. Universally responsible business would actually negate the need for all these policy changes, complexity, and reporting requirements. Until we collectively realize such a reality, the overhead will remain.

The legal profession and ESG

The law exists to ensure the proper functioning of society, protection of rights, and the prevention and remedying of harm by and upon it. Lawyers, therefore, hold a pertinent place in the ESG equation, in the role they play, the leadership they provide – or not – and the duties they have in relation to the law and to those seeking to navigate and avail themselves of it.

However, often forgotten in a commercial context, lawyers have a duty to the rule of law and administration of justice that ultimately sits higher than their duty to a single client. Legal services regulation is focused on "trust in the profession" because without it the system breaks down, as we see signs it is. The professional and regulatory duties of integrity and independence require an approach that should set and hold a standard for us all. Those duties were ESG obligations long before ESG became a thing. They are baked into the social and legal contract lawyers have with the state, and the legislation upon which legal services regulation itself is founded.[1]

This puts law firms in a great position to lead on ESG, not as a meaningless mantra or an add on to service lines, but consciously and demonstrably to place integrity and responsibility at the core of it all. For a few, this will already be the why of their existence – to break from what they see as the toxic, self-serving norm. For others, it will simply make great business sense as they look to the future. For the rest, it will be of less interest, until financials force the matter.

A law firm that has evolved its own vision and strategy in response to societal, economic, and global developments is a more valuable partner to clients than one of lower maturity. A law firm that has evaluated its own context and commitments on sustainability and responsibility, and that understands the operational challenges and opportunities, is a more valuable advisor than one that has not. Those who consider afresh the role a law firm plays in modern business and the needs of their clients in the context of current and future service offerings, position themselves at the high value end of the market, where relationships hold a premium as they have in the past, and clients look to those relationships as key assets in the success of their business.

Who is the client?
In order to understand the client view on ESG, ask first, who is the client?

For most law firms in a corporate and bigger business context, the default here is the general counsel. In practical terms, that will often be the deepest relationship and most direct reporting line. If the GC is not happy, the law firm doesn't get work and doesn't get paid, and the opposite is also true. But the GC is not the client. In typical terms, the organization the GC represents is the client. Most often, this will be a corporate entity made up of shareholders, represented by a board, but it may be a number of other structures. The exception is where it is a personal appointment to advise a GC, such as on their regulatory duties and professional governance and liability – something that is increasingly common and required.

The reason that clarity on this point is critical is that the interests and perspective of the GC and those of the ultimate client may not be aligned. By virtue of professional obligation, the GC must remain independent from their client, while acting in their best interests. As articulated by Professor Stephen Mayson in his Independent Review of Legal Services Regulation, this creates *"inherent tension"* in the relationship, which can create *"a chilling effect of potential reprisal"*.[2] Conflict will arise, where the GC is under pressure to sanction or facilitate a course of action with which they have concerns; where they discover failings, misconduct, or illegality in the business by decision-makers; where the client has an entirely different perspective to the GC on risk and commercial outcomes; or indeed where conduct or advice of the GC is problematic.

Few law firms have given this much thought or have governance infrastructure in place to deal with it. It is wise to apply both. To do so requires acknowledging the symbiosis that exists between law firms and the in-house legal world and the unhealthy dynamics that can arise from that symbiosis. Over-reliance by GCs on external counsel is disempowering for the in-house legal team, keeping them insecure about their capability and thinking they need an insurance policy or to "double check" externally when they do not. This impacts how the internal legal team see themselves and their role, and the level at which they operate. In reverse, law firms that focus solely on the GC's needs block their attention to the broader business context and opportunity, fueling the cycle of law firms being reactive rather than strategic in their approach to clients and also capping the potential positive impact of the GC operating at the top table. These dynamics across the profession.

There are three recommendations in approach:

1. *Backing.* Always have the GC's back. Enable them to do their job really well and look good while they are doing it. Right size your work and keep billing responsible and contained. Help build confidence and business influence, not paranoia, and be creative when they are pushing water uphill with decision makers. Be hyper conscious of conflicts they may be experiencing and help them navigate that too. This includes where they are "double-hatting" with multiple roles or being outright bullied.[3]

2. *Upstream.* Understand that you and the GC have the same client, and it is the client's needs that you are serving, always subject to the bigger societal and stakeholder picture beyond short-term commercial goals. Make sure you (and the GC) understand what is important to the client organization and its stakeholders, as well as the GC. Be prepared to speak truth to that power, even if it risks losing a client.

3. *Boundaries.* Understand the rubicon of your regulatory duties and who you are acting for. Have processes in place for when those boundaries are in question or breached. This includes understanding when a concern or conflict means you need disclosure direct with business decision-makers, a GC needs separate personal advice, or you need to cease to act.

Some law firms will do a lot of work directly with business owners and founders, or individuals seeking personal advice. Advising individuals is less within the scope of this chapter, but some of the points remain applicable. For business owners and founders engaging directly with firms, they are usually at an earlier stage of business growth without the resources to hire an in-house lawyer, or who have not yet seen the need to. In this case, the "Who is the client?" question is still relevant from a legal and beneficial ownership point of view. For founder-led businesses like start-ups and scale-ups, it is easy to see the CEO as the client and the only one that matters, especially in the case of strong personalities. This may not, however, be the case. The CEO will be the client if the organization is wholly owned by them, but if it is not, there will be a governance structure that sits behind the CEO that must be assessed. The client is the legal entity, for example owned by shareholders under its constitution, typically represented by a decision-making board. To be clear on these points of detail is not only part of the "G" (governance) that law firms need to follow, but can also be critical to supporting sound ESG outcomes. A CEO or other executive driving a piece of work may not have the full backing of the business or have considered sufficiently the interests of their stakeholders.

What is driving client maturity?

Clients arrive at different points on the ESG spectrum based on different drivers. Understanding their location on that spectrum and the drivers behind that is key to understanding what they want as well as what they need.

As mentioned, larger businesses, certainly listed businesses, and those operating in regulated spaces will already be subject to a range of ESG-related requirements and aware of further regulation coming down the track. They will be at the higher end of compliance maturity, and ESG will be a matter of hygiene and "have to" in terms of drivers. There are smaller organizations that emulate or compete with listed businesses or who choose to map their governance to listed requirements for market confidence or risk mitigation. These may be scaling businesses or steady state.

Within both categories there will be those who choose to do the bare minimum. Drivers for this will include:

- Cost;
- Philosophical outlook; and
- Lack of awareness and experience.

In both categories there will also be those who choose to go further and deeper with ESG than basic compliance. Drivers for this include:

- Personal values of leadership, where decision-makers want to "make a difference";
- Reputational matters, where an ESG narrative is helpful to brand positioning, differentiation from competitors, or appeal to stakeholders such as impact investors and top talent; and
- Direct alignment with business outcomes – revenue impact, innovation, and risk mitigation fall into this category.

There are also those in between the two ends of this spectrum who don't want to be "out there" leading but want to do more than the minimum and haven't yet decided what that should be. These "on the fence" organizations are often waiting to see what everyone else is doing before they commit, either because they don't want to be at a competitive disadvantage, or because they haven't yet prioritized or accessed the expertise to help them decide or deliver. Understanding clients by industry, size, regulatory categorization, stage of growth, and drivers can be extremely helpful, without forgetting that every client is also part of a supply chain of some kind, for which segmentation is also relevant.

When you view your clients through this maturity spectrum lens, you can help them better, by starting exactly where they are with what they next need. You can also help move them along the maturity curve to where they will later need to be, or where they can consider going sooner to grasp a market opportunity.

What clients want on ESG

Tone from the top

What stands out like a sore thumb in law firm strategy and engagement with clients is lack of authenticity. When things are done for show or have no lived quality behind them, they register as flimsy and ineffective. Clients see straight through that and it sours relationships. The trend in the ESG context towards talking about purpose without doing the work to connect with what it is and what that means in real terms for values, strategy, and conduct, has escalated in law firms as it has in business. The impetus is correct, in that purpose is most definitely where it's at, but the approach taken has been knee-jerk and self-serving.

Firms would do well to pause before taking that path. You can talk about purpose until the cows come home, but if it is not common ground from a leadership point of view and integrated into how staff behave, whether people are genuinely cared for, how decisions are made, and all the tell-tale signs operationally of what is considered important, then it will count for nothing. It is not about token gestures, rebranding, or making grand claims. It is about understanding why you exist, why that is valuable for clients now and in the future that is coming to them, and how that meshes with the societal context of legal services. This work can only be undertaken in a meaningful way at the top of a firm. It is not to have an ESG or HR professional roll out some beehives, an EAP, chill out zone, rubber stamped waste management, or inclusion initiative and claim the job is done. It is a leadership responsibility and something on which leadership is desperately needed in the legal profession. When you get to the G (governance), not having this direction and clarity in place will also make decision-making and oversight harder, slower, and more fragile, which has knock-on effects for clients.

Set the purpose, strategy, and tone from the top and communicate it to clients. Settle on your values as something core and congruent, not just words on a wall. Put it in RFPs. Share your progress. Engage on the issues. Clients will be delighted to learn you have done the actual work on what advancement looks like and you can extend, rather than just meet, their approach – whether or not they have asked you to articulate it.

How law firms address ESG is also understood by clients to be contextual. Materiality will depend on the nature of the firm's operations, client base, and stakeholders. It is better to have fewer clear and concentrated ESG commitments that are genuinely undertaken and demonstrable in financial terms, than a long tick list that won't deliver impact over time. For example, eradicating misogyny, resourcing work in a sustainable way, embedding ethics infrastructure, and providing clients with the reporting data they need would be a powerful start.

Law firms that sell ESG-specific services to clients will need to go further than those that do not. The same will be the case for law firms acting for clients operating in industries subject to a high degree of ESG regulation and scrutiny, such as carbon intensive sectors, finance, FMCG, and healthcare. Some firms will have social enterprise clients, and act for those for whom commitments to the UN Sustainable Development Goals[4] and Global Compact[5] or ISO environmental management[6] and ISO social responsibility[7] certification will be important. For others, clients will have specific ESG standards for all services suppliers. Whatever the level of investment, it must come from the top.

Ultimately, what clients want to see is capable partners that have thought this all through and are prepared to put their money where their mouth is. Tone from the top also means your financials speaking the truth of your investments, otherwise it's just noise.

Get your house in order

All the strategic work in the world does not negate or delay that clients need their law firms to have their own house in order in respect of ESG. This means applying the same basic standards on ESG as the rest of the business world. Certainly, if they meet regulatory thresholds – but for all firms if they want to have credibility in the market. Law firms of all sizes – including at the smaller end of the scale – will want to ensure they are up to speed.

Where law firms do not meet the baseline standards, this negatively impacts clients in practical and confidence terms. For example, inaccurate carbon footprint reporting where law firms are part of the client supply chain; inability or difficulty meeting internal procurement procedures that cause friction for client representatives internally; and delays in the leadership and culture change that clients seek or drivein industry, and across the legal profession.

The baseline basics that clients need from their law firms are as follows, which will adjust over time.

Environment

1. *Sustainability reporting.* Reporting on carbon emissions, energy use, and efficiency, plus wider ESG risks, activities, and impacts in line with relevant regulatory frameworks.[8]

2. *Substantiating claims.* Ensuring environmental claims are evidenced, avoiding ambiguity and exaggeration in how services are described, especially where those claims influence client decision-making.[9]

Society

3. *Wellbeing.* Commitments evidenced in metrics around sustainable working hours, fair work allocation, and treatment of staff. Of all the baseline areas of focus, this is the one given least current attention by law firms and that is coming most to the personal fore for GCs and in-house legal teams. High profile stories of harm and death linked to toxic workplace practices and a business model built on the billable hour have had a big impact in the community. Countless research papers[10] evidence the toxicity, health issues, and harm, particularly within "big law", and show it is within the control of law firm leadership to address.

4. *Equality and diversity.* Work on DEI and publication of data to address disparities in pay and treatment between male and female employees, as well as around fairness in ethnicity and socioeconomic representation, recruitment, retention, and promotion.

5. *Social justice.* Preventing slavery and human rights impacts across activities and supply chains, including working practices and outsourced operations for law firms.[11]

Governance

6. *Corporate governance.* Reporting on risk management, independence, and responsibility towards stakeholders, even in a limited liability partnership context.[12] This extends to all areas of governance, including technology use, treatment of client data, bias mitigation, professional duties, and fair billing.

7. *Ethics and anti-corruption.* As an extension of corporate governance, this is about robust systems and controls to prevent unethical practice and involvement in misconduct and corruption. This goes well beyond anti-money laundering and takes account of the spotlight on the legal profession as enablers of misconduct.[13]

This baseline can be seen through a compliance lens, but it goes further in the minds of many clients. This is not only about what is legally required and nor is it about disproportionate or unrealistic investment and disclosure. It instead goes to demonstrating actual commitment and transparency. When a law firm wants to support a client – particularly on ESG – but does not have the basics in place, this weakens its reputation in the mind of the client. The client may work with the law firm on urgent needs such as aspects of compliance but will not think of it for the strategic or more integrated ESG work.

Deliver the goods

Clients are focused on outcomes – revenue, growth, and problems solved. At the end of the day, they want necessary work done and they want it done well. They don't want it for the sake of it; they want it because of where they are trying to go and what that moment requires – reporting compliance, regulatory risk assessment, or crisis management, for example. Give them what they want as quickly as practicable and at a sensible price point. They will often, of course, be in a reactionary rush, dealing with something that has become impossibly urgent.

This means understanding immediate needs versus things that can be done later – and having the discipline to communicate them in that order. So far, so simple. But what about execution? Law firms excel at giving advice, but what clients need is the job done. This is where the legal services market roundly misses a step.

Translating advice into action is an activity in itself, one that is often left at the client door. Forming policies, rolling out processes, data infrastructure, reporting frameworks, and oversight monitoring needs to be done by someone, somehow, sometime after the advice is received. Assuming advice has been made super practical – which should be but often isn't – the missed step is to provide a team that can go in and effect that implementation – taking the advice and "operationalizing" it. Some clients will be resourced enough to go that massive mile themselves, but many will not, and it will either languish in an "important, not urgent" pile, get done but poorly, or be contracted to a consulting company that can send in people to deliver it as a separate exercise. When the core of the work is legal, why not have a multidisciplinary team within the law firm that can get it done itself end-to-end, at the time it's needed?

This is not a secondment situation, with the intransigence law firms now approach that, nor is it a number of fee earners back at the firm, doing what they do by the billable hour. This is a swat team structure at a sensibly priced project cost, where, for example, specialists in project delivery, data science, and regulation "go in" to the company to build the internal transformation that the context and compliance requires – until it's done. Having such an approach would move us all faster out of states of complexity, versus making a decades-long meal of it as we did with embedding privacy regulation into business operations.

Bring the big picture
Clients need context – for their decision making and execution. This is the case whether law firms are working on specific matters or strategy. This is a fundamental part of incorporating ESG into legal practice. It is about giving clients what they need as well as – or in fact sometimes instead of – what they want.

Of course, above all things, clients want the job done, done well, done fast, at the right price point, as covered above. That is table stakes, though sadly not always reality. They don't want the upsell, the gilded lily, or the over-cooked initiative. However, they also do not want to bowl down a particular path to discover a foreseeable pothole along it or to realize a development was on the horizon that meant it would have been wiser to wait. Nor do they want to present onward proposals themselves that are not rounded as to market practice or that don't sufficiently account for where the organization is trying to go over the long-term.

Clients need an expert who knows and won't be learning on their clock (repeat, not learning on their clock), but they want a specialist who knows and who understands and advises in the context of their bigger picture. Obvious perhaps, and yet not yet nailed. This is across two aspects.

On live matters, the opportunity is for advice and execution to be way more consultative than transactional, accounting for client organizations' purpose, strategy, and market environment. Whether clients ask for this specifically, they need law firms to have a great grip of their context and link in what is relevant.

Contextual research is common in the consulting world, where evaluation will be undertaken before pitching for work or undertaking a project, as well as keeping track over time. Typical dimensions are client strategy and competitive landscape, industry threats and opportunities, financial performance, supply chain and operations, organizational structure and resourcing, communications, risk, innovation, and geopolitics. This is not chargeable or exhaustive work – it is simply what is required for advice and decisions to be properly informed and for work to be good – on anything but "quick questions" of law. Law firms largely miss this step, relying on clients to brief them – which they of course also must – and what they assume they know – which they may discover they do not, or not sufficiently. With developments in technology, this is now low-effort, high-impact to do.

Having the fish-eye view is about linking that into delivery. Understanding that an organization has a new chair or executive team with a particular ethos – and knowing that is where the advice is destined – means advice can be framed in a way that will be most useful to effecting an optimal outcome with and for that audience. Knowing what is driving stakeholder activism will inform recommendations and prioritization. Knowing about geographical footprint, financial markets exposure, and expansion plans will offer a more globally relevant view. Joining dots between what look like disparate legal requirements, but are deeply connected in client context and overall compliance, will make all the difference down the line. The point being, the bigger picture is critical, and over a longer timeline than the client might be thinking. It presents important angles for more informed, responsible decision-making, makes it less likely things will be missed, and makes it more likely a client will extend their instructions to broader or future work.

Law firms can usefully broaden their own horizons too. There is a race to the ball with carbon reporting, and it is understandable to focus chronologically on regulatory roll out, but there are other issues implicated and "in the bucket" too. Thinking through risk and reputational considerations, how organizations can practically be approaching human rights, societal impact across supply chains, and the implications of sustainability and responsibility in finance are just some elements that should be more common in service offerings. Not to mention looking now, as reporting infrastructure is being developed, at other requirements on the inevitable horizon. Even just thinking about the recipients of advice and implementation through the client's supply chain would be a basic bonus. Add to this, helping clients remember, understand, and fulfil their statutory commitments to stakeholders and society, such as those baked into section 172 of the UK Companies Act. This is about a rounded definition of success for modern business, which is actually the foundation of the right to operate.

This also brings in the criticality of adjacency in a more consultant-style approach to legal services. We are past the point of being able to say here is a corporate lawyer, here is a tax lawyer, or real estate, or employment lawyer, and here is the regulatory lawyer who does ESG and you have to pay for each and all of their time by the hour. The siloed working of the past doesn't cut it. It's not about the law firm's point of view, where clients need to understand their world to navigate their services. It's about service offerings that align across industries and map bespoke to client needs. Like tech transformation, law firms that do this well will have ESG capability across the firm regardless of fee earner primary specialism, have a guild of ESG experts to drive and be deployed where needed, and create service offerings and teams around client sector and segmentation, priced creatively.

The future of legal services is consultative, as well as commoditized (on the latter see "Technology" below). The sooner law firms respond to that in their practice with clients, the more effective for everyone.

A client is not just for Christmas

Relevant across ESG dimensions is the role of the law firm as a client partner. Law firms talk about this a lot but mainly leave it to the client to trigger, unless billing is so big to instigate otherwise. A leading indicator is what happens after a piece of work has been completed. Typically, the work is seen in one-off pieces, maybe a series, but not as a continuum. However, it is, can, and must be a continuum. Work doesn't stop when advice is delivered – certainly not for the client. This goes to the fundamentally transactional attitude baked into law firm psychology. You don't pick up and put down a client like a hobby or wait until Christmas – and it does feel like that.

There are a number of facets to this. The first is linked to the swat team approach covered above, which is about what happens after advice is given. It applies equally to when a transaction or other activity is completed. There are operational aspects of how that lives on in the organization that are often a stretch for clients to undertake from a resourcing point of view and something on which they would value support at the right price point. This goes particularly to ESG-related activities where internal teams may have limited expertise. There are also technological opportunities not yet embraced, covered in more detail in the section below, where law firms can help clients automate business operations during legal work, in a way that removes manual steps for clients down the line, supports ESG compliance, data insights and oversight, and provides ongoing touchpoints for law firms.

Along a similar vein is the opportunity for law firms to prepare a suggested roadmap when they advise or complete specific pieces of work, for clients to get a sense of follow up or future work that would enable them to achieve growth or innovation outcomes and manage risks over the longer-term. That longer-term work may be undertaken (or not) transactionally at future points in time, but the delivery of a program management framework that the client can use to map and tackle it is a valuable adjacency for clients to the advisory work law firms undertake. This is not about waiting to be asked for such a thing, but to deliver it because it would be of value for a client to be able to visualize the horizon and plan beyond the short-term. The upside being they are likely to think of you to help them with the work if they decide to do it.

A further behavior valued by clients – and missed in its absence – is providing contextual suggestions about action a client should be taking or considering based on their activities and announcements. This is at any time, on any day of any week – not just when an instruction is underway. Risks or innovation ideas to cover off are hyper-valuable, based on what is happening in the client industry or geopolitically. This is the industrialized equivalent of what great client relationship partners sometimes still do, which is pick up the phone and say, "Hey, I saw you are doing X, have you thought about Y?". Like that bigger picture conversation you have over the lunch that doesn't get cancelled, from which many ideas flow. This is a great area on which to task technology. In ESG-related work, this is particularly valuable, because the information overload is noisy, innovation is in demand, and "what's market" is not yet settled. "Thought leadership" is not just for press releases.

There is now no such thing as what law firms call "value add". There is just value (or not) in the relationship. Unless you're fired or you fire them, once a client is your client, treat them always as that, however much time might go by between instructions. This goes to the role a law firm itself plays in ESG as well as to actual ESG instructions from clients. Conferences and email bulletins might be great but don't cut it – certainly not as the legal sector tracks towards transformation. Clients are insourcing work, increasing in sophistication, and availing themselves of data insight and automation. In a competitive and fast-moving environment, suppliers of all specialisms need to up their game. Relationships and relevance will be what wins out in this landscape.

Finally, to add that few if any law firms are leading on the obvious links between the legal sector and responsibility – which is to say integrity, sustainability, access to justice, the rule of law, ethical decision-making, human rights, and more. We see some great initiatives in the sector around gender, socio economic diversity, and pro bono, but overall the progress is limited. Yet these are subjects of great interest and passion for many in-house counsel inside client organizations in particular, and at a time of heightened profile and relevance of all such topics in society. The subject of ethics alone is rarely discussed and yet of daily relevance to the in-house legal context. What are the ESG lessons from the appalling examples of corporate and institutional misconduct such as the Post Office Horizon Scandal?[14] How are law firms responding? How can clients respond? There are many legal sector ESG issues on which the community would want to see engagement and themselves engage but that have to be activated and coordinated to happen.

Training

As mentioned, awareness around ESG will be at different levels for different organizations and for different leaders within them. Training to increase or more evenly distribute that awareness is fundamental to any client strategy and makes it easier for subsequent work to be decided and delivered. This is the case particularly for ESG where there is a lot of noise, misconception, and unsettled thinking. The critical backdrop being that client organizations are often reactive and likely to be behind where the GC or ESG lead want them to be in terms of progress and investment. Training can help bridge that gap.

Training is something on which in-house legal or ESG/sustainability teams can lead but which it is invariably more valuable to have an external provider deliver. This is because of the optics of external specialism and the boost of bringing a cross-market perspective, plus the reality of how busy in-house teams typically are. Law firms are well positioned to provide that training. They don't necessarily need to provide it for free. In fact, to charge is likely to focus minds on both the required impact of training and its priority.

Recommendations include:

- *Train the board first.* Training done well will be a context-rich work-shop (or series) at the top level that provides the executive and decision-making boards with a space to think strategically and engage with what ESG means across their reach. Getting this right first will make all subsequent work smoother.
- *Be creative for everyone.* Information-dense sessions or cookie cutter video explainers can be a total turn off, working against the training

aims. This is a subject of relevance to every single person in the organization and can be brought to life as such. Collaborative preparation with internal teams is critical to achieve this.

- *Make it practical, not ideological.* With many values and views in the room, it would be easy to get bogged down in what's trending or what one person thinks versus another. That may be useful for separate ethics sessions in the business. However, the first priority is ensuring people understand the E, the S, and the G across all relevant dimensions and how that applies practically to the client organization's objectives, responsibilities, and operations – legal and otherwise.

Use best in class technology

Globally, we are moving in leaps and bounds on technology. The law has become one of the most cited opportunities for tech disruption, particularly in terms of use cases for generative AI, which is of great interest to cost saving CFOs, growth-focused boards, and GCs building legal operations. ESG is no exception, offering an opportunity to take legal up the value chain inside an organization.

Clients are underway with "digital transformation". They do not want to spend money on tasks that technology can eradicate or build out processes that do not account for their future needs. Innovation in service delivery is a client procurement expectation, along with the priority to capture and harness valuable, audit-grade, business data. Further, ESG compliance is a data-heavy undertaking with an emphasis on reporting. All of which points to the fact that clients cannot address ESG well without technology. The same is true for the law firms that advise them.

An important consideration is the trajectory in legal services towards commoditization, where anything routine will be standardized into low-cost, technology-led products and processes. A range of ESG activity lends itself well to this, such as production of reports and checking or updating contracts and policies for ESG compliance.

A further trend of obvious necessity is using technology to help clients prevent harm. As with predictive analytics in healthcare and content moderation technology for social media, technology can be deployed to help organizations monitor and mitigate ESG-related risks before they crystallize. Risk prediction based on live data, trend analysis, operational anomaly evaluation, "Grammarly" style compliance co-pilots, safety sensors, and other risk indicators flagged up for manual review are all examples. These types of tools sit nicely alongside more complex ongoing work and help inform its direction. Examples are as follows:

- *Reporting.* Tools that help with data collection, analysis, and report production, such as for emissions tracking, sustainability, and supply chain metrics combined with other business data, mapping to various ESG frameworks.
- *Risk and regulation.* Tools that support governance, risk management, and horizon scanning. This is one of the most popular areas of enquiry for in-house lawyers seeking to get a handle on the expansion of ESG related obligations and geopolitical and legal developments. AI governance tools also sit here, where tech is helping to govern tech.
- *Agentic technology.* Tools that anticipate and undertake tasks for you, such as pre-populating reports, synthesizing data from live sources, reminding you to take actions, monitoring compliance, and fulfilling contract obligations. This is one of the less developed areas of technology and a great opportunity for law firms, because it can be embedded "upstream" at the point of document production and provide value long after a transaction or project has closed.

From a client's point of view, their technology needs for delivering on ESG strategy and compliance will require an evaluation and mapping exercise in itself. There are numerous ESG solutions on the market with a range of features and functionality. For law firms to be valuable to their clients in this space they will need to have a good grasp of what is out there and keep track of the "universe of the possible" in technological terms. It would be irresponsible to provide a service to a client for which a tech solution already exists or to charge bespoke rates when a commoditized approach is available for some or all of it. Indeed, many law firms are building technology solutions or partnering with technology providers to meet their clients' needs. This is a valuable development for clients and one that will grow in breadth and scale.

For tech deployment, firms will need to understand client guardrails on use of technology, for example working with a pre-approved tech stack or something easy to integrate that maps to their security needs. Largely, clients won't care in principle about the model used (e.g. partnership, white label, bespoke or licensed), provided they have freedom to operate and well governed risk at a sustainable cost.

It is worth noting the options for clients to have their needs met on ESG expand in scope and the competitive landscape shifts. Consulting practices are adding legal and tech dimensions to their service offerings, understanding client organizations' need and want to leverage sustainability and responsibility as a strategic asset. Technology companies are adding service lines to their product offerings and expanding further into law. Law firms will need to innovate to stay relevant.

The use of technology also has societal and governance implications, bringing practices squarely into the ambit of ESG. Whether or not a law firm is advising on ESG specifically, not using technology where it is entirely viable to do so (and where to do so decreases risks) would likely be seen as both a professional failure and insurance exposure. For example, if as a law firm you can scan 100 percent of a document set in a due diligence exercise using technology (not to mention in a fraction of the time and at a fraction of the cost) versus having paralegals review, say, a ten percent sample of those documents and using that to extrapolate risk, have you taken reasonable care? On the other hand, if you rely excessively on technology without correct assurance and oversight, have you taken reasonable care? These are ethical questions as well as competence and cost ones, when legal services regulation is heading towards technology capability being a feature of competence and insurers are costing tech into premium discounts.

There are obvious rule of law and ethics implications of using technologies such as AI in a legal context, because of the highly sensitive nature of the data, decision-making, and large downstream impacts that legal work implicates. Yet use them we must, to serve clients well and harness the many benefits. Governance therefore becomes an obvious imperative. For every RFP that asks law firms to set out their tech and innovation strategy, there will be a need to articulate the governance and assurance that sits behind that and for it to be robust. There are a number of best practices and frameworks to apply in this regard and a whole raft of regulation of which to stay abreast.[15]

Legal services regulation itself is also implicated, with legal professionals required to retain supervision over legal work, which includes work produced using AI, and comply with applicable laws, which includes fair use by law firms of client data in R&D, not, for example, using client data to fine tune an AI model without the legal rights to do so.

Governance – the next frontier
Done well, governance is what helps organizations move swiftly, responsibly,

and with confidence. Clients have long drawn on legal support for their own governance. As governance requirements shift worldwide in response to geopolitical and regulatory dynamics, along with the span of oversight clients are becoming subject to, and the never-ending growth imperative, governance is becoming a new frontier in innovation. Law firms can get ahead of this in their service offerings for clients. Technology has a relevant role to play, both in respect of the need to govern its use, and also in its use as part of modern governance infrastructure.

However, what has changed now is that lawyers need to strengthen and demonstrate governance of their own. This is in response particularly to criticism of lawyers in the public arena, where they have been involved in high profile wrongdoing or associated with clients or activity that cast a shadow over the profession.

Historically, governance in legal practice has been focused on conflicts and AML checks. What is precipitating now is a wholescale re-evaluation of what governance necessitates in and of the legal sector. Two particularly potent topics as previously mentioned are integrity and independence. To what degree are lawyers acting with integrity in all they do, and remaining independent from their clients, as their regulatory duties require of them? These are topics on which the in-house legal community is increasingly focused and on which many questions are now being asked of law firms – by them, by academics, by public inquiries, by regulators, by policy makers, and by the public at large.

What is required is governance infrastructure around these and all duties and commitments – infrastructure that assures their fulfilment and holds that solid when the pressure is on. Examples of governance frameworks that support in-house counsel can be found in the GC complaint to the Solicitors Regulation Authority,[16] and across the profession in the upcoming output of the Post Office Project.[17]

There is work to do to ground ourselves afresh in the standards we are required in legal services to uphold and to establish and maintain the governance infrastructure that will enable us to do that – all the time, every time. This is an important growth area. Clients and their stakeholders need this for themselves and need it from their law firms – both of which legal service providers can and must attend to.

Impact, not ideology
Ethics is also part of ESG, including what may be legal but harmful. This

encompasses who you represent, how you conduct work, and all manner of related aspects. It is not about piggy backing on media narratives or grabbing on to a pendulum of political pervasion. To retain the confidence of clients, law firms will need to have done the work on what they stand for and ensure they run their business with integrity. Legal ethics is an integral part of this picture, on which Professor Moorhead's 2024 Hamlyn Lectures are essential consumption.[18]

Clients care. Questions will arise. They will take an interest in who you are acting for and the positions you are taking. They will care what is written about you in the press and being seen to be aligned with you. What you do is absolutely their business, up to a sensible point of business and client confidentiality. If you are involved in facilitating harm, misconduct, abuse, discrimination and all their relations, even in a far-flung client location or distant department, you will find they have no tolerance for that. You will need to choose a side. To an increasing degree, what you do is also specifically relevant to clients' legal compliance. You are part of their supply chain and the projects you support or liability you create may become material to their reporting.

That is not to say that law firms must always agree with clients or take positions they favor. In fact, across a range of clients, it would be impossible to agree with them all. Clients appreciate their suppliers can take positions as a business on who they work with, as can any other business, within the confines of the law and professional regulation, correctly applied. Moral judgments or otherwise will be a matter for law firm leadership to decide upon, along with a range of other factors based on their values. But know they will be interrogated by clients and have financial implications. Particularly when passionate GCs hold the purse strings and share views in community networks. It will be a question of market forces as to which law firms become or remain successful over time based on the decisions they make.

Representation and conduct are separate aspects to be controlled as such, but they are closely connected in this regard. By representing companies in legal but controversial industries and contexts, law firms can, through their conduct, help improve the landscape and address pervasive problems, or they can aggravate harm and delay correction. This includes much-maligned oil and gas companies (whose impact on our environment needs uncompromisingly to be addressed but without whom we do not yet have enough fuel to survive), gambling, alcohol, defense, pornography, tobacco, and all raft of industries with considerable ethics issues. The same applies in contexts where controversy is not initially obvious, as the Post Office and other scandals have demonstrated. It goes deeper and wider than optics.

What this comes down to is the quality of decision-making, as an outcome of great governance, aligned around clarity of purpose. Ignoring issues, turning a blind eye to how advice is used, or hoping "wokewashing" will fix it is not where it is at for clients. ESG is about advancement that is enduring. What clients will look and more precisely feel for, is integrity – or not – demonstrated by the firm and whether the approach actually means something – whether it helps or harms. This is about impact, not ideology.

Ultimately, clients want to know that their suppliers and partners are taking material matters seriously and tackling issues responsibly, and where they stand, so there are no surprises. The key is to address things head on and be transparent. Slippery slopes are dangerous for a reason. Clients may introduce or require policy alignment on certain subjects that go beyond law and regulation. The same approach applies. Agree or not with the policy, but consider it thoughtfully and discuss it early and openly so relationship decisions can be made undramatically.

Conclusion

Responsibility is becoming as important as revenue. Whatever title is given to describe that, the fact is not going away. Law firms are now operating at the intersection of clients' operational needs in respect of ESG, and clients' interest or obligations in respect of how their suppliers and supply chains operate. Both will feature heavily in why and how clients instruct law firms and other advisors and what they expect from them from here.

The key for clients is that their external advisors need to have done the work to understand what ESG means for their practice and their people. Whether they yet specifically ask for it, clients need maturity from their law firms in practical terms – partners that understand their own purpose and values, that meet basic business standards, and have baked ESG into their strategy and operations in a way that helps rather than hinders them as clients. This is practical, not ideological. Whether or not law firms want to advise clients on ESG specifically, ESG and any of its successor terms will be unavoidable. As legal service providers, they are part of the client supply chain and will need to engage as such to engage at all.

Clients will be at different stages of their own ESG maturity, many focused on short-term needs and the washing machine of regulation that can seem like a never-ending spin cycle. Law firms need to respond to that, while also understanding and navigating the broader landscape and horizon that will influence their clients' success over the longer term. Stakeholder and geopolitical influences are important considerations, along with ethics and the role technology and governance will increasingly play. This requires a more broadly informed and innovative mindset on the part of external advisors and a more consulting-style approach to legal work that goes beyond traditional business models, specialisms, and thinking.

Climate-related regulation has taken a front seat, but responsible business is about much more. This can be seen as an overhead, but it is also an opportunity. There is a blue ocean out there. Clients are grappling with risk and complexity, transforming their business operations, and innovating for growth. Supply and demand cycles are shifting and they have to respond to that too. They need steady legal guidance and powerful delivery teams alongside them to help them chart that path – a path that is sustainable as to growth and responsible as to society. There is a lot of work to do.

At a time when the world is experiencing vast changes and volatility, people are getting sick of abuse and corruption, and the call is for the evolution and care we all deserve, it is for the legal sector to respond, along with the rest of the world. As clients transform their businesses, so they look to law firms to transform theirs – across value proposition, ethics, methods of delivery, technological capability, attitude, governance, and revenue models. Sustainability and responsibility are what the legal sector should naturally be about. By virtue of their duties to society that underpin the license to practice, it is something on which lawyers should actually lead, not follow.

In what may seem paradoxical but is one hundred percent not, this is a movement both back – to the original purpose and value of law and lawyers – and forward – to the significant and valuable role they can play in the future of business and society. That is something from which we can all enjoy the benefit.

References

1   In the UK, section 1 of the Legal Services Act 2007.
2   Para 4.12 of the Independent Review of Legal Services Regulation:
    www.ucl.ac.uk/ethics-law/sites/ethics_law/files/irlsr_final_report_final_0.pdf
3   *Ibid*. See also The Eagle Club and Mishcon de Reya, "Agents of Change" whitepaper on
    toxic practices: www.mishcon.com/eagle-club/agents-of-change-white-paper
4   https://sdgs.un.org/goals
5   https://unglobalcompact.org/

6   www.iso.org/standard/60857.html
7   www.iso.org/iso-26000-social-responsibility.html
8   Such as under Streamlined Energy and Carbon Reporting (SECR), European Sustainability Reporting Standards (ESRS), Corporate Sustainability Reporting Directive (CSRD), Corporate Sustainability Due Diligence Directive (CSDDD), Global Reporting Initiative (GRI), Integrated Reporting Framework (IIRC), Task Force on Climate-related Financial Disclosures (TCFD), and Task Force on Nature-related Financial Disclosures (TNFD).
9   The CMA Green Claims Code.
10   Such as the IBA Report on mental wellbeing: www.ibanet.org/Mental-wellbeing-in-the-legal-profession; LawCare report on wellbeing: www.lawcare.org.uk/latest-news/life-in-the-law-new-research-into-lawyer-wellbeing/.
11   Modern Slavery legislation, CSDDD.
12   Corporate Governance Code for large companies: www.frc.org.uk/library/standards-codes-policy/corporate-governance/uk-corporate-governance-code/; section 172 of Companies Act 2006: www.legislation.gov.uk/ukpga/2006/46/section/172.
13   IBE Ethics Taskforce: www.ibe.org.uk/resource/ibe-launches-taskforce-to-examine-legal-services-to-oligarchs-and-kleptocrats.html; Post Office Project et al: https://postofficeproject.net/.
14   Post Office Horizon Inquiry: www.postofficehorizoninquiry.org.uk/; Professor Richard Moorhead Post Office blog: https://richardmoorhead.substack.com/; Post Office Project: https://postofficeproject.net/; GCs' regulator complaint and activity: www.jeniferswallow.com/posts/in-house-lawyers-a-bell-has-been-sounded.
15   Such as the NIST AI Risk Management Framework: https://nvlpubs.nist.gov/nistpubs/ai/nist.ai.100-1.pdf and the EU AI Act: www.europarl.europa.eu/topics/en/article/20230601STO93804/eu-ai-act-first-regulation-on-artificial-intelligence.
16   https://docs.google.com/document/u/1/d/e/2PACX-1vTsOgvhoqvOWK_kFXUUnqBct5bxHQuV3jzhDU9QwSbUUY59rJx4vjD1Pc5e9RSbZOt94emhyTrWNERS/pub
17   https://postofficeproject.net/
18   2024 Hamlyn Lectures: https://law.exeter.ac.uk/about/thehamlyntrust/lectures/

Chapter 7:
What clients look for in panel selection – diversity and culture

By Joanna Day, commercial business leader

Be it an annual exercise or one that takes place every three years, in most organizations it seems as though no time at all has passed since the last panel selection process took place. Whilst the process varies from firm to firm, it generally requires a minimum of six months' lead time. Gone are the days when it was the role of the general counsel to simply determine which firms would be on the panel. For a number of years now, the panel selection process has been driven by the procurement function – although this isn't always the case.

These days, nearly all organizations have procurement expertise or functions, and the panel selection process is a collaboration between procurement and legal. Whilst procurement can add real value in terms of request for proposal (RFP) preparations and in the detail of the selection process, they are not subject matter experts in terms of legal services. For that reason, it is incumbent on the general counsel to lead procurement rather than the other way around.

The need for diversity
What the general counsel wants is diversity. Diversity does not simply mean the number of firms on a panel – it means the interplay between a number of things, such as technical breadth, depth, tactical expertise, sector knowledge, and a proven track record in a given area. Flexibility is key. For this reason, the starting point is always the size of the panel, as clearly the larger the panel, the more choice there is in terms of determining which firm can do what. From the law firm's perspective, they want as large a slice of the pie as is possible. Historically, some organizations have claimed to have only one firm on their panel, but how realistic is that? It surely can't be a panel.

There is inherent tension between procurement and legal in any panel selection process and this is because procurement will be focused on cost (demonstrating to the business the savings to be made from the previous panel selection process) and legal will naturally want the best firms to provide the best legal service to supplement its own internal legal resource. Any procurement process is primarily aimed at reducing costs and then keeping those costs under control. Therefore, procurement-led processes will be tied into stringent cost management processes and disciplines, which can make it difficult when external legal resources are needed urgently in an unforeseen crisis. What the legal counsel will want is an established relationship with a direct line to the right advice at the right time. It is often these urgent pieces of work that are difficult to scope, quote, and budget for before the advice has been given. It's not difficult to see how tension arises.

Categories of work

So, where to start? Before even thinking about who should be invited to pitch, there are plenty of things for the in-house legal function to consider. The structure of the panel is all important and the starting point should always be the "categories". These are the areas of law that the client is looking for in terms of support and they can cover a whole spectrum of specialisms, including the traditional areas of law such as corporate, commercial, employment, and so on. It is not as straightforward as simply defining legal categories of work but making sure that the right firms are asked to pitch for the right category. This might sound obvious, but if for example a client is only looking for one firm to provide support on litigation, there needs to be a differentiation between heavyweight, strategic litigation, and simple debt recovery, not least because of cost considerations. If you can, try and establish the client's business model, as often commoditized services, such as debt recovery, sit in another business area, outside of legal. The distinction between "volume" and "strategic" litigation is hugely important for the client and it is not just about cost. The real consideration is knowledge and expertise as, on many occasions, a client has been disappointed when seeking tactical or strategic advice because it is difficult to advise on the bigger picture when the firm has no idea of how the small claims play out in the courts. This is especially the case with consumer litigation.

Interestingly, many law firms are focused purely on selling their services, and therefore conversations at relationship meetings with general counsel center around what the law firm believes it can do for the client. However, it is impossible to confidently say what you can do for a client without truly understanding their operating model. All clients will want legal advice and services tailored to their specific organization, rather than being sold what works for the law firm. Take the time to try and understand the client's operating model and how they deliver legal services within their organization. By doing so, you can create a real win-win for both the law firm and the client.

In the financial services sector particularly, there are other considerations that need to be taken into account, depending on the product range of the client. Whether the client is a monoliner or a multi-service, multi-product organization, the areas of specialism are often niche depending on the delivery channel and specific product. Due to increasing regulatory oversight, all financial service organizations have a constant need for expert advice and support on highly individual and specific areas of law and regulation, and it doesn't always sit within the same law firm. An area where financial service providers continue to desperately seek the right law firm partners is product terms and conditions. Is your firm adept at drafting them or defending them? Can you really separate the two? Do you have the technical resource to support the whole product range? Bear this in mind when completing and/or pricing your proposal tender or bid. All these are good reasons for diversity.

Playing to strengths

In addition to categories, there are other considerations such as geography and jurisdiction. I shall speak to my experience working in the UK. Is the panel to be purely for the UK? Is Scottish law a requirement? Most organizations will have separate panels for overseas work and indeed even Scottish law whilst some have sub-panels that may, or may not, be going out to tender at the same time as the main panel. Sometimes there is a split between London and national firms. The driver for this is usually cost, as generally London rates are higher than in other parts of the country. This is another area that warrants attention. If your firm operates out of both, it is pretty certain that you will be expected to charge out at the lower rate. Again, think of who within the firm is going to be providing the services. Is it more effective for that piece of work to be delivered out of a regional office? This might not be a major consideration for a particular tender but is it going to enable you to provide a competitive rate?

Another consideration is the number of firms that are to comprise each category. The usual assumption is that the law firm that comes in lowest on price ranks first in the given category with those ranking say, second or third, coming in below. In reality, this should mean that the firm that won the number one position in a given category is in the prime position. It is always worth checking this assumption as whilst this is helpful for the client if there is a conflict or the number one firm doesn't have the capacity to deal with a particular piece of work, the client has flexibility and can go to one of the other firms. However, this situation is not always transparent to the law firm, especially the one that ranks in first place. Make sure that you understand how this ranking operates in practice as it is clearly an area that could potentially undermine the panel process. There is nothing more frustrating for a law firm than winning on price but not getting the lion's share of the work – or indeed any work.

In practice, the manner in which the particular panel is to be structured should be clearly explained in the RFP, although there will always be questions for the firm to ask. The most important thing is to think long and hard about which category your firm wants to pitch for but in doing so, really look to understand the client organization's structure and its existing legal resource. These matters should be set out in the RFP but often misunderstandings occur because not all organizational structures are the same.

Most RFPs set out the client's expectations in terms of management information and reporting, which are largely geared to work types, billing etc. It is not usual to see the provision of management information go both ways, i.e., for the law firm to be provided with monthly reports on what work has gone to which firm (although this type of information is often provided in relation to historic instructions at the outset of the panel selection process). If it is not going to be provided, you should ask if it could be, as this is one of the few ways that the law firm can ensure true transparency around the effectiveness of the panel.

Once you have successfully gone through the RFP stage, the inevitable beauty parades commence. Most clients recognize that law firms are extremely slick when it comes to responding to RFPs and many of the larger firms have teams devoted to nothing else. However, there have been examples of beauty parades or pitches that have fallen flat because a senior partner wants to impress the client or believes it is his/her right to do so but what the client wants is to have confidence in who is going to be delivering the services. This doesn't mean to say that you need to include all those individuals in the pitch, but do think long and hard about who is going to be making it. You can include the finer details in the "glossy" to be handed out at the beauty parade itself.

The auction process

Once a firm has gone through these stages in the panel selection process, the next is usually the dreaded e-auction. If a client organization uses an e-auction or e-bid as the defining tool in its panel selection process, we can stop talking about categories and instead think of "lots".

Many Magic Circle firms view the e-auction process with disdain. Corporate M&A activity as a "lot"? A horrific concept! Increasingly, more and more Magic Circle firms are refusing to participate in the process, which is a real challenge. There have been numerous examples of such situations mentioned in the legal press in recent months. Whilst there may be an established relationship with a firm that goes back for years at the most senior level, there are only two outcomes that arise from this dilemma. The first is that the firm is no longer used for refusing to participate and the client suffers by losing that expertise and knowledge. Alternatively, it may be the case that the general counsel or even the CEO has used a certain firm for a number of years and has absolutely no intention of going elsewhere. This may be all very well, but the position is only sustainable as long as that personal relationship exists – and even then it is accompanied by an administrative burden. Increasingly stringent cost management systems and processes make it virtually impossible to obtain a purchase order for a firm not on a "supplier list". There are clearly risks for both parties, so do think long and hard before declining to participate in a panel selection process.

For most organizations going through a full-blown panel selection process, it will be impossible to escape the electronic bidding platform. This is when the importance of determining which lot a firm proposes to bid for becomes apparent. The firm should focus on what it is really good at in a given area and resist the temptation to have a go at everything. Firms will have been provided with the "rules of the e-bid" beforehand and, whilst this might sound an obvious point, it is crucial to carefully study these rules as failure to follow them can result in disqualification. In this context, I am not referring to technical aspects on the day itself but guidance in terms of what lot to bid for. There are numerous examples of where this has played out badly for a firm. For example, I know of one firm that insisted on applying to bid for each and every lot rather than specify the suggested categories. For that reason, the organization itself decided which lots the law firm would be entered for – needless to say, this meant that the firm did not achieve the result it was looking for.

Being realistic

In addition to determining which lot a law firm is going to bid for, it needs to work out its break-even point in terms of rates. Most panel selection processes use an hourly rate as the determining factor in terms of winning a bid. Of course, there may be further weighting that may have been taken into account beforehand but on the big day itself, it all comes down to that hourly rate. Again, make sure you are clear about the rules, as some organizations will ask you to bid on a blended rate whilst others will be asking for the rates for a range of levels of legal expertise/roles/PQE (and in this regard, do ensure that your firm and the organization are aligned in terms of what these actually are, as they vary from firm to firm).

It seems madness that everything hinges on an hourly rate, as in the majority of cases work is quoted for on a fixed fee basis, or is at least subject to a cap – but there has to be at least one element to the equation. Procurement is unable to estimate the number of man hours required to produce a given piece of work or transaction – it is difficult enough for the lawyers to do so – but there has to be at least one point where it is possible to achieve certainty and that is it, the all-important hourly rate.

There are a variety of novel approaches that can be taken in terms of hourly rates, which contribute to realizing a competitive rate. For example, some firms do not charge at all for paralegals as their time can be absorbed in the hourly rates of other fee earners. Realistically, how likely is it that a senior partner is going to be providing services in a given category? If they aren't, don't include their hourly rate in the blended rate. Whatever your approach, do ensure that what you are proposing works for your firm. Try costing out a dummy piece of work that might typically arise with a couple of different pricing models – it can really be worth the time and effort as you can then gain a view of what you stand to win, or lose.

If you have never seen an e-bid take place (either from the perspective of the law firm or the client), it is something you should do at least once in your career. It is positively nail-biting and can only be described as watching a stock market crash. If you are permitted to observe, you are not allowed to leave the room once the e-bid commences, and mobile phones are not allowed. A strong stomach is needed to sit in front of the screen watching the rates tumble to a point where it is difficult to comprehend how on earth a firm is going to be able to deliver any form of quality service at such a low rate. This is why it is so important for the law firm to remember its bottom line and stick to it.

As explained earlier, it is the hourly rate that is often the determining factor in terms of winning the e-bid, but other weightings are also taken into account. One of these falls under the heading of the old cliché of "added value", which usually means free secondees to the client. This can often prove a difficult area as everyone is financially challenged these days and there is huge demand for secondees where clients face the never-ending shortage of in-house lawyers to meet organizational demands. There have certainly been numerous instances of secondees succumbing to the attraction of going in-house and accepting offers of employment with the client, despite the most carefully worded non-poaching clauses. For a law firm, there are risks in accommodating clients in dispatching a steady stream of secondees (some of whom never make it back to the mothership), although there are undoubtedly advantages to be gained in that secondees can obtain first-hand experience of working within a business, as it helps them become more commercial.

A good cultural fit

Another important aspect is culture. You often hear general counsel say that they regard their panel firms as an extension of their internal legal resource. This means that there has to be a good values-based relationship between the law firm and the client. Culture is increasingly becoming weighted as part of the RFP process as a client organization strives to find law firms with the right "cultural fit". This is not always easy to meaningfully define. Naturally, this works two ways, and it is possible for a law firm to have a feel for the client organization from previous interactions with it or how it is perceived externally. It is therefore important to understand whether both parties share common values. This might all seem a bit soft in what is essentially a tough business environment, but it really is important as truly effective panel arrangements are a form of partnership. More and more organizations set out the values they espouse in the RFP and if a firm is able to respond to the RFP in a manner that demonstrates understanding and alignment in terms of those values, they are going to be considered far more of a cultural fit than those that simply dive straight into the bottom line. Culture is becoming increasingly important when doing business and, again, it is often another area that is weighted.

Both law firms and organizations realize and appreciate the fact that panel selection processes are hugely time consuming and require a significant amount of time and effort. If they are conducted thoughtfully and thoroughly by both parties, then they are workable, but disappointingly many law firms have put in the effort and have not gained any work from that effort. The only way to resolve this situation is through active and meaningful panel and relationship management as there is no point in an organization undertaking all that work and then leaving things undisturbed until the next panel review. It is also imperative that the general counsel ensures that the panel arrangements are not undermined by ensuring that all legal spend is only incurred with its panel firms.

However, it is all very well planning how to participate in the panel selection process, successfully bidding, and getting onto a given panel, but the key question is how to build that relationship before the panel selection process begins. How do you even get an RFP in the first place?

Another question has to be, are panels here to stay? The answer is yes – probably. Even if formal panels become less attractive in the future, there has to be some way of selecting a preferred legal supplier – and cost is likely to be a key factor.

Chapter 8:
Effective panel and relationship management

By Joanna Day, commercial business leader

What is a panel?

It might be helpful to introduce this chapter with a definition of "a panel" and the various types of legal panels that have evolved over the years. Depending on the type of business that your firm undertakes, some may be familiar to you and others less so. In its simplest form, a panel is just that – a group of law firms that, having gone through an organization's procurement process, are pre-approved to provide legal services to the client organization. There are distinct advantages to having a panel – the most obvious being that it drives value for money – but it also helps the organization ensure that it obtains the best possible service. The process involved in preparing a request for proposal (RFP) means the client organization has really drilled down into understanding and considering its legal requirements in granular detail before asking the law firms to deliver on these.

In the last chapter, we talked about categories (or "lots") into which various areas of legal expertise or support are classified. The fees assigned to each will invariably differ based on the nature of the category – for example, corporate work will attract a higher level of hourly rate than say, commercial contracts. The fee can either be based on a discounted hourly rate that is applied to an estimated number of hours when instructing a specific piece of work or, in some cases, for example real estate work, there can be a fixed menu of fees relating to specific transactions. There may be discounts to be applied when reaching a certain number of instructions on the fee menu or a ceiling of fees and/or spend has been reached. This is how a basic panel structure works and is designed. There will usually be management information requirements and key performance indicators in place that will be used to monitor the amount of instructions in the respective categories and the related spend.

An organization may have separate panels for geographical locations or jurisdictions. Sometimes there can be "sub-panels", which are typically used where there is high volume routine work (and here I am not referring to heavily commoditized services such as debt recovery). An example of where this type of arrangement can work effectively is real estate work, where the organization has a substantial property portfolio, or even Employment Tribunal work. The main reason for having a sub-panel is to have one firm that can provide economies of scale through thoughtful processes and delivery and compare the position to the main panel where there is usually more than one firm in any given category. The appointment of that firm will often follow a form of mini tender where all the firms on the main panel are afforded the opportunity to pitch should they wish to do so. It is important for the client organization to offer the opportunity to existing panel members to bid before opening it up more widely and it should, ideally, only do so where there is insufficient expertise in a given category on the main panel.

Sub-panels can work well where the client has a business area that is well versed in understanding the nature of the work, both in the context of its specific business requirements and also the nature of the legal support needed. A good example of this is where a designated contact within the HR function liaises with the law firm direct on outsourced Employment Tribunals. This can work really well as, for example, the HR function can aid the preparation of witness statements, collation of documents etc. as they have the knowledge and expertise of the issue and know their own business intimately. In addition, this approach allows the law firm to build a picture of where things typically go wrong in the organization's processes and policies. The law firm is therefore well placed to provide valuable input into setting HR policy to address these pitfalls going forward. There are, however, two things to be aware of in this type of arrangement – one being that the general counsel does not lose sight of the work being undertaken by the law firm, although this can be monitored through the provision of management information and regular attendance at review meetings. The other thing to be alive to is the fact that the law firm undertaking the work on the sub-panel should always be given the opportunity to undertake any strategic or more substantial piece of work when it arises. Not only does this ensure that the firm is rewarded for what would undoubtedly be lower margins on high volume matters, but it also benefits the client organization as they have a law firm that truly knows their business and can work best for the client on a more strategic piece of work, which would undoubtedly attract a higher fee.

All of the above examples relate to work being undertaken for the client organization "directly". This means that the legal fees come from the organization's legal or project budget directly. This might seem an obvious point, but I want to emphasis it because, in the world of financial services especially, there is something known as "third party spend". Why is this important? Often, the third party spend is far greater than the "direct" legal spend. Third party spend relates to legal fees that are paid to a law firm by a business or corporate customer of the financial service provider when taking out a loan. Like a residential conveyancing panel for mortgage lenders, the general counsel does not typically have much involvement in these arrangements as they may be managed by a risk or a business/corporate banking function. There will, of course, be some "high level" oversight from the general counsel or the legal function in terms of the operating parameters, but the detailed management and oversight will often be undertaken by the business area itself. In order to ensure the appropriate management of reputational and operational risk, this "high level oversight" will consist of the regular reporting of pre-determined management information so that key performance or key risk indicators can be effectively monitored. Given that in nearly all businesses and organizations, legal risk is "owned" by the general counsel, he or she is likely to have been involved in agreeing and developing these key risk indicators in line with the organization's overall risk appetite.

The area of third party spend in terms of business or corporate loans is interesting and worth mentioning. This is because the value of the overall relationship to the law firm, in financial terms, will consist of both types of spend. From the law firm's perspective, it may receive a significant amount of third party spend but not be on the main panel. This could be a good way of effecting an introduction to the general counsel to explore other opportunities available to the law firm and, depending on the law firm's area of expertise, there could be synergies that would benefit both parties. It is always difficult for a law firm to get in front of a busy general counsel, but if the third party spend is significant, there must be a good relationship between the business and the law firm and the lender's relationship manager could prove helpful in effecting such an introduction in a meaningful way. It is often the case that the GC will also gain valuable insight into the organization's business through a different commercial or operational lens. This could also provide an opportunity to the law firm to be considered by the GC for inclusion when the next RFP is sent out.

From the client organization's perspective, a holistic view of all the law firms on whatever panel is crucial. Not only is it important in terms of quality assurance, managing operational and reputational risk (for example, if a small firm runs into financial or other problems), it also allows the GC to understand what exposure the organization has in terms of a specific firm. Given that the panel arrangements relating to direct spend are driven through procurement-led processes, there are unlikely to be the same levels of due diligence applied when a business contact proposes a specific law firm to go on to the third party spend panel. It is not unknown for these relationships to develop as a result of the law firm being a business customer of the financial institution itself – another reason that there should be effective governance and oversight.

Panel management

Panel management is not a matter of monitoring how the instructions flow and how the invoices are paid. It is not about the client dictating its requirements, monitoring service levels, querying invoices and so on. To be effective, it requires a great deal of effort from the client organization. I mentioned in the last chapter that it is essential for the law firm to be plugged into its client's vision, strategy, and plans. The onus should not simply be on the law firm to use precious time in relationship management meetings, painfully drawing out information about what the client organization's next biggest challenge will be so that it can resource appropriately. Neither should it be a hurried recital of what the general counsel is tied up on at that precise moment in time. Focus should always be on the long-term important challenges, not the immediate urgent ones, although those will always be there.

So how does the law firm get to know what its client's strategic direction and biggest challenges are? There are examples of where this can be done exceptionally well. One large organization held annual "partnership days" where representatives from all the firms on the panel were invited to attend a session of presentations from various business heads. The idea behind the exercise was not to be legally focused – it was so that the firms could hear, first-hand, what was important to the client organization from the business heads themselves. They were also given insight into the trading environment, market risks, sector issues, and other relevant matters. The GC added context where needed and it enabled the law firms to gain insight through the lens of the business. The session was followed by an opportunity for follow-up questions on a more informal and fluid basis.

Why do I mention this? Not because it demonstrates a nice opportunity for a chat over a coffee and a biscuit but because in a large forum where all the law firms are sat together there is often a reluctance to ask questions publicly. The format really encouraged meaningful dialogue and an understanding of common issues. Organizing such an event requires a significant amount of time and effort but it is worth the investment and can be really effective. It also serves to demonstrate to the law firms that the client organization itself is committed to the relationship and wants both parties to get the best out of its panel arrangements.

It is important to appreciate that there is a real difference between panel management and relationship management. Panel management is the responsibility of the client organization to quality-assure its law firm partners and to ensure that legal services delivery comes in within budget, on time, and is delivered within the organization's risk appetite. Effective panel management can be time-consuming and complex, depending on the nature and size of the client organization, but it should always be looked at holistically. Relationship management is a two-way effort and applies both to firms on the organization's panel and firms that may not (yet) be.

Relationship management

So, what is relationship management? It might be easiest to start off by saying what relationship management isn't. It isn't about lunches, suppers, dinners, and different forms of corporate hospitality. Law firms might be pleased to hear that those features are fast becoming consigned to history, at least in terms of what is regarded as effective relationship management. How many times have you taken the time and trouble to set up a lunch or dinner at an expensive restaurant, only to find that the GC has had to cancel at the last minute because of a busy schedule or sheer exhaustion?

Whilst relationship management is obviously about the law firm understanding the needs of the client organization, it is about listening, not selling. It is also about building and sustaining a meaningful relationship with the client and, as stated previously, it has to work two ways. As is the case with any relationship, be it business or personal, it needs to be based on trust. To demonstrate how it is possible to build a strong and effective relationship whose foundations are built on trust, it is helpful to consider this aspect in the context of the universally recognized Trust Equation (also mentioned in chapter five), which is:

$$\text{Trust} = \frac{\text{Credibility} + \text{Reliability} + \text{Intimacy}}{\text{Self-orientation}}$$

Credibility: Your firm will have been selected to participate in an RFP based on its reputation in the market, reputation for legal expertise, sector knowledge, and most likely testimonials and/or references. This could apply whether you are an existing provider of legal services to the particular client organization or not.

Reliability: In terms of a new incumbent to an organization's panel, this is something that can be ascertained as part of obtaining references when selecting a firm, for example seeking the views of other clients. However, reliability is really something that is developed and built upon as the relationship evolves. For example, does the law firm consistently deliver on time, ahead of time, on budget, or even under-budget? Does it deliver what it says it is going to deliver and as briefed?

Intimacy: This is crucially important for both parties, and it is about that investment in mutuality, which needs time and effort on both parts. For the client organization, brief the law firm properly, anticipate what it is they need to know to be able to deliver the specific piece of work in a way that truly meets the organization's expectations, provide feedback on a regular basis and especially at the end of a given piece of work, and ask for feedback from the law firm (were instructions clear, how did the team do etc.?). By doing this, both parties can truly build a relationship feeling secure in their knowledge of what the other party wants and their ability to deliver it. Importantly, and again for both parties, be transparent about what you know and don't know about the project or delivery requirements. The client doesn't just want another firm on its panel, it wants a trusted advisor.

Self-orientation: This can apply to the individuals leading the particular relationship, although the principles apply equally to everyone engaged in the relationship because self-orientation is all about focusing on the needs of others rather than yourself. The most obvious example is being concerned with delivering what the client needs and wants over personal kudos for the lawyer delivering the piece of work. There is no place for egos. The client organization knows that it is working with a law firm partner that it can truly trust.

Finally, effective panel management ensures the seamless instruction and delivery of legal services on an ongoing basis. Combined with effective relationship management, based on trust, it brings longevity and value to a truly meaningful partnership.

Chapter 9:
Fees and billing – a transparent approach

By Joanna Day, commercial business leader

Whilst fees and billing may sound straightforward, in reality this is the area that often places the biggest strain on the law firm/client relationship. If a firm is on a panel, there will be a rate card in place that will not be deviated from for the duration of the panel appointment (unless there is provision for annual adjustment). Usually, the client will ask for a quote for a specific piece of work and the law firm will provide that quote based on an estimate of the number of hours to be expended, and by whom. However, we all know it is not as simple as that. There are a number of reasons why this often goes wrong. Here are a few.

Lack of clarity / failure to scope appropriately

After the quote has been accepted and at the commencement of a specific piece of work, the law firm will be allocated a purchase order number that sets out the amount that has been allocated and authorized for that particular piece of advice or work. It is therefore crucial for both parties to ensure that proper thought and attention has been given to scoping as the general counsel will want to ensure that the law firm comes in on budget. Apart from anything else, the administration involved in revising a purchase order is never welcomed. If you are not entirely sure what is to be covered in the scope, do ask – there is nothing more frustrating for the client than working through a long list of assumptions.

Given that the rates will have already been agreed for a panel firm, the law firm will not have to compete against another firm via a tender process, so make sure that the quote, so far as possible, accurately reflects the work that is to be delivered. If this is not possible due to the nature of the instruction, try and break it down into individual components with the relevant cost clearly attributed to each. Some components may be missed, others may require further breakdown, and others might not even be necessary as the work progresses, but this at least helps the client have confidence that it will only be charged for what is actually delivered. Remember, for the client organization, the important thing here is not a fixed fee but certainty as to cost. There is a difference.

Always ensure that you are clear as to the instruction at the outset and re-check the scope and client expectations if necessary. The client would far rather the law firm asked for clarification (and more than once, if necessary) than have a dialogue justifying the invoice when it comes to payment. If it looks as though a piece of work is going to be more involved than originally anticipated, go back to the client at the earliest opportunity, let them know, and agree a revised figure. Arguably, over-quoting is better than under-quoting, as it is a far better look to come in under budget than over budget – providing, of course, you have delivered what you have said you are going to deliver.

Watch out for scope creep. It is not unusual for a client to come back with additional requirements once the work has commenced as it may not have been possible to fully scope requirements at the start due to various unknown factors. Perhaps the law firm itself may recommend additional elements as the matter progresses. Scope creep is not a problem so long as it is relevant and addressed at the earliest opportunity and not simply when the invoice is submitted.

The key thing to remember is "no surprises". If there is good, effective relationship management between the law firm and the client organization, either directly through its general counsel or another suitably empowered contact, the client should be comfortable that it has full transparency over fees.

Help, it's urgent!

It happens all the time – the general counsel needs an urgent piece of advice and urgent, more often than not, means complex. Although the law firm may say it needs further information to be able to accurately quote, this is the last consideration when the health of an organization depends on swift legal resolution or certainty in relation to the particular problem it is having to deal with at that moment in time.

However, and not surprisingly, it is with these urgent instructions that the legal advice or services are likely to be more expensive, due to the involve-ment of the most senior and/or highest level of technical expertise. Both parties are naturally focused on the issue itself rather than how much it is going to cost (arguably, quite rightly so) and therefore the now secondary matter of the legal fee does not become apparent until the piece of work is completed. Even a ballpark figure at the outset would be helpful. A self-contained but urgent request for specific legal advice is relatively easy to quote for, but with an unusual or complex transactional matter, or one where circumstances are dictated by a third party, such as a regulator, it is less so. Such situations are usually unplanned and therefore there is no allocated budget for legal support, making it doubly important to ensure there are no major surprises when it comes to receiving the invoice.

With unexpected instructions of this nature, it is not always going to be possible for the law firm to achieve the result that the client wants from a commercial, regulatory, or some other perspective, meaning that the advice and/or outcome might not necessarily be welcomed by the client organization. This is a tricky one as a client is more amenable to accepting a hefty invoice for legal fees when achieving a positive outcome, but no one ever wants to pay for something when they did not get the outcome they hoped for. However, the invoice still needs paying because the work has been done.

With this type of urgent and/or complex instruction, significant work is often undertaken up front. Unless you are billing on a regular basis, it is important that, in the absence of a definitive quote, the client is kept abreast of cost developments to avoid an unpalatable surprise further down the line. This might sound obvious, but this is one of the most common scenarios that leads to souring of the relationship and/or delayed payment.

If you are undertaking a piece of work that is likely to span several months, agree monthly billing with your client. Not only is the firm not carrying more work in progress (WIP) than is necessary, but regular billing cycles also enable you, and the client, to track progress against the budget and both accounts departments will thank you for it.

Perhaps the most important thing for the client, other than receiving good quality legal advice, is transparency over costs. This is not always easy to achieve. Whilst the law firm will be able to demonstrate from its time recording system how many billable hours at what rate have been expended against a particular piece of work or project, this does not necessarily mean that the client feels as though they have received real value for money.

When it comes to invoicing, it is not simply a matter of the general counsel validating an invoice. In client organizations, it is assumed that the GC understands the organization's legal, regulatory, and governance needs and knows where to source the right advice at the right time. He/she will have an agreed budget for meeting these requirements but there will be occasions when the cost of legal advice or services will not come from the legal budget but from a project or provision line. This places an additional onus on the GC to ensure that these additional and "out of budget" expenditures are properly controlled and continue to demonstrate value for the organization. That is why it is imperative that he/she is able to accurately demonstrate what has been spent, when, and why.

Lack of effective relationship management

As you will have gathered from the previous chapters, the effective relationship and panel management of law firms is a topic in its own right. Whilst most of the points mentioned below might seem obvious, they are often the areas that cause problems. Here are some of these relationship "hot spots" so far as they relate to fees and billing.

Make sure the instructions come from a recognized contact. If the GC has delegated to a member of his/her team to ask for a quote or engage on a matter, or the instructions come direct from a business area, make sure that that person is able to give full instructions and answer any questions in relation to the scope of the work. Ensure that the GC is copied in on the instruction and quote to ensure there is no scope for misunderstanding.

One of the challenges often faced by client organizations is where business areas bypass the legal function and go directly to the law firm, as it then becomes difficult to control costs. Most law firms know how to handle this situation, but make sure that the legal contact at the client organization has authorized any nominated business (or other) contacts as this is an area that gives rise to unaccounted-for and additional fees. It is also painful for the law firm to be bombarded with uncoordinated questions and requests. In some instances, instructions may come direct from a business area, such as HR or property functions, where they may have agreed a menu of services and costs with the previous legal incumbent.

When it comes to invoicing, send a draft invoice or narrative to the GC for validation before submitting the invoice itself. This should happen in any event but, depending on the client organization, a busy GC, who may not have been involved in every aspect of the interaction with the law firm, may not be able to get to this before the law firm physically submits its invoice and invariably will need to involve a member of his/her team (or the business area) in order to validate the work that has been undertaken. This is especially important where the legal fees are being paid from a central project or provision line where internal validation is required in order to authorize payment.

Billing

Most law firms have sophisticated and efficient billing systems in place, so that lawyers don't need to spend their time raising and processing invoices themselves. However, systems can only process the information put into them. It's important to ensure that any changes to the scope of work or anything else that affects the output is carefully recorded. Do not simply rely on the system to generate the invoice or a junior member of the team to review the narrative – always ensure that someone actively engaged in the work reviews the narrative before it is sent to the client. There is nothing worse than an incorrect invoice entry where work undertaken for one client has accidentally been allocated to another.

Many law firms submit the narrative to the client for agreement before generating the invoice, which helps avoid any embarrassing errors of this kind. It also means that the invoice itself will not be a surprise to the client. Try not to present a client with an invoice accompanied by 20 pages of narrative, abbreviated and showing units of time at a rate that may, or may not, tie back to the agreed rates. Make sure it is both meaningful and understandable. Whilst system-generated narrative may be helpful for the law firm in terms of its own time recording or accounting purposes, it might not be the most appropriate way of invoicing a client. There are two different objectives behind the narrative output – one being the allocation of billable hours to a particular fee earner and the other to apprise the client of the work that has been delivered. The approach for one might not work as effectively for the other.

Regardless of what billing system is used, different law firms have different approaches. Ideally, once the piece of work has been delivered, an invoice is submitted for the agreed fee, the invoice matches the quote, which matches the purchase order number, and everything goes smoothly. However, this is often the exception rather than the rule, so always make it clear to the client how you will be billing (assuming that has not already been dictated through the panel terms and conditions). Determine whether the invoice will be submitted on completion of the particular piece of advice or work, or at monthly intervals.

Most firms now invoice on a monthly basis but sometimes, for whatever reason, the invoice gets missed or is delayed in submission. The reality is that the client will want to receive the invoice promptly each month, or whenever agreed, so that it correctly sits within its budgeting and payment processes and cycles. Submission of the invoice should ideally be preceded by a draft invoice or narrative for agreement or validation.

What would really assist clients is to see a running total of work in progress and how it is tracked against the original fee quote so that both parties can see the rate at which the costs are being incurred, what is left to be done, and the amount of budget remaining. It may be that you have accounting software that allows you to set an alert for all fee earners when the fees are within a certain amount of the agreed fee being reached. Using this type of alert will allow you to track progress versus fees and if, based on your knowledge of the transaction, you know you are going to exceed the agreed fee, it will allow you to have that conversation with the client sooner rather than later. This allows the client to adjust the budget and/or purchase order. If the agreed fee was £20,000 and you deliver a bill for £25,000, the client is unlikely to pay £20,000 and argue over £5,000. It will instead withhold the whole bill. These kinds of issues often take a number of weeks to resolve, which will compromise your cashflow or fee deliverables and/or targets. Stepping in early creates good discipline for the fee earner and also helps with the realization that it's not all about individual fee earner targets – it's about managing the client relationship. This type of budget forecasting is not often seen, either in the context of a billing system or through active relationship management. However, that does not necessarily mean there is a lack of transparency around fees but rather, it is more a matter of how they can be communicated to the client in a succinct and meaningful way.

It is usual for the client's management information requirements to be dictated in the RFP, but a law firm should never feel unable to ask the GC whether these requirements or information work in practice. Innovation is always a criterion for panel selection!

Another area that is often difficult is in relation to abortive fees – although it is recognized that this is more of an issue in relation to transactional matters. Always ensure that you state the position at the initial instruction stage as, whilst it might simply be a matter of paying hourly rates up until time is called on the transaction, there may be other aspects or implications, especially where the fees have been broken down into the delivery of individual components, not all of which have been delivered. No one wants to think about abortive fees when there is the enthusiasm and optimism of a new project or transaction to get off the ground – but it does happen, and it may save both parties time and effort by addressing this issue at the outset. Having the ability to recover abortive fees is not necessarily the same as billing them. To foster a good relationship with your client, you may discount or waive some of the fees as the client has not achieved its goal. This approach always goes down well with clients – but always ensure that they are subtly reminded of this type of concession when it comes to panel renewal time!

I mentioned earlier the example of clients being accidentally billed for work attributable to other clients, but what about non-accidental billing? What is your firm's approach to chargeable hours? It is always important that this is clear from the outset. Many panel terms and conditions specify what is chargeable and what is not. This is another area where assumptions are often made. From a client perspective, there is nothing more galling than having a relationship meeting with a number of the firm's shining stars or senior partners and then receiving an invoice (or a line in an invoice) charging for the meeting. This does not mean to say that relationship management meetings should not be charged for, but if they are, manage the client's expectations, restrict the number of attendees, and ensure there is a clear client-focused agenda. Of equal irritation is when a phone call is made to a senior partner in a law firm to see if they can assist with a specific piece of work in a non-standard area and then being charged, at partner rate, for the discussion. If the primary purpose of the call is to see if the law firm can assist and thus receive additional work, the client should not be billed.

The above are just a few examples of where things can go wrong. Hopefully, they provide a balanced insight as to how to potentially avoid these pitfalls. Throughout this chapter, I have talked about billing in the context of a panel arrangement where the rates, and other aspects of billing, have already been agreed with procurement input. These same basic principles apply to non-panel arrangements to ensure complete transparency.

Disbursements

Transparency is something that should also apply to disbursements as any quote is going to be with the addition of VAT and disbursements. So far as you can, ensure that any disbursements (certainly those over a given threshold) are accounted for at the commencement of the engagement. If the law firm is going to sub-contract any aspect of the instruction, assuming that this is permitted under the panel arrangement, it will still be accountable as the primary contractor and therefore responsible for controlling these costs, which should be made known to the client at the earliest opportunity. If there is a need to obtain counsel's advice, let the client know as soon as possible and again, obtain details of those fees – do not simply include them on the invoice under the heading of "disbursements" without explanation or the client being aware. On occasions, disbursements themselves exceed the legal fees, and whilst there might be a perfectly sound justification for this, it will come as a breathtaking surprise to the client. It is for the law firm to ensure that, if disbursements are going to be incurred with a third party, they are a known quantity as the client will not necessarily have any control over that third party relationship.

Transparency does not just apply to the amount of the fees, the billing/invoicing arrangements, or disbursements – it applies to the whole relationship. If sub-contracting is permitted under the terms of the law firm's panel appointment, the sub-contracting itself is not an issue – but a lack of transparency is. Let's use an example. When undertaking a substantial piece of work, a law firm outsourced a sizeable chunk of that work to a third party "factory". The client was not made aware of this fact by the law firm itself, which charged the client its usual hourly rates. However, the "factory" undertaking the work approached the client directly to enquire about undertaking volume work going forward, and it transpired that the law firm was making a significant margin on the work. Such an enterprising approach is not a problem in itself, but there was a lack of transparency in this example that impacted on the overall relationship. Most client organizations are amenable to innovative approaches to delivery and would leap at the opportunity to share any reward (and the margin).

Risk reward is not necessarily considered in any detail once a law firm is on the panel because of the rigor of the procurement process. Most RFPs will include at least one question about innovative approaches to charging, so there is an expectation for something different if the situation arises. It is recognized that the sharing of risk and reward does not lend itself to each and every transaction but there may be situations where an unexpected piece of work arises that lends itself to the opportunity to share the upside (such as the "factory" example above). The more traditional methods of incentivization, such as bonuses for completing a piece of work earlier than agreed, are less common these days but that does not mean to say that real value should not and cannot be rewarded.

Added value

Typically, added value is not something that clients expect to see included on an invoice. The most obvious form of added value is the provision of free secondees, or even secondees at cost – and there are pros and cons of secondment arrangements either way. There are, however, other examples of added value. One that is becoming increasingly popular for organizational clients is the use of a law firm's facilities for team meetings and other events. This saves the client the expense of hiring an external venue when the majority of law firms are geared up to provide external hospitality, and is also a good opportunity for the legal team and the external lawyers to meet and exchange views. Many firms provide other forms of added value that bring cost savings to clients, such as the sharing of resources, databases, precedents etc.

Never underestimate the value placed on training and presentations to in-house legal teams where budgets are often constrained. Give careful thought to them, based on your interaction with the organization. Can you provide something bespoke that will benefit both sides of the relationship?

Cost management

From the perspective of a client organization, there are different ways of managing and controlling legal spend. I mention this because the cost management model employed by an organization often puts a certain dynamic on the money available for legal spend. Generally, legal spend is managed horizontally, meaning the general counsel has a legal budget and can spend or allocate this however he/she needs, so long as it meets the organization's objectives. There are the obvious nuances around budget management that everyone will be familiar with, such as budget cycles, accruals etc., and in a productive law firm partnership the law firm will be aware of these factors and take them into account when receiving and delivering on instructions. However, it is becoming increasingly common for legal spend to be managed vertically (i.e., through a central unit) or, in some instances, both horizontally and vertically. Vertical cost management is where there are a number of spend types or cost management units within a business and individual executives will be accountable for that category of spend, wherever it comes from within the organization. It does not necessarily follow that there will be a legal cost management unit managed by the GC as there could be a wider one, such as consultancy, managed by an executive other than the GC. For this reason, it is helpful for the law firm to understand the cost management structure of a given organization.

Conclusion

The approach to fees and billing is far from black and white and the success of how this works in a given law firm/client relationship is very much dictated by systems and processes. However, there are ways to make it a natural and positive conclusion to the delivery of legal advice or a legal service. Above all, transparency is key.

Chapter 10:
Matter management – collaborative working

By Dr Heidi K. Gardner, distinguished fellow, Harvard Law School and CEO, Gardner & Co., and Csilla Ilkei, insights director, Gardner and Co.

> *"Just being a strong technician no longer cuts it. And being 'responsive' is client service 101. No gold star for that, either. I expect my advisors to have a deep grasp of my business, and how the industry dynamics do and will affect us. Bring me insights. Help me see around corners."*

That's how a Fortune 50 general counsel summed up what he looks for in outside counsel. And he's not alone. Our 400-plus interviews with GCs and chief legal officers in the last couple of years consistently turn up the same themes – clients want proactive, future-focused insights on complex issues – the kind that are only possible through *smarter collaboration*.

Smarter collaboration involves specialized experts – like law firm partners – working together across traditional business silos – like practice groups – to tackle more complex problems than any could achieve on their own. It's not easy, but it's incredibly rewarding.

Our decade-plus of research at Harvard University, and private work through Gardner & Co. with hundreds of companies and professional service firms worldwide, unequivocally shows that better collaboration means more comprehensive and innovative advice, deeper client relationships, and more engaged talent.[1]

Taking a step back – how legal needs are shifting

> *"For too long my legal team was like the clean-up crew following the horses in the parade, sweeping up the mess that's left behind. We want to move to the front of horse, helping to guide the decision making rather than waiting to 'respond' once people get into hot water."*

This is the (admittedly inelegant) explanation offered by a GC at a recent Global Leaders in Law event for the shift his team needs to make. In this section, we outline two key trends in in-house legal departments that are driving the need for regular cross-silo collaboration – by them and their outside counsel.

Increasing demands to "move up the value chain"

The demands on in-house legal leaders are ramping up significantly. Over the last few years, our research with senior executives across a wide range of companies and geographies has unearthed two clear patterns:

1. In-house legal departments are under pressure to deliver more value; and
2. Their progress toward truly accomplishing this has been slower than desired.[2]

Whereas many legal departments were previously viewed as cost centers – in the worst cases as "business blockers," the "department of 'no'", or "necessary evils" – they are increasingly expected to act as thought partners who operate on par with the best business leaders. This heightened role demands that they contribute new ideas – rather than just providing legal advice in a reactive, transactional manner they must become deeply involved in the strategic and decision-making processes of the business. They need to help the company make informed, balanced decisions by considering not just the legal landscape but also a host of other aspects, including operational, financial, and market considerations.

This is a step forward, but not enough. Lawyers need to be seen as "value creators" – co-inventors of strategies that promote competitive advantage with acceptable levels of risk. This requires them to be curious and collaborative across disciplines.

Becoming a "value creator" often involves taking on responsibilities beyond purely legal ones, including finding ways to enhance their own service levels and then taking that learning out to the business. For example, at Heineken, the legal department uses a GenAI-fueled "PowerBot" to save time on routine tasks and enhance the quality of debate during meetings.[3] They have learned a lot about barriers to GenAI adoption, including a perceived lack of time and a lack of trust in GenAI, and how to overcome them. They have also come to understand the role of leaders in creating the context where GenAI can be a contributing "team member". Lawyers who are innovation-focused can take knowledge like this and lead the way in their company. In the next section, we specifically outline how external counsel can help their clients move toward being value creators.

But it's important to note that taking on "extracurricular" tasks doesn't guarantee a move up the value chain. Being more proactive and future-focused is the way to get a seat at the strategy table.[4]

This includes having deep contextual knowledge about the business, understanding its key threats and opportunities, and developing forward-looking solutions. For example, to understand more about the business it can be helpful to take field trips to different departments and offices. Once in-house legal leaders have a seat at the strategy table, they need to make the most of it – by demonstrating "authentic gravitas", working to deepen trust, and effectively leveraging external counsel.[5]

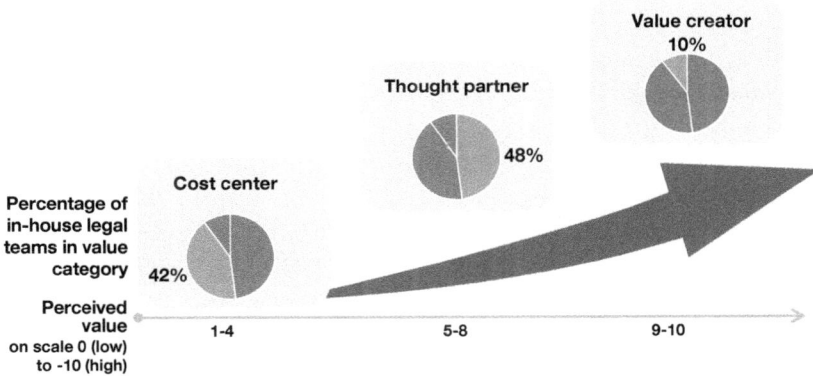

Figure 1: Executives' view of in-house legal departments. Source: Gardner & Co., 2024.

Necessity of in-house collaboration across four "vectors"

More and more, clients describe their environment as VUCA – volatile, uncertain, complex, and ambiguous.[6] They recognize that addressing the legal challenges arising in such a world often demands expertise across various disciplines in their own legal department, and the broader business problems require them to collaborate with other functions and their business partners.

When analyzing who needs to collaborate with whom, and how much, we refer to it as a collaboration "vector" (i.e., a line with direction and magnitude). We've identified four collaboration vectors for legal teams:[7]

1. Within the legal department.
2. With other functions.
3. With the board / executive team.
4. Outside the organization.

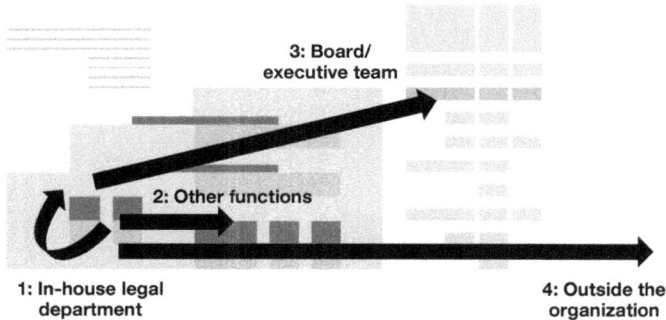

Figure 2: Four vectors of collaboration. Source: Gardner & Co.

In-house lawyers need the same thing from their professional service providers, for them to collaborate across silos. This includes collaboration across practice groups and sometimes jurisdictions. It also means gathering input from across sectors – companies are increasingly engaged in a range of industries, defining themselves on a spectrum instead of in a single SIC code.[8] Furthermore, the strong role of private capital in many companies and industries requires superior cross-functional working. Day in and day out, these clients need a broad range of deep expertise at their fingertips.

As one European GC put it:

"They need to understand the world we operate in, including our invest-ments and our obligations. We need to know that all our bases our covered... they are essentially our safety cushion."

Implications for external counsel – how firms can respond to stepped-up demands

"I don't care how much you know until I know how much you care."

This quote from Shawn Solon, GC at the Detroit-based fintech group Rocket Companies, stood out amongst our interviews. He emphasized that no amount of legal expertise is welcomed by him unless his external counsel consistently demonstrate that they will invest in the joint relationship. Moreover, he said that this was a company-wide philosophy that was long embraced even before his tenure.

Since David Maister coined the term "trusted advisor" in 2000,[9] partners have been striving to become their clients' consiglieri – the one on speed dial for everything matter of significance. But what has clearly changed in the ensuing decades is that no single partner can cover a GC's most valuable, complex issues and opportunities. Today, being "trusted" means that a partner will freely open up the full force of her firm to serve the client – and ideally, do it proactively to address issues and opportunities before the client even knows to ask. (Again, it's helping the GC "see around corners" like the opening quote.)

Based on our research, here are two ways external counsel can better serve their clients.

Ramped up sector-based expertise

One way law firms have adjusted to growing client demands is by developing more specialized go-to-market organizations based on their clients' sectors and sub-sectors (like renewable energy, medical devices, or luxury goods). As Orrick chairman and CEO Mitch Zuklie put it, *"The simple act of defining yourself in terms of a client's business orients you around solving the client's problems rather than staying in the comfort area of your expertise".*[10]

The next step is "Sector 2.0", which means working across traditional sectors to integrate expertise from multiple industries. For example, the more sophisticated legal work regarding data centers requires partners to bring together insights from the infrastructure, energy, real estate, and technology sectors. Gathering market intelligence and other know-how across sectors allows external lawyers to generate novel insights and even truly breakthrough ideas.[11]

By delivering sector, or multi-sector insights, partners help their GC become a much more valuable resource for their company's decision-makers. This integrative, contextual knowledge equips them to transcend narrow legal advice and provide more strategic inputs.[12]

Focus on proactivity over mere responsiveness

It's incredible, but true – when asked what differentiates them from their competitors, many law firm partners boast, *"I'm incredibly responsive to my client's needs"*. Sorry to break it, but that's the bare minimum service level that keeps professional services providers from getting fired. Instead, a truly differentiating factor is how much partners invest in a relationship when they haven't been directly asked – and when they're not immediately getting paid for every minute. It means helping clients understand issues *before the client even thinks to ask about it.*

This could involve simply picking up the phone to a client to discuss, for example, how a news event or regulatory shift will affect them. (Yes, clients often prefer a quick phone call rather than the hundredth email to hit their inbox.) Of course, it means inviting them to firm-sponsored social events or CLE sessions. But what's more valued is the more personalized outreach that helps them directly "see around corners" and move toward their ambition of adding greater value to their business.

During our smarter collaboration diagnostics with new clients (or diagnostic tune-ups with existing ones),[13] we typically see that law partners over-estimate how good they are at collaborating to provide this kind of service. Let's be clear – any partner who wants to be truly proactive will have a much easier, quicker time of it by teaming up with peers and business development professionals who can feed them ideas and insights that they pass along.

We measure both partners' and their clients' assessment of their "on matter" client service (when actively engaged by a client) versus "off matter" (in between paid assignments).

In Figure 3, the size of the bubbles represents how partners at a typical firm feel they collaborate during the different client stages. The triangles, on the other hand, show their clients' view. A gap is clear – in the wrong direction!

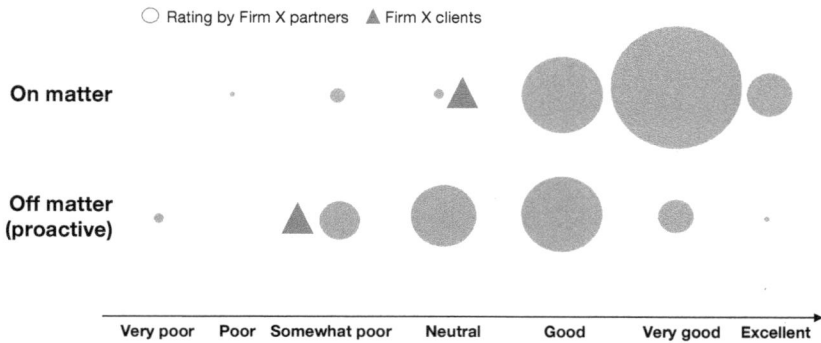

Figure 3: Effectiveness, consistency and frequency of partners' collaboration. Source: Gardner & Co., 2024.

That said, those lawyers who have committed to – and are actually practicing – smarter collaboration so that they can provide proactive service to clients are winning more lucrative work in the long run. Equipping their clients with future-focused insights is critical to demonstrating real value, and clients truly appreciate it.[14]

As one GC said:

"Don't treat me like an ATM, where you only engage with me when you want me to spit out money."

Top ten reasons clients value smarter collaboration

"I want door openers, not gatekeepers. It's infuriating when I need some kind of specialist, go on one of my existing firm's websites, and find out that they have the exact lawyer I need... but the partner has failed to introduce them to me. If someone is overly protective about our relationship they risk losing it."
Country general counsel, global consumer goods company

Our 400+ interviews with GCs and CLOs from leading global companies, as well as insights from their C-suite counterparts and other internal stakeholders, show that smarter collaboration is becoming more of a demand than a "nice to have".

Of course, the issue at hand needs to be complex enough to justify involving multiple experts.[15] Without that complexity, as one client put it, *"If my lead partner knows the answer and still brings in others, he's either incompetent or intentionally over-lawyering me".* When that criterion is met, then clients value their external partners' collaboration for a host of reasons.

1. Access to the firm's best knowledge and experts
Clients facing the toughest, most complex problems expect their outside counsel to tap into the right expertise wherever it exists.

Seems obvious, right? Yet, many partners hesitate to admit to clients that they don't have all the answers. *"If I'm supposed to be their trusted adviser,"* one anxious partner said, *"won't they expect me to be more than just a go-between for the firm's 'real' experts?"*

Actually, the answer is no. Clients consistently say they don't trust someone who claims to know everything. And collaboration isn't just important to the most sophisticated clients – it's essential for in-house legal officers at small and mid-sized companies, nonprofits, and public sector organizations too. Their own teams are lean, and they rely on outside lawyers to leverage their broader network of legal expertise.

2. Deeper understanding of their own business

For most outside lawyers, at least some of their clients operate in deeply siloed organizations. If their colleagues are advising on different parts of their business, sharing that business intelligence within their team can help them bring valuable insights to their clients. For example, has one division recently secured a discounted contract with a cloud services supplier that other divisions could also benefit from?

In-house lawyers are increasingly expected to act as "business partners" to their internal clients. If their outside counsel can help them excel in that role, they'll earn significant goodwill. The same goes for insights across the sector. As one GC put it during a panel, *"If you can tell me just one thing my competitor is doing better than we are, I'll give you all the time you need"*. External lawyers must consider how effectively they are leveraging insights from colleagues who work with other clients in the same industry.

While many firms claim on their websites to serve a dozen or more industries, only a few go beyond lip service to build truly valuable, sector-focused practices.[16] One GC we spoke with credited her firm for standing apart, saying: *"Considering the great sector expertise they have, I would be happy if they called me and brought up emerging topics a lot more often"*.

3. More innovative and tailored guidance

When clients encounter a new challenge, they approach it with a team. Many are well-versed in the business press and management best practices, and they're aware that research consistently shows teams outperform individuals in terms of innovation.[17] They often apply this same approach to their expectations for external advisers.

Even if the situation doesn't call for groundbreaking solutions, it's still important for external counsel to adapt their standard advice to fit the client's specific context and limitations. *"They should tailor their advice to be more practical for us"*, one manager in the pharmaceutical sector said, expressing frustration with his outside law firm. *"We have to invest too much time to make it usable."*

Considering how challenging it is to stand out in the legal field, why shouldn't external lawyers collaborate with their colleagues to deliver advice so precisely tailored that it exceeds their clients' expectations?

4. An international perspective that offers new possibilities

If lawyers are part of a multi-country firm, even clients without international ambitions might still expect them to offer a global perspective. A leader of a European regional retail bank once shared that his organization didn't do any business in the US and had no plans to. However, he said:

"But I want my lawyers to help me understand the regulatory environment there. It'll better prepare us for what might eventually come our way. At the very least, I need reassurance that there's nothing to worry about. It's the unknown that causes anxiety. I want my advisers to help me feel more at ease."

5. Firm's suitability for future, higher-value collaboration

Clients often see how outside lawyers interact with their colleagues as an indicator of their overall ability to collaborate. General counsels need to trust that they'll be a reliable thought partner and a smooth, low-friction adviser who can effectively work with their internal teams. In addition, as clients look for cost savings through disaggregation and outsourcing, they expect their advisers to collaborate seamlessly with other firms.

6. A consistent, headache-free experience

Partners are well aware of how frustrated clients get when a colleague ignores billing guidelines, or they are charged for time spent re-explaining the same issue to different partners. And nothing looks worse than when a client has to inform a partner that a colleague from their own firm is already working on the matter.

Generally, clients are willing to pay for complementary perspectives, especially if it ensures open communication now and long-term service continuity. On that note, law firm leaders might want to consider "laddering" – pairing their professionals at each level with client counterparts of a similar age – to facilitate smooth generational transitions.

This was the practice at one law firm, which paid off for a global beverage client, according to their GC:

"We are the beneficiaries of having a stable, well-functioning, collaborative legal team – that is how they build institutional knowledge."

7. Simplicity in the "vendor base"

Clients are always looking for simplicity, and one way they achieve it is by sourcing a wider range of services from a smaller pool of providers. More than a decade ago, this approach was mostly seen among the largest, most sophisticated clients with strong procurement teams.

Now, the trend has spread to smaller clients, many of whom are adopting what's often referred to as a "core provider" model. When collaboration expands the client's perception of a firm, it helps reinforce or elevate their status as a core provider.

8. Efficiency and economy

This has two key aspects. First, involving multiple experts across a firm ensures the client receives top-notch advice swiftly. Second, with the right systems (and, naturally, the right experts) in place, it should be more cost-effective for an expert to handle an issue than for a nonexpert, who needs time – and compensation – to get up to speed.[18]

9. A greater sense of support, acceptance, and wellbeing

Collaboration makes the work experience much more enjoyable, for lawyers and their clients. As one client recently told us:

"A problem shared is a problem halved – it is reassuring to have the right expertise on hand. I feel more supported and less anxious about the responsibility I carry."

And there's real science to back this up. When people engage in healthy, trust-based relationships, their dopamine levels go up – giving them a surge of positive emotion.[19]

High-performing collaborators also thrive because they bring their authentic self to conversations, both with clients and within the firm. Simultaneously, underrepresented colleagues feel less free to present their full self – and it is exhausting.[20] Fortunately, smarter collaboration – and all the mindsets, skills, and behaviors that are part of it – creates the ideal environment to invite, understand, and fully embrace diversity.

10. Greater influence and career growth

As mentioned earlier, in-house lawyers become more valuable to their organizations when they bring forth comprehensive, business-focused insights formulated through smarter collaboration. This allows them to gain knowledge, status, and power (including financial power) much more quickly. Plus, the connections they gain through smarter collaboration open up more opportunities for career growth going forward – including new job opportunities, board positions, and prospective clients.

Let's face it – no single client identified all the benefits of smarter collaboration. In fact, many clients don't fully grasp how effective collaboration within their firm can help them. Our research strongly suggests that many clients are not just open to collaboration, but eager to find external lawyers who can help them solve their problems by putting narrow legal expertise into the broader context of their biggest challenges. However, many don't know where to begin. With the potential to add value, deepen relationships, and boost profits, isn't it worth starting that conversation?

Then again, in some firms, the critical conversation needs to start with the partnership. What's the business case for smarter collaboration? Is it worth the effort?

Proving the point – outcomes of smarter collaboration for law firms and partners

Our decade-plus of work with hundreds of law firms shows the enormous, quantifiable benefits of smarter collaboration – time and time again. For example, smarter collaboration boosts revenue and profitability, client stickiness, and partner performance.[21]

As for the financial benefits, we have conducted a particular analysis across dozens and dozens of law firms around the world. Essentially, it shows that cross-practice service produces significantly highly value to clients – and is therefore tremendously more lucrative for the firms that operate this way. In essence, revenue generated from clients served by two practice groups is typically three times higher than either of those groups would have generated alone (i.e., 1+1 = 3); revenue from clients served by three groups is five times higher (i.e., 1+1+1 = 5). The math clearly shows that clients are willing to pay more when offered a joined-up solution that tackles their more complex challenges. We also see profits go up due to the increased sophistication of the engagements.

Increased client stickiness, meanwhile, results from partners' deeper understanding of their needs, the market they operate in, and the trends that will impact their business. As shown in Figure 4, clients that are served by a sole relationship partner are overwhelmingly (72 percent) likely to switch providers if that partner departs (e.g., moves to a competitor, or retires). In contrast, clients served by two or more partners are sticky – 90 percent would stay with the firm if one of the relationship partners departed.

"If your relationship partner departed, would you seek another provider?"

■ Remain with firm
Seek another provider

Single-partner clients   Multi-partner clients

28%   90%

Figure 4: Link between client portability and solo – versus multi-threaded relationships.
Source: Gardner & Co.

As for partner performance, our "twins" research has shown that smarter collaborators (people who regularly and deliberately collaborate with people in their networks) perform four times higher than their less collaborative counterparts. Performance covers a variety of measures, including revenue, profitability, and client satisfaction. The smarter collaborator – "twin 2" – gets a lot of benefits that "twin 1" does not. This includes information (e.g., insight into the firm, clients, and markets), new opportunities from his network, the ability to focus on what he's best at (since he takes advantage of his colleagues' expertise), and more relationships with people who are familiar with his work and know that they can trust his competence and his character.

For a comprehensive review of the business (and talent) benefits of smarter collaboration, we encourage partners – and other legal professionals – to read *Smarter Collaboration: A New Approach to Breaking Down Barriers and Transforming Work*[22] and/or *Smart Collaboration: How Professionals and Their Firms Succeed by Breaking Down Silos.*[23]

If it's so in-demand and lucrative, why is it still so hard? Challenges to collaboration in law firms

"Collaborating with other partners is too time-consuming: I must figure out who to reach out to, and then there's a ten percent chance they'll actu-

ally respond – or get back to me quick enough. My other fear is they steal the client away or I lose credit for my involvement... our compensation system is so antiquated..."

Sound familiar? This AmLaw 50 partner touched on several collaboration barriers we commonly encounter in our work with law firms.[24] Here's an overview of the top seven blockers:

1   *Lack of time.* "I am drowning in client work – I can barely keep my head above water, let alone take the time to brainstorm joint BD opportunities."[25]

2   *Lack of collaboration skills and confidence.* "I don't know that collaboration is all it's cracked up to be: I end up feeling more confused than before."[26]

3   *Lack of interpersonal trust.* "Ever since two partners bad-mouthed me to the client, I'm hesitant to bring them – or anyone – into my engagements."[27]

4   *Lack of competence trust.* "The only partners available to help are the ones whose expertise I question. There's a reason they are free."[28]

5   *Knowledge of colleagues' expertise.* "Since our merger two years ago, I can't keep track of who does what."

6   *Incentive system.* "We are not rewarded for collaborating, so why would I?"[29]

7   *Less-than-collaborative culture.* "People barely talk to each other – even in the office. It's the strangest thing."

The next section offers a number of "how-tos" for overcoming these barriers. Law firm leaders should keep in mind that the specific remedy depends on the specific top barriers that their firm face, which can be achieved through a smarter collaboration diagnostic.

Exceeding clients' demands – practical, smarter collaboration how-tos

"Collaboration is like a muscle – the more you train it, the stronger it gets. Like any training regime, it might feel tough at first. But once collaboration propels your performance and growth to new heights, there's no turning back."
Healthcare sector leader in a Magic Circle firm

In this section, we offer a number of concrete tips to tune up law firm partners' collaboration muscle. Law firm lawyers can pick one or two areas to start with, and then see how it affects the quality of their client and colleague relationships. Then they can make adjustments as needed and extend their efforts to other areas when ready.

Exercise "convening power"

Most law firm partners seriously fail to use their superb networks for the sake of clients. Remember, many GCs and other senior executives are siloed inside their own organization. They deeply value the chance to meet with their peers in informal, off-the-record settings where they can compare ideas and discuss non-confidential issues they're facing. What attracts them most is a combination of (1) the quality of other participants, and (2) a hot topic that they are really keen to discuss with peers. Organizing this kind of roundtable event is relatively low-cost and low-effort, and the returns are massive. Not only do the host partners demonstrate their willingness to build client relationships, but they also showcase how savvy they are by picking the right participants and topic. Moreover, if they listen carefully during the event, they will learn enormous amounts about what matters to each attendee. Many, many GCs have confirmed with us that they understand that partners will follow up with them post-event – and that they welcome those conversations.

Focus on knowing strategic clients through and through

We encourage partners to identify the firm's most strategic clients – those that are interested in operating in the collaborative, business-partner-like way we've been describing. They should invest in understanding and serving them in a truly differentiated way and should obsess over their business as much as their clients. Here's an exercise we often do with law firm partners:

"Picture in your mind your most important client. In the next two minutes, write down everything you know about their company strategy. Then jot down the general counsel's key performance indicators – the metrics that determine her bonus or performance assessment."

Too often, we find the partner's page is still pretty empty at the 60-second mark.

Figure out an operating model for non-strategic clients

Most law firms have a "long tail" problem – entirely too many clients that are served by a single practice group, generate insignificant revenue (and possibly even negative profits once administrative costs are factored in), and have no desire to move toward a more strategic relationship with the firm. Oftentimes they pop up in conflict situations and block the firm from taking on more strategic work with better clients. Perhaps the biggest problem with them is that these bitty clients drain time, energy, and resources that should be aimed at strategic clients. Every firm needs an approach to segmenting the small clients by their potential, and then either offloading the non-strategic ones or using them as a training ground for up-and-coming lawyers.

Use innovative approaches to connect with clients

One firm, for example, invited their top 30 GCs to take the Smarter Collaboration Profile, a psychometric tool that helps people crystallize their preferred ways of collaborative working.[30] The lead client partners for each account did the same, and then teams compared their results to find novel ways of working that leveraged each person's strengths – especially focused on clients' preferences. For instance, one team discovered that both their lead partners were highly complex thinkers – that is, they loved exploring the abstract, almost theoretical aspects of the law. The GC was similar. It opened up a conversation about how to ensure that the advice was concrete and pragmatic, the sort of advice that translated easily into the "so-what" points for the business.

Put the client at the heart of a "hook"

Outside lawyers must not wait for the GC to ask about the latest, thorniest challenges in their industry or business environment. Instead, every lawyer needs to sit in the driver's seat and initiate a conversation on a new development – centered on "What it means for you, dear client". By fully putting oneself in the client's shoes, it's possible to explore the issue – and potential solutions – from the client's perspective.

After this conversation, they need to go back to their firm, find the relevant experts to tackle the issue, and prepare for a co-creation session with the GC and their executives. In a recent client conversation, we heard about a missed opportunity for a proactive "hook". According to the CLO:

"I really would like them to pick up on AI – I don't know where to start. I

don't know what I need. The team could help me to digest what it means to our department. Guide me."

Get comfortable with discomfort

The best collaborators develop comfort around being uncomfortable when the conversation gets outside of their natural expertise area. That is the beauty of smarter collaboration – people don't have to know everything. What is more important is recognizing one's strengths, fostering a high-quality network of people with different skills and specialties, and leveraging these contacts when it makes sense.

Tap into network connections[31]

When appropriate, partners should bring outside contacts into their client work. One GC complimented a particular law firm for consulting with key industry experts:

"Over the past year I've seen an uptick in you showing us the strength of your network and how this can be utilized for our business."

But don't get into the "look at me, I know so many people" state of operating. It's best to bring in network connections when it fills a specific gap or offers a distinct opportunity.

Reward strategic thought leadership activities

We advise law firm leaders to encourage, incentivize (if possible), and recognize strategic thought leadership efforts. This includes packaging up the "firm's point of view on XYZ" and sharing it with relevant, high-value clients. While these activities take time, requiring different subject matter experts to work together, they guarantee that the GC gets the comprehensive guidance they want – and need.

Looking ahead

Our research has revealed what GCs and CLOs truly want from their outside law firms – advice that's deeply grounded in their business and industry insights. To get that in today's complicated environment, they need to practice smarter collaboration – bringing together the right highly specialized experts, at the right time, to generate highly integrated, tailored, and forward-looking counsel. Smarter collaboration isn't easy, but because of that it's a stupendous opportunity for law firms to stand out and wow their clients. A few principles to keep in mind are to focus on strategic clients, be OK with relying on others for help, and embrace the power of listening.

References

1   For empirical results showing the effects of smarter collaboration on business and talent performance, see Gardner, H. K. and Matviak, I. (2022) *Smarter collaboration: a new approach to breaking barriers and transforming work*, Boston, Massachusetts: Harvard Business Review Press; Gardner, H. K. (2020) *Smart collaboration for in-house legal teams*, Woking, United Kingdom: Globe Law and Business; Gardner, H.K. and Gillespie, A.E. (2018) *Smart collaboration for lateral hiring: successful strategies to recruit and integrate laterals in law firms*, Woking, United Kingdom: Globe Law and Business; Gardner, H. K. (2017) *Smart collaboration: how professionals and their firms succeed by breaking down silos*, Boston, Massachusetts: Harvard Business Review Press; "By Failing to Collaborate, Law Firms Are Leaving Money on the Table", *American Lawyer*, www.law.com/americanlawyer/2018/10/04/by-failing-to-collaborate-law-firms-are-leaving-money-on-the-table/; and "When and Why Clients Want You to Collaborate", American Lawyer, www.law.com/americanlawyer/almID/1202757856001/

2   Gardner, H. K. (2020) *Smart collaboration for in-house legal teams*, Woking, United Kingdom: Globe Law and Business.

3   Gardner, H. K. and Bienstein, H. (2024) *Collaborating with GenAI: Heineken legal department's use of the "PowerBot"*, Gardner & Co.

4   Gardner, H. K. (2024) *General counsel: how to gain and use a seat at the corporate strategy table – with help from your external lawyers*, Gardner & Co.

5   Newton, R. (2019) *Authentic gravitas: who stands out and why*, New York City: TarcherPerigee.

6   Crocker, A., Cross, R., and Gardner, H. K. (2018) "How to make sure agile teams can work together", *Harvard Business Review*. Available at: https://hbr.org/2018/05/how-to-make-sure-agile-teams-can-work-together

7   Gardner, H. K. (2020) *Smart collaboration for in-house legal teams*, Woking, United Kingdom: Globe Law and Business.

8   Gardner, H. K. and Matviak, I. (2022) "Collaborating through a sector lens", *Smarter Collaboration: A New Approach to Breaking Down Barriers and Transforming Work*, Boston, Massachusetts: Harvard Business Review Press, pp. 139-157.

9   Maister, D. H., Green, C. H., and Galford, R. M. (2000) *The trusted advisor*, London: Simon and Schuster.

10 Gardner, H. K. and Sine, R. (2020) *Supporting a sector strategy at Orrick*, Harvard Law School.

11 Gardner, H. K. and Matviak, I. (2022) "Collaborating through a Sector Lens", *Smarter Collaboration: A New Approach to Breaking Down Barriers and Transforming Work*, Boston, Massachusetts: Harvard Business Review Press, pp. 139-157.

12   Gardner, H. K. (2024) *General counsel: how to gain and use a seat at the corporate strategy table – with help from your external lawyers*, Gardner & Co.

13   Gardner, H. K. and Ilkei, C. (2023) "Is your firm ready for smart collaboration?", *Legal Management*. Available at: www.alanet.org/legal-management/2023/april/columns/is-your-firm-ready-for-smart-collaboration

14   Gardner, H. K. and Matviak, I. (2022) "The Business Case for Smarter Collaboration", in *Smarter Collaboration: A New Approach to Breaking Down Barriers and Transforming Work*, Boston, Massachusetts: Harvard Business Review Press, pp. 13-36.

15   Gardner, H. K. and Matviak, I. (2022) "The Overcommitted Organization", in *Smarter Collaboration: A New Approach to Breaking Down Barriers and Transforming Work*, Boston, Massachusetts: Harvard Business Review Press, pp. 227-245.

16   Gardner, H. K. and von Nordenflycht, A. (2023) *Go-to-market trends: How law firms are embracing and prospering through a sector-based approach*, Litera. Available at: https://info.litera.com/rs/046-QLX-552/images/230207%20Sector-based%20Go-to-market%20Benchmark%20Report.p

17   Briggs, L. and Everett, S. (2020) "Smart collaboration and innovation, with Dr Heidi K. Gardner", Lawyerist Podcast. Available at: www.youtube.com/watch?v=xfkSiEkhkRA

18   Gardner, H. K. and Matviak, I. (2022) "The Business Case for Smarter Collaboration", in *Smarter Collaboration: A New Approach to Breaking Down Barriers and Transforming Work*, Boston, Massachusetts: Harvard Business Review Press, pp. 13-36.

19   Krach S., Paulus F.M., Bodden M., and Kircher T. (2010) 'The rewarding nature of social interactions', *Frontiers in Behavioral Neuroscience*. 2010 May 28;4:22. Available at: https://pmc.ncbi.nlm.nih.gov/articles/PMC2889690/ (Accessed: October 10, 2024)

20   Gardner, H. K. and Matviak, I. (2022) "Watch Out: The Illusion of Inclusion", *Smarter Collaboration: A New Approach to Breaking Down Barriers and Transforming Work*, Boston, Massachusetts: Harvard Business Review Press, pp. 193-210.

21   Gardner, H. K. and Matviak, I. (2022) "The Business Case for Smarter Collaboration," *Smarter Collaboration: A New Approach to Breaking Down Barriers and Transforming Work*, Boston, Massachusetts: Harvard Business Review Press, pp. 13-36.

22   Gardner, H. K. and Matviak, I. (2022) *Smarter collaboration: a new approach to breaking barriers and transforming work*, Boston, Massachusetts: Harvard Business Review Press

23   Gardner, H. K. (2017) *Smart collaboration: how professionals and their firms succeed by breaking down silos*, Boston, Massachusetts: Harvard Business Review Press

24   Gardner, H. K. and Matviak, I. (2020) *Implementing a smart collaboration strategy, part 1: building the case for change*, Harvard Law School Center on the Legal Profession. Available at: https://clp.law.harvard.edu/wp-content/uploads/2022/10/Gardner-Matviak_Implementing-a-Smart-Collab-Strategy_Part-1.pdf

25   Gardner, H. K. (2022) "No time to collaborate? Make some.", LinkedIn. Available at: www.linkedin.com/pulse/time-collaborate-make-some-heidi-k-gardner/

26 Gardner, H. K. and Ilkei, C. (2023) "Do you measure up? Equipping leaders to promote smarter collaboration", *Modern Lawyer*. Available at: https://globelawonline.com/article/730/do-you-measure-up-equipping-leaders-to-promote-smarter-collaboration

27 Gardner, H. K. (2022) "Consistency, empathy, and openness: three keys to interpersonal trust", LinkedIn. Available at: www.linkedin.com/pulse/consistency-empathy-openness-three-keys-interpersonal-gardner/?trackingId=YYtqXEpVSd6A3zH1y56vgg%3D%3D

28 Gardner, H. K. (2022) "Yes, your colleagues can deliver. (Why did you roll your eyes?)", LinkedIn. Available at: www.linkedin.com/pulse/yes-your-colleagues-can-deliver-why-did-you-roll-eyes-gardner/?trackingId=kVCoMJU2TRq7D%2FHIvjEzXA%3D%3D

29 Gardner, H. K. and Matviak, I. (2022) "Performance management shouldn't kill collaboration", *Harvard Business Review*. Available at: https://hbr.org/2022/09/performance-management-shouldnt-kill-collaboration

30 Gardner, H. K. and Matviak, I. (2022) "Individual and Team Diagnostic", *Smarter Collaboration: A New Approach to Breaking Down Barriers and Transforming Work*, Boston, Massachusetts: Harvard Business Review Press, pp. 75-93.

31 Gardner, H. K. (2022) "Growing your network: bigger isn't better", LinkedIn. Available at: www.linkedin.com/pulse/growing-your-network-bigger-isnt-better-heidi-k-gardner

Chapter 11:
Active listening – do you know what your clients are asking for?

By Claire Rason, Client Talk

The best way to find out what clients want is to ask them. That sounds simple, doesn't it? It can be. Paradoxically, it is also increasingly complex. With corporate clients comprising multiple individual buyers and touch points, and with technology starting to influence the way lawyers gather and analyze information, client listening has taken on a new dimension. In this chapter, I discuss the shift from passive to active client listening and how this needs to drive a step change in law firm client listening programs, whose aim is to find out what clients want.

The old way of client listening
Before we look at the "new way", let's set out the "old". The old way of client listening combined the gathering of quantitative and qualitative data. The quantitative was information gathered through surveys. Often an annual exercise was conducted to find out how firms were getting on, sent to a central database, usually seeing poor response rates. Qualitative data gathering was also undertaken in a structured way – at set points across the year, or at significant milestones – usually by independent listeners who had a set list of questions to go through. These interviews were dubbed client research, but they were in effect a market research interview.

Given that the starting point for both quantitative and qualitative research was a set list of questions, both of these approaches can be thought of as "firm-led". Clients answered the questions that firms wanted to ask. What was important to the firm was the starting point (the question set). In this way the client can be seen as passive. They were able to provide answers based on what was asked, but often not on what they might have liked to have been asked. This was particularly true of quantitative research. Furthermore, clients provided feedback at a time that suited the firm – not necessarily at a time when they had something pressing to say.

Interviewers, if external, were trained in statistics and in market research.

Some of the larger market research agencies had junior researchers, learning how to ask questions and analyze the answers on behalf of their law firm clients. Few had individuals who had ever been firm-side, and much less client-side.

This approach to client listening did not train interviewers in active listening – a skill that extends beyond market research and has seen rapid growth due to the popularity of coaching as an industry. The market researcher didn't necessarily need to listen well, they just needed to have the confidence to ask the questions and the skill of recording the answers.

This passive approach was, in part, driven by the technology available at the time client listening programs were devised. Notes from qualitative interviews had to be typed up by someone. In order to make sense of what was said, a human needed to read across the multiple interviews that had been conducted. These highlights were often fed into CRM systems – if they allowed for it. This was a mammoth task made easier by question standardization. Even with question standardization, firms often had to wait weeks – if not months – to get a big-picture understanding from multiple interviews.

This old way worked to an extent. Clients were asked what they thought. They responded. Insights helped firms shape their services. However, the "old way" had shortcomings. Surveys are notoriously hard to get answers to – low response rates affect the outcomes of quantitative research and the aggregate is more likely to have sampling bias.

Having market researchers use a set list of questions in a face-to-face interview generated more nuanced results – however, if clients didn't feel listened to in the exercise, and if they sensed they were being led in a certain direction, the answers would be unlikely to show the full picture. Of course, clients and their advisors would be in dialogue, but the shortcoming was that the data from the conversations was often not shared beyond the core client team.

The old way gave a sense of what clients wanted, but it did not give the full picture.

What's the new way?

The "new way" of finding out what clients want is something I describe as "active client listening". Active client listening is client-led and empathy-driven; it enables the listener to truly drill down into what it is that clients want. In what is said, but also what is unsaid. It is a human-centered approach to client listening that is tech-enabled. It enables the listener to build a rapport with the client and go deeper than a market research exercise. It reduces the need to rely on questions and surveys (not eliminating them altogether, but really questioning their use and employing them only when it makes sense).

The ability to be brave and start with an invitation to the client to find out "What is on your mind?" is a new way to approach qualitative feedback. If the old way can be thought of as passive, the new way embraces what the client wants to share – and when they want to share it.

Active listening

Active listening is at the heart of the new way. Active listening is what happens when you listen consciously and deliberately, rather than by habit. You listen for what is said, as well as what is unsaid. Active listening is what Stephen Covey (the author of the well-known book *The 7 habits of highly effective people*) describes as level 5 listening, or empathetic listening. Stephen Covey told us many years ago that highly effective people seek to understand before being understood. He was on to something!

The truth is we rarely go to level 5 in our daily lives. It is a level that we often miss in our personal and professional lives and not something that we are consciously aware of not doing. Some professionals – therapists and coaches in particular – spend many years honing their ability to listen. However, even they need to focus before embarking on the exercise of actively listening, and even they will fall short in many of their conversations.

One of the reasons why it takes therapists and coaches so long to learn to listen is that they first need to listen to themselves. To untangle their biases, to hear what their thoughts and limiting beliefs are, to listen to and understand their feelings and emotions. Why? Listening at level 5 requires that we understand how we listen, how we become connected to the person we are listening to, and through mirror neurons (the part of our brain that fires when we are connecting with another) how we can even feel what the person we are listening to is feeling. What at surface level appears to be a simple skill – we listen much of the time – hides multiple levels of complexity.

Whilst it is not proposed that everyone who undertakes a client listening exercise take years learning how to, I believe that there are some lessons that can be learned from those who are professional listeners. The skill of active listening can be harnessed to powerful effect when it is understood. Actively listening builds empathy and rapport. It also means that we are alert to what is not being said. It makes it more likely that we will feel alongside the person and notice incongruency between those feelings and the words that are being offered.

One of the peculiarities of gathering feedback in law firms is that the feedback tends to cover not only information that is subjective and external to the professionals (fees, technology, facilities) but also information that is personal to the lawyer delivering the service (understands my business, service delivery, relationship). It is here that many of the things that get in the way of deep listening arise. Given this personal element to client feedback, understanding the psychology – and how we listen – can help lawyers get more from the insight gathered in client listening exercises.

What lessons carry across from active listening into active client listening?

When I speak to clients, one of the most common frustrations I hear is that advisors don't listen well enough. Have you ever come up with a product or service that you thought the client wanted, only to find out that it didn't quite hit the mark, or worse, was not needed at all? How many times do you think someone has heard you, only to find out later that what they thought they heard wasn't what was intended at all? Or vice versa?

The first lesson to be learnt from active listening is that we need to be listening more intently to our clients – more of the time.

In order to achieve this first lesson, we need to start with ourselves and an understanding of how we listen. By understanding our preferences and biases, we are more able to set them to one side, and to be conscious of them when we do listen. If we are more aware of how we listen, we can be better placed to flex our style depending on the situation we find ourselves in. As a result, we can become more empathetic listeners.

In 1995, psychologists Watson, Barker, and Weaver[1] sought to identify how individuals listen. They created a listening style profile that sets out four different listening preferences. The preferences set out the default way we listen and can be remembered with the acronym PACT.

- *People-oriented*. The person receiving the information seeks to understand the emotion and feelings of the speaker. The person is the preference. They are empathetic and look to both the verbal and non-verbal signals. The person-oriented listener is better at reading non-verbal signals and great at nurturing relationships. However, they might be seen as intrusive and can be over-empathetic.
- *Action-oriented*. The focus of the person receiving the information is the task at hand. They are keen to get to the bottom line. The action-oriented listener is great at getting to the heart of the matter and looking for inconsistencies. The preference is what needs to be done.

On the other hand, they often second-guess and minimize relational issues and concerns.

- **C**ontent-oriented. The person receiving the information focuses on the details. They are good at looking for inconsistencies. The preference is the content. Advantages to this style are that they welcome challenging information and look at all sides of an issue. However, they can become too detail-oriented and can intimidate in their questioning. The content-oriented listener also downplays relational issues.
- **T**ime–oriented. The focus here is how long the task of listening will take. Listeners will often start with sentences such as "We have five minutes to discuss....". The time-oriented listener is great for setting guidelines for meetings – there will be no running over here! Conversations are focused. However, they can rush speakers and interrupt and relationships are less likely to be nurtured.

As we can see, there are pros and cons to each of the listening styles, and as with all preferences, there is no "right way". In addition, often the style we adopt is context-specific. However, hopefully you can already see how understanding what your preference is might help you think about how you can develop your listening skills. We can think about how our style might mean that we overlook some of the data that we receive when we talk to clients. We can also think about how the client responds to the way we listen and flex our style accordingly. How we listen shows up in the way we ask questions and in what we choose to focus on.

A powerful question that we could all ask ourselves is: "How might we conduct an interview such that the client doesn't see what our preferences are?"

Having a preference in the way we describe above isn't the only way that our listening can be biased. Heuristics pop up all over the place – the mental shortcuts that we all have in order to effectively and efficiently navigate the vast amount of data and decision-making that we have to do as humans. They are what Daniel Kahneman[2] describes as fast thinking. However, there is a reason the shortcut isn't the road, and heuristics can lead to cognitive biases. When we become aware of our shortcuts, much like with our listening preferences, we can reflect on their impact, and we can treat them as hypotheses to be tested rather than assumptions of truth.

There are a number of common heuristics and biases that pop up in client listening. I will share two of these now, in order to show how they work.

The first example is confirmation bias. This heuristic makes us seek out information that confirms our beliefs, expectations, or hypothesis. It makes us more likely to focus on information that agrees with us and dismiss information that does not.

It does not take long to see how this type of bias could hamper the gathering of feedback or making sense of feedback when it is being reported back. If we focus on the information that confirms our beliefs about the client relationship, we might not give adequate weight to information that does not, or we might probe further into one area at the expense of another.

This is not just about looking for the positives. Think of a scenario where we believe that a client is unhappy with our relationship because we are more expensive than the competition. We can think about how this might play out. We might ask, *"How do you feel about our pricing?"* They might respond, *"Whilst you offer good value for money, you are more expensive than the competition".* Confirmation bias would lead us to focus on the second part of what the client has said and downplay the importance of the first part of the response. Rather than ask, *"And what do you think makes us good value?"* we might ask, *"And how much more expensive are we?".* These follow-on questions would produce different feedback and could lead to two very different conversations – this would be interesting when it comes to analysing "what clients want" off the back of it.

A second example of a common heuristic is the fundamental attribution bias. This is the tendency to over attribute other people's behavior to personality-based factors, while over attributing one's own behavior to situational factors.

Think about this in the context of feedback. A partner seeking feedback about his team might hear that one of the other partners lacked understanding of the deal. The same feedback might also have been received about him in relation to an understanding of the sector. This bias could lead the partner to attribute his colleague's behavior to the fact that he is lazy and likes to focus on what he knows. In contrast, he might attribute his behavior to the fact that he was busy on numerous deals and did not have the time to demonstrate what he knows about the sector.

This bias is important when gathering client feedback because it might mask what the real issues are or prevent the team from truly uncovering what lies at the heart of any particular problem. In effect, it stops the firm and the lawyer hearing what it is that the client actually wants.

There are many other preferences and biases that exist within us.

Understanding that they exist and noticing when they might be at play can help you to be better able to hear what your client is telling you. However, we have said that you do not need to become a trained psychologist in order to be able to actively listen to clients. So, how do you find out what clients want?

What is it that clients want?

The second lesson to be learnt from professionals is that we must give clients our undivided attention – at least some of the time.

Few would say that they enter a room for a client listening exercise without giving the client their undivided attention. However, how do we achieve this in practice? One of the ways you achieve this is through focus. How many times do we enter a conversation with our own agenda, or with other thoughts playing on our minds? How many times do we use a client listening exercise, not as one to learn, but as one to influence (at best) or to sell (at worst)?

Active client listening involves entering the exercise with a clean sheet of paper, and no agenda. It means we are better able to hear what the client is trying to tell us. We can say, "What do you want to tell us?" rather than, "This is what we want to hear". Professional listeners often take a moment to center themselves before they walk into a listening session. This can be as simple as taking a few breaths and noticing how they are feeling and what thoughts are present. This is something that professionals in other areas could do more of.

Tricks of the trade

The third lesson comes from some tricks of the trade – these are tools that professional listeners use to help the client feel listened to and understood, even if they are slipping in and out of level 5 listening.

Open-ended questions are a key tool in any listener's toolbox. Lawyers will understand the concept of "leading the witness" and be familiar with the value of open-ended questions. The old way likely contained open-ended questions too. *"What do you think of our billing process?"* is a firm-led open-ended question.

Open-ended questions should be used to dig deep and should be as open as possible. They should be client-led, open-ended questions. An example might be, "Talk to us about [our firm], how are we doing?". This enables the client to raise what they think is important – which might be billing, or it might be something else. It can be their agenda. By keeping things as open as possible, you hear what the client wants you to hear. You might be preoccupied with billing – however, if your clients don't raise it, the likelihood is that they aren't. This is where the silence is data.

Another tip to listen better is to summarize. You will hear coaches use phrases such as, "So what I am hearing is....", "Can I just summarize what I have heard..." – they may even play back words that stand out. Summarizing is a great trick. It makes the client feel heard, it helps the interviewer remember and clarify their understanding, it also removes some of those preferences and biases we have been speaking about. By consciously repeating and asking the client to confirm you have heard correctly, it gives space for modification. Things are not lost in translation.

Summarizing has another benefit that might not seem obvious on the face of it. It builds empathy. Empathy is another one of those simple but complex constructs. There are multiple types of empathy, from cognitive empathy (where we understand what the other is thinking) through to the highest level of empathy, compassionate empathy. This is where we both understand and feel along with another. Not only that, we know what they need and are driven to act.

For client listening exercises to really deliver what clients want – and this was as true in the old way as it is in the new – there needs to be some action and change following the exercise. Empathy is a driver of action.

Informal conversations and empathy

We have mentioned that technology enables this new approach to client listening. By using artificial intelligence, volume and variety is possible. Artificial intelligence means that note-taking and summarizing vast volumes of data is made easy. It also has the potential to help strip out bias from reporting and it can provide real-time thinking. In the following chapter, my co-author Paul Roberts will set out how it can be used to read across datasets and enhance and enable this broader approach to client listening. What it fundamentally does is strip away the reasoning that sat behind standardized questions. AI doesn't need the questions to be in a particular format to make sense of what has been shared.

In this chapter, I've focused on more formal ways to listen. However, to truly embrace an active-approach, lawyers should be asking clients much more frequently what they want. Again, the structured ad hoc nature of the old way was driven by the complexity of manually reading across large datasets. Those conversations that were lost can now be captured and added to the dataset, teaching the firm real-time what clients want.

Active listening works in formal settings, but it is a skill that can be deployed at any time. The benefits are as true if it is deployed to an informal setting. Empathy is built. Rapport. Understanding. Using active listening in the first five minutes of each client interaction not only strengthens the relationships lawyers have with clients, but also provides ongoing insights that can be gathered and shared across the law firm.

Technology makes it possible to know what clients want today, how that changes tomorrow, and to take into account yesterday.

References

1   Watson, K. W., Barker, L. L., and Weaver, J. B. (1995). The Listening Styles Profile (LSP-16): Development and Validation of an Instrument to Assess Four Listening Styles. *International Journal of Listening*, 9(1), 1–13.
    www.tandfonline.com/doi/abs/10.1080/10904018.1995.10499138
2   Daniel Kahneman, *Thinking Fast and Slow*, 2011.

Chapter 12:
An empathy-driven approach to client listening

By Paul Roberts, founder, MyCustomerLens

How well do you really know your clients? Do you know them well enough to spot their emerging needs, shifting priorities, and changing expectations? "I know my clients" is a common refrain in the legal sector. But forward-looking law firms are realizing that unless this knowledge is centralized, they don't have the evidence they need to fuel organic growth.

Modern-day law firms are constantly seeking ways to differentiate themselves and drive sustainable growth. While expertise and results remain crucial, an often overlooked yet powerful driver of success is the ability to truly understand and connect with clients.

In this chapter, I discuss how empathy is transforming client listening from a passive research project to a dynamic source of business intelligence. I explore how adopting an empathy-driven approach to client listening can help law firms to transform their client relationships and deliver organic growth.

The purpose of client listening
Client listening has been around for a long time. But why firms do it is changing. For the modern law firm, client listening is how they:
- Measure the strength of their client relationships;
- Identify ways to improve client experience; and
- Discover opportunities that can lead to new work.

When done well, client listening is a competitive advantage. Every department has their finger on the pulse – they know what clients are experiencing now, what they want to happen next, and how their team can contribute to that.

This is a significant shift in purpose. Client listening has moved on from periodic research projects that focused on the largest or happiest clients. Now it's about building a real-time understanding of the needs, expectations, and experiences of all clients. An understanding that the whole firm has access to.

The twin drivers of this shift are a more empathetic approach to client listening and new technologies that enable empathy at scale. Hybrid working, generative AI, and stalling growth are all impacting how clients want to do business with law firms. In response, firms are developing an empathy-driven approach to listening. This ensures they make decisions based on evidence, rather than assumptions, about what their clients want.

In the previous chapter, my co-author Claire Rason describes this new approach as active client listening. Rather than firms asking closed or standard questions, they are actively seeking to understand their clients' perspective. This creates a more positive experience for the clients, as it shows them that the firm is actively listening. It also gives the firm invaluable insights that guide strategic decisions, improve client satisfaction, and build loyalty.

Imagine having a single source of client and market intelligence that enables:

- Business development to see how to win more bids.
- Marketing to see how to enhance thought leadership and brand differentiation.
- Lawyers to see where they can strengthen their relationships and reputations.
- Client teams to see how delivery and market trends are shaping client expectations.
- Operations to see how to improve process efficiency and reduce complaints.
- People teams to see how to adapt their recruitment, training, and culture to ensure they develop and retain the best talent.
- Your board or SMT to gain a real-time view of how the strategy is impacting clients, colleagues, and profitability.

By embracing an empathetic always-on approach to client listening, all these benefits are possible. Insights become generated "outside-in", as the firm becomes more curious about their clients' perspective.

Traditional client listening lacks empathy

Few would argue that listening to clients is a good thing, vital even. Yet when push came to shove, many firms limited the scope and frequency of their client listening programs. There were three main reasons for this:

- At an individual level, lawyers felt they knew, or would be told by the client, everything that they needed to know to do their work. The assumption that "I know my clients" led to many fee-earners not engaging with the process.
- Client listening was assumed to be a burden for clients, and that communication was better kept to the matter in hand. "It is not the right time" became an excuse to exclude busy or unhappy clients.
- Client listening projects were inefficient. Collecting, analyzing, and reporting on the data was a slow and manual process while outsourcing to consultants was expensive.

In short, the client listening process was not seen as a value-add to clients or to lawyers, and therefore cost restricted its scope and impact. It became a periodic research project where relationship partners "opted-in" the clients they were happy to be included.

This traditional approach to client listening lacked empathy. Internal assumptions outweighed the curiosity to discover the client's perspective. Interviews would get under the skin of client needs and experiences, but they were limited to a handful of top clients. Meanwhile, surveys were filled with closed questions that asked about the things important to the firm.

This approach did not send a good message to clients either. Unless they had a one-to-one interview, clients felt like they were being researched rather than listened to. They received a survey each year, or sometimes every few years. These surveys took a long time to complete because it was the one chance the firm had to gather data.

To keep the analysis manageable, the surveys were filled with closed questions. Ratings and tick boxes focused on the topics the firm wanted to measure. The voice of the client was missing. Closed questions left no room for clients to explain what was on their mind and what was important to them.

Without the client's voice, the insights were limited. No matter how the results were cut, it was hard to discover what clients wanted and why clients felt the way they did.

To compound the problem, traditional client listening ignored "non-research" sources of the client voice. Clients were sharing their needs, expectations, and experiences in complaints, reviews, testimonials, pitch feedback, emails, feedback forms, and everyday conversations. But all these potential insight sources were managed in different teams and siloes.

It was hard for firms to show empathy when each team had selective hearing.

Designing a client program outside-in

In contrast, an empathy-driven client listening program is designed outside-in, by putting yourself in the client's shoes. It starts with the question "What do clients want us to know?" rather than "What do we want to measure?".

Firms that adopt an outside-in approach to client listening:

- Make it easy for clients to share feedback when they have something to say, not just when the firm is ready to ask.
- Use a broad range of feedback sources.
- Ask open questions to discover the other person's perspective.
- Gather feedback across the client journey, when the firm still has time to act on it.
- Include all of their clients in the listening program.
- Make the insights accessible to all decision-makers.
- Show clients they are listening by closing the loop.

Make it easy for clients to share

Many client listening programs are restricted to periodic interviews and surveys. As a result, clients are asked to reflect on expectations and experiences that happened a year or more in the past. While they may remember the feelings of frustration and unexpected delight, they are unlikely to remember what caused them.

Making clients wait to share feedback risks losing the very insights that firms are seeking. It also suggests to the client that their experiences and needs are not that important to the firm. The alternative is to make it very easy for clients to share unsolicited feedback, at a time and place that works for them. For example, create a very short feedback form and put it front and center in your client portal; or link it to the company's default email signature.

Broaden your sources of client voice

The voice of your clients is already being shared in many places, but they may not be considered "client listening". For example, testimonials are often ignored because they are comments from happy clients reflecting on positive experiences. But look deeper. What aspects of your brand and service delivery do your best clients focus on, when they know the comments are attributable? Do they say anything that wouldn't be equally applicable to your competitors? Do they collectively mention all aspects of your brand, or is their silence around an area you consider a key selling point?

Similarly, reviews and complaints tend to be managed in different teams and considered in isolation. Yet they both reflect the experiences and priorities of clients who want to impact your service delivery. When you combine reviews and complaints with your other feedback sources, you will see early warning signals start to emerge. This helps you go from managing complaints to driving continuous improvement.

A third way to expand the voice of your clients is to centrally capture informal feedback. These are the unsolicited comments that clients make in emails and conversations. Sometimes these get sent to marketing to live in an email folder labeled "feedback". More often they get talked about and then forgotten. Instead, create a simple form that enables fee-earners to quickly capture the informal feedback separately from matter-related discussions.

Ask open questions

Consultants, coaches, salespeople, journalists, and therapists are all taught to ask open questions. Open questions give people the space to share what they want to say. In contrast, closed questions, such as multiple-choice survey questions, restrict responses to the options the firm has offered.

Open questions demonstrate empathy, by showing that you are interested in what the other person has to say. You're not making assumptions about what is important to them. As Claire discussed in the previous chapter, open questions are the foundation of active listening. This doesn't mean turning all the closed questions into open questions. It means using one open question to reveal the answer that several closed questions are fishing for. In the process, you learn what is most important to the client, while giving them the space to mention something you hadn't thought to ask.

Ask more empathetic questions

To increase empathy, start by standing in your client's shoes and looking at service delivery from their point of view. Then write open questions that give them space to share their needs, expectations, and experiences. I've had great success with asking two simple questions:
- What did we do well?
- What could we do better?

Notice that neither question starts with "why". Many surveys limit open questions to asking why someone gave a specific rating. Such a question lacks empathy because it asks people to justify their rating. In contrast, by probing for both the positives and negatives, you get richer and more balanced responses from clients. Happy clients will feel comfortable telling you about minor frustrations and unhappy clients will note that some elements of delivery are very good.

Listen while you still have time to act

The two most common places that client listening is deployed are after a pitch process and after a matter. In both cases, the discussion looks back over a process to learn what the firm did well and what could have been done better. These are good insights, but it is too late to act on them. I've heard of firms that do not send out their survey until after the client has paid the final invoice. Nothing says "we value your opinion" like asking for feedback when everyone has moved on to other projects.

Forward-looking firms check in on progress and ask for feedback when they still have time to act on it. They look at the whole client journey and ask themselves, "What do we need to know at each stage to ensure we can meet client needs and deliver a great experience?"

For example, at the start of a matter, it is helpful to understand the client's expectations for this specific piece of work. Do they need more regular updates? Or are they expecting to see the firm leverage Generative AI (GenAI) or specific individuals? During a matter is a great time to briefly check-in on progress, and to ask whether expectations are being met and whether new needs have emerged. By mapping listening touchpoints to the overall client journey, firms can generate insights that help them to actively manage each client's experience.

Listen to all your clients

When a prospective client reads a proposal or website that says the firm puts "clients at the heart of our strategy", they would be forgiven for thinking that their voice would be included in that firm's listening program. But that's rarely the case with traditional research-based listening. Many firms still operate an "opt-in" approach to client listening, where clients are handpicked for inclusion.

This approach creates significant blind spots. While the relationship partner may feel they already know what the client would say, this is not completely true. New questions prompt new insights. At a firm level, exclusion reduces opportunities to discover and learn from cohorts of similar clients.

Forward-looking firms – the ones practicing active client listening – do the opposite. Their program is "opt-out". All clients are part of the listening program by default. This approach enables the firm to learn from small, emerging, and innovative clients whose needs and expectations can signal broader market trends. This also helps delivery teams to understand and proactively respond to the expectations of each client, which will lead to stronger word of mouth endorsements.

Give decision-makers access to real-time insights

We've already seen how firms can practice empathy when listening to clients. However, insight creation is a waste of time unless decision-makers have access to the results. The traditional output of client listening has been PowerPoint slides and pdf reports. These tools are good for sharing static knowledge, but quickly become stale and unused.

The alternative is to create real-time insights that decision-makers can access themselves. Once you start listening to more clients, at more stages in the client journey, you develop a continuous flow of insights. Modern client listening platforms can instantly aggregate and analyze these different data sources to create a single source of truth. Interactive dashboards then ensure that decision-makers across the firm see the relevant cross-section of insights they need to make evidence-based decisions. Enabling decision-makers to "self-serve" from a shared understanding of actual client needs improves the firm's ability to make client-led decisions.

Show clients you are listening

The final stage of empathy-driven client listening is to close the loop and show that you were listening. This step is often misunderstood to mean following up on any specific issues or actions raised.

The biggest driver of survey response rates is not fancy emails, incentives, or relentless chasing. It is something far more human – does the recipient believe that participating is worth their time? Asking empathetic open questions is a good start. But then you need to close three open loops:

- Respond to individual feedback by addressing any issues or actions raised.
- Share the key themes and results with all clients, whether they were asked for feedback or not.
- Share all the themes and actions with your internal teams.

Sharing with all your clients what you've learned and how you've responded is a vital signal of empathy. It shows the market you are genuinely listening, and reminds clients that their peers are engaging with the program and being rewarded with action. Sharing insights and actions across your firm also has important benefits. It helps challenge outdated assumptions and broaden client understanding. It also shows those still reluctant to engage with the program that the firm is taking it seriously.

If closing the loop sounds too hard, or too risky, consider how leisure centers solve the problem. They put an A-frame display in reception that staff and customers have to walk past. On the display is a sheet with two columns – "You said" and "We did" – plus a link to their feedback form. You may not want an A-frame in your lobby, but you can use display screens, noticeboards, client newsletters etc. You could even publish the results online, as Mills & Reeve does with its "Fearless Feedback" program. The important thing is to show, not just tell, clients that their voice is important to how the firm delivers their service.

Listen differently – adopt an always-on approach

Firms seeking a more empathetic listening program are adopting an "always-on" approach to client listening. The five hallmarks of always-on client listening are:

1. Always be listening.
2. Centralize the data.
3. Automate the analysis.
4. Give results context.
5. Close the loop.

Together, these hallmarks create what I call a "Feedback Flywheel" (Figure 1), as early success builds momentum that leads to further success. More insights lead to more action, which leads to more engagement that generates further insights. An effective flywheel can future-proof law firms by ensuring that they are making evidence-based decisions when seeking to attract, grow, and retain clients.

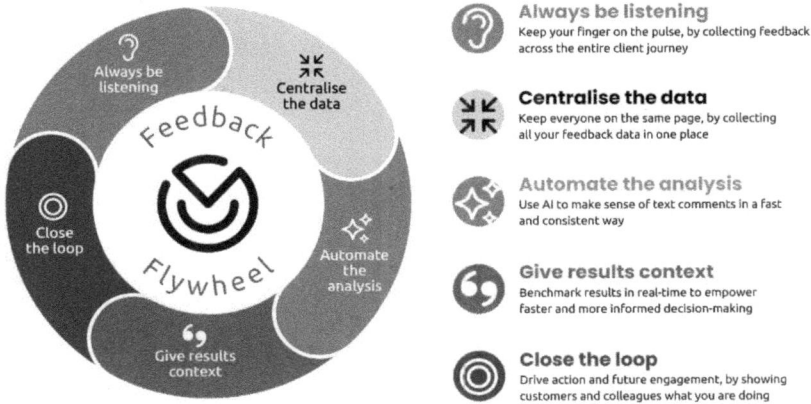

Always be listening
Keep your finger on the pulse, by collecting feedback across the entire client journey

Centralise the data
Keep everyone on the same page, by collecting all your feedback data in one place

Automate the analysis
Use AI to make sense of text comments in a fast and consistent way

Give results context
Benchmark results in real-time to empower faster and more informed decision-making

Close the loop
Drive action and future engagement, by showing customers and colleagues what you are doing

Figure 1. The Feedback Flywheel.

Always be listening

Clients want to be able to share their needs and experiences at a time and place that is relevant to them. To support this aim, firms have repositioned formal research to be a small piece of a bigger puzzle. Client and market intelligence is being collected through a wide range of sources, from informal conversations to formal feedback processes.

To help your firm to always be listening, start by listing all the existing feedback and data sources across the firm. Complaints, testimonials, CRM notes, and operational data can all provide valuable signals about current client experiences and future priorities – but only if they become part of a unified client listening program. Then consider adding an "instant feedback form" to your email signature or website. This form should have two open questions and no ratings or multi-choice questions. Ask them what the firm is doing well, and what it could do better, then get out of their way.

Centralize the data

Voice-of-the-client data is often captured in different systems and managed by different teams. These silos limit the insights that can be created. Once client listening teams can access all their voice-of-the-client data in one place, it becomes easier for them to see trends and patterns across different clients, sectors, and data sources.

This centralization doesn't mean putting all feedback into a CRM system. CRMs are great at summarizing and reporting on structured data such as the names and dates of recent client interactions. But they're not designed to aggregate and report on unstructured text data. Client feedback and intelligence data is best centralized in a modern client listening platform with the flexibility to handle different data formats.

Automate the analysis

Manually tagging text data, whether digitally or with highlighter pens, has been the main barrier to expanded client listening. It is neither a consistent nor scalable process, leading to firms restricting the use of open questions and the frequency of reporting. Hiring more people, or outsourcing the analysis to consultants, is prohibitively expensive.

Forward-looking firms are turning to AI-powered analysis to keep their flywheel spinning. AI-powered text analysis can do in seconds what humans do in a day. The question is whether to use proven Natural Language Processing (NLP) algorithms or the new Large Language Models (LLMs).

LLMs have grabbed the headlines with their ability to do everything from summarizing data to creating new music. The problem with LLMs – at the time of writing – is that they are unpredictable. Prompting remains a dark art and there is no knowing how it reached conclusions, which is crucial when looking to make sense of client comments.

The better way to implement AI-powered text analysis is using Natural Language Processing (NLP), which is a less exciting but more robust way to analyze text. NLP analysis can identify what clients are talking about (topics), how they feel about it (sentiment), and why it is driving their behavior (value drivers). It also enables benchmarking of text insights, because it consistently delivers the same results.

Give results context

Automated analysis does the heavy lifting, but it can't provide a definitive "so what". That's because two firms could hear the same comments from a client but take different actions. For example, a client could tell both firms they are expensive, but a premium-priced firm will respond to that very differently from a price-matching firm.

This is where the client listening and account teams come in, adding context that turns insights into actions. These actions may be specific to one client, or they might indicate opportunities across a similar segment of clients. They might give clues about how to win future pitches, how to differentiate the brand, or how to improve the experience clients have with a specific process.

Giving results context can feel hard. It can sometimes require deep thought and collaboration. But it's also crucial to demonstrating empathy. If actions don't follow client listening – even if that action is just to keep doing something well – then clients will feel that they were not heard.

Closing the loop

Closing the loop is what turns passive listening into a flywheel of active listening. The true value of client listening lies in the actions you take in response to what you heard. Clients need to see tangible evidence that their input is valued and acted upon. This "closing the loop" process is essential for building trust and demonstrating the real impact of your client listening program.

Start by closing the loop with the specific client. Acknowledge the feedback shared by an individual, so that they know it was seen by humans, not just a machine. Say thank you for taking the time, comment on any nice words, and follow-up on any specific actions or issues raised. This response builds trust and increases the likelihood that the client will share feedback in the future.

Then close the loop with your wider client base. Look at the insights and resulting actions in aggregate. Uncover the stories most relevant to broader segments of your clients. Share some of the praise, and a few improvement areas that you plan to address. This shows all clients that their peers are sharing feedback, and that it's worth their time to do so. When sharing, keep in mind that only sharing praise makes the communication feel "salesy" and less believable. Instead, be authentic and show how your firm is innovating and driving continuous improvement.

Finally, close the internal loop by sharing the impact of client listening with all your teams. Don't just share the numbers. Highlight the teams getting positive feedback, and examples of where your brand positioning is appealing to clients. Without naming names, share the improvement areas and the actions that are being taken as a result. This demonstrates the firm is acting on what it's hearing. Plus, someone in your firm will probably know why any system or process is causing friction, and how it can be improved.

Always-on client listening in action

Murgitroyd, a leading IP law firm, has expanded the voice of its clients by creating a form to capture unsolicited feedback emailed to attorneys. It also has an "instant feedback" form promoted in its default email signature to make it easy for clients to share their experiences. To close the loop, the firm has created social media graphics and posters that show how it has taken action in a simple "You said, we did..." format.

UK firm Tozers has developed centralized product, relationship, and end of matter surveys that collect insights alongside testimonial and reviews data. By listening at more points along the client journey, it can more quickly respond to emerging client needs. By centralizing data, and automating analysis, it can see what's driving word of mouth and how the firm is positioned.

Does AI automation reduce empathy?

With the rise of AI and automation, there is a concern that these technologies might diminish the personal connection in client listening. This concern is understandable, as it reflects broader fears about AI taking jobs from humans. At the same time, customer service delivered by chatbots and automated call systems remains a frustrating experience.

It is worth remembering that artificial intelligence is an evolving science rather than a new technology. It's been around for a long time, slowly growing in capability. The field of natural language processing began in the 1940s, while the term "machine learning" was coined in 1959 to explain computers that seemed to teach themselves. But "AI" captured the public imagination in 2022 when the first Large Language Models such as ChatGPT were released. Suddenly, consumers had the ability to create images, summarize large documents, and write poems, songs, even books. Over the following 12 months, every piece of software seemed to add a "now with AI" badge.

But AI is just a feature, a technology to enable more efficient or effective processes. So how it impacts empathy and client listening depends on what type of AI is used and how firms choose to deploy it.

My view is that firms will have the greatest success when they use AI to enable, rather than replace, people within the client listening process. For example, using AI chatbots to conduct client interviews would reduce empathy because clients would feel less valued. But using AI to draft a transcript of the conversation so that the interviewer can follow up sooner will increase empathy.

Similarly, using an AI model to analyze and report on client listening trends, without human oversight, will lead to generic insights and confusion caused by the inevitable hallucinations. But leveraging AI-powered text analysis to discover emerging themes, new opportunities, and urgent issues will enable firms to better understand their clients and respond faster.

Even the most expensive LLMs would need constant updating to be able to make strategic decisions relevant to each firm. So blindly using AI to create actions from feedback would likely lead to some actions being too generic or even strategically damaging. However, giving internal experts access to AI-powered analysis will help them make faster and more informed decisions that benefit their clients.

AI is a powerful tool, but empathy-driven firms must keep humans in the loop – not just to check outputs but to provide the additional context and reasoning required for informed decision-making. AI can analyze vast amounts of data instantly and, if it's properly trained, deliver relevant and actionable insights. But firms don't treat every client the same, and therefore shouldn't blindly use AI outputs. Client listening teams are becoming more, not less, important but their role is evolving. Thanks to AI, they will spend less time finding and crunching data, and more time deciding "So what?" and driving the resulting actions and improvements across the firm. For clients, this will make the firm feel more responsive and empathetic.

Key takeaways

An empathy-driven approach to client listening goes beyond gathering data – it represents a powerful opportunity for law firms to transform their client relationships and drive sustainable growth. By shifting from traditional, research-led projects to an always-on approach, firms can create richer insights and build deeper, more meaningful relationships.

To achieve these benefits, client-centric firms are designing their client listening programs from the outside-in. Firms are collecting the voice of the client from a range of formal and informal sources, with touchpoints at all stages of the client journey. They are asking more empathetic, open ques-tions to let clients share what's most relevant and important to them. Thoughtful integration of AI-powered analysis is enabling client listening teams to drive more engagement and action across the business. Finally, the proactive sharing of insights and management of actions is enabling client teams to add more value and demonstrate the RoI of client listening.

This approach creates a flywheel of momentum with more insights leading to more action and more engagement. This benefits clients too, as more empathetic listening creates a more client-centric conversation and ultimately a more compelling client experience.

Do not worry if this all sounds too overwhelming, or too far removed from your firm's current process. Empathy-driven client listening requires process and cultural changes that take time. The important thing is to start the journey and celebrate your progress.

Benefits accrue along the way, not just at the end. Starting points include:

- Shortening your surveys by replacing multiple choice questions with an open "How?" or "What?" question.
- Adding a short form that clients can use to share unsolicited feedback.
- Combining existing data sources in one central place.
- Using dedicated NLP algorithms to analyze open text comments quickly and consistently.
- Have a Board or SLT discussion about making client listening "opt-out".

Chapter 13:
The strategic necessity of personalized client relationships

By Helen Hamilton-Shaw, member engagement and strategy director, LawNet

In an era where the legal sector is increasingly driven by technology and efficiency, law firms must recognize that the human element is a critical component for success. Personalized client relationships are a strategic necessity that can shape a firm's reputation and long-term trajectory.

Clients are demanding more from their legal advisers, seeking partners who understand their needs, communicate transparently, and offer genuine care. This personal touch is a key factor in building trust and long-lasting relationships. For law firms, the rationale is clear – those who invest in creating a personalized service will not only enhance client satisfaction but also gain a competitive edge.

Traditionally, many areas of the legal profession have been seen as transactional, with service delivery focused on resolving specific legal issues, rather than building long-term, personal relationships. Until recently, this saw many law firms offering a matter-based service model, delivered through professional specialism silos, rather than a holistic approach. There has been a fundamental shift in recent years, driven by changing client demands.

Expectations and service standard demands have been driven by retail and online brands, setting new benchmarks. New technology has helped drive this – it has also helped address the previous imbalance in the flow of information. Clients now have access to more information, a wider range of choices, and public platforms to express dissatisfaction if they are unhappy.

This has translated into a shift in the power dynamic between client and lawyer. Firms are expected to prioritize client care, with clients demanding greater transparency and enhanced service from providers.

Clients are increasingly looking for legal partners who can offer more than just technical advice. They want strategic partners who understand their industry, or personal situation, anticipate potential issues, and work collaboratively.

Against this backdrop, the evidence shows that firms stand out when they commit to developing relationships founded on an understanding of a client's individual needs – this fosters trust and loyalty, which in turn builds and reinforces their reputation. A client who feels genuinely cared for is more likely to remain loyal to a firm, recommend its services, and return for future legal needs. In this way, personalized service can become a competitive differentiator in a crowded marketplace.

Clients receiving positive experiences and outcomes can swiftly become advocates, harnessing public platforms such as review sites and social media – that can so easily be weaponized by dissatisfied clients – to deliver powerful testimonials.

Research from social psychology[1] illustrates that people often form interpersonal connections with brands that exhibit similar dynamics to those in their personal life. These relationships involve reciprocal exchanges that provide tangible benefits, including a sense of perceived commitment. There are some obvious fundamentals that apply universally – the importance of honesty, being treated as an individual, and keeping promises in order to build trust.

Personalized service provision by a law firm involves taking a proactive approach towards understanding client concerns, offering support, and delivering an experience that addresses the unique needs and preferences of each client.

Just as clients have different needs and expectations in their different personal relationships, so they may want and expect different things from their different organizational relationships, requiring sensitivity to establish exactly how they would like the relationship framed.

Clients are looking for more than just legal outcomes – they seek partners who care about them and are focused on their wellbeing, whether that is to achieve a positive financial outcome or by providing considerate social interaction during any exchanges. As the *Harvard Business Review*[2] notes, trust-based relationships lead to long-term success because they go beyond the immediate transaction and reflect the firm's commitment to its clients as individuals.

Fundamentally, this is grounded in the culture of the firm, as the right culture has a direct impact on a firm's ability to deliver personalized client care. McKinsey's[3] report on organizational culture emphasizes the importance of leadership in shaping workplace culture. Law firm leaders must actively promote values that encourage and enable staff to build relationships, such as open communication, respect for clients, and professional development.

Building a culture that instils a sense of "psychological safety"[4] for staff will pay dividends in client care, as staff will feel confident in sharing problems or making mistakes, without fear of embarrassment or criticism, knowing they will be supported to learn or change in pursuit of improvement.

Demonstrating that the firm values teamwork, empathy, and collaboration not only improves employee satisfaction but also creates a ripple effect that enhances the client experience and helps ensure that client care remains at the forefront of everyday practice.

Firms that foster this sort of positive, supportive workplace will create an environment where employees naturally go the extra mile for their clients. Conversely, firms that neglect their internal culture often see higher turnover rates, lower employee engagement, and poorer client care outcomes as a result.

Gallup[5] research on employee engagement shows a direct link between how employees feel about their workplace and how they treat clients. Engaged employees are more motivated to provide exceptional client service, whereas disengaged employees may prioritize tasks over relationships.

Investing in people development is not just about improving technical legal skills – it's about fostering the interpersonal skills that lawyers need to provide high-quality client care. Law firms that prioritize training and development in these areas can create a workforce capable of building strong, lasting relationships with clients.

A client-centric culture – the foundation of personalized relationship building

Client-centric businesses across industries, including legal services, consistently outperform their competitors in terms of retention and profitability, according to research by the Chartered Institute of Marketing.[6]

But many organizations, including law firms, often fail to distinguish between client service, client experience, and true client centricity. While client service focuses on meeting immediate needs, and client experience focuses on interactions throughout the service journey, client-centricity demands a more fundamental shift. It requires rethinking how the firm operates at every level, ensuring that the client's interests are the driving force behind all decisions and actions.

Becoming truly client-centric involves aligning the firm's culture, processes, and values around the client's needs, placing their perspective into every facet of the firm's operations. This type of culture encourages every employee, from fee earners to administrative staff, to put the client at the heart of all decision making. Having a client-centric approach as a central ethos is essential for law firms striving to create a consistent, personalized experience that fosters deep, long-term client relationships.

This central ethos can only grow and be sustained if it is developed and led from the top, promoted at every level, and supported from the bottom up. Leaders need to actively promote policies and behaviors that prioritize the client experience. Also essential is multi-directional listening that analyses and reacts to feedback from all staff within the firm. According to the McKinsey report,[7] organizations with a strong client-centric culture have leadership that champions client-focused initiatives, empowers employees to make decisions with the client in mind, and rewards behaviors that improve client satisfaction.

To further reinforce a client-centric culture, some of the SME law firms in our collaborative network have introduced tangible ways to ensure the client's perspective is never overlooked in decision-making. For example, having a designated "voice of the client" champion in meetings ensures that the client's views and experiences are actively represented. In some cases, firms have gone a step further by placing an empty chair or a place card at meetings to symbolize the client's presence, serving as a visual reminder that every decision must consider its impact on the client. These simple yet powerful gestures help embed client considerations into the firm's daily operations and strategic planning.

Consistency is critical in developing and maintaining a client-centric culture, the Chartered Institute of Marketing research[8] found. It's not enough to adopt a client-first approach at only certain points in the client journey – it must be a continuous commitment across all touchpoints, from the initial client interaction and enquiry to the final resolution of a case. Adopting this approach will take firms to the next level, better able to meet client needs and leading to stronger, more enduring client relationships.

Law firms can cultivate such a culture by critically reviewing every process and client touchpoint, identifying improvement opportunities and investing in tactics and training programs that emphasize client engagement to foster an environment where empathy and communication are valued.

We have observed concrete benefits from adopting a client-focused approach across the firms in our network. Each firm is required to meet and maintain our ISO standard, which includes a key metric for client care, known as the LawNet Excellence Mark. Maintaining this standard involves participating in external assessments of the client experience, which offers our members a clearer view of how clients perceive their journey and where improvements may be needed, complementing the firm's own internal research.

The assessment includes both in-depth client experience evaluations – using anonymous walk-ins, telephone, and online visits – and digital satisfaction surveys. Each year, the feedback gathered from the client experience reviews is used to inform decisions on improvement initiatives, training, and ongoing development within member firms. Over the past 11 years, this has become the largest client experience research initiative within the UK legal sector, with close to 10,000 experience reviews and almost 100,000 satisfaction surveys completed, providing a substantial source of data and insights for continuous enhancement.[9]

Measuring and evaluating client experience and its impact on a firm's success presents several challenges, but it's only through a comprehensive review of performance that genuine improvements can be made. The evidence shows this holistic approach leads to substantial gains – by implementing targeted actions and focused training, firms saw their average score in client experience reviews rise from 52 percent in the project's first year back in 2013 to 76 percent in 2023/24, with our highest performing firms scoring up to 88 percent.

This positions our member firms well above the sector average, indeed between 30 and 50 percent higher depending on the enquiry entry point, with telephone calls consistently more challenging for firms throughout the sector. But, while LawNet's efforts have positioned the network well ahead of their competitors, potential clients often measure service quality against top-rated consumer organizations in wholly different sectors. It is no longer enough to be excellent at what you do compared with your peers – firms today must match up to retailers and other consumer-facing companies such as John Lewis, Nationwide Building Society, and key-cutting, shoe repairing Timpson. These organizations held the top three slots in the July 2024 UK Customer Satisfaction Index (UKCSI)[10] ranking, with an 85 percent+ satisfaction rating.

We see the customer-centric focus reflected in the storytelling of these major brands. John Lewis' iconic Christmas adverts, for example, never focus on products but rather evoke emotions and feelings. Similarly, banks discuss the life changes that come with buying a home rather than focusing on mortgage rates, and Nationwide emphasizes its community focus, how it is keeping open its local branches.

This kind of storytelling seeks to connect with customers at an emotional level, by demonstrating a deep understanding of what really matters to them and the focus of their journey with the organization. It embodies client-centricity and personalized experience and can lead to stronger client engagement. It applies equally to consumer and business clients, who, despite their professional roles, are individuals with their own emotions, fears, and aspirations. It demonstrates the importance of empathy.

Empathy and understanding – the human element in legal services

Empathy is a vital component of client-centric legal service delivery and too often is overlooked in the race towards matter completion and the balancing of finite resources against client demands. But when lawyers understand the emotional and practical challenges their clients face, this can create a fundamental shift in the overall client experience. Law firms that encourage empathy in client interactions create an environment where clients feel heard and understood. This personal connection can reduce client anxiety, especially in high-stress legal situations. As Daniel Goleman's[11] research on emotional intelligence suggests, the ability to recognize and manage emotions in both oneself and others is key to building meaningful relationships. In legal services, empathy enables lawyers to see beyond the legal problem and consider the person behind the case.

The relationship-building skills of fee earners – lawyers, partners, and other client-facing professionals – are increasingly recognized as critical to the success of law firms.[12] Clients want more than just technical expertise – they want to work with professionals who can build rapport, understand their business, and offer strategic advice that goes beyond legal problem-solving. Developing these relationship skills can significantly enhance a lawyer's ability to attract and retain clients, the evidence for which is growing.

Research by the US-based Association of Corporate Counsel[13] found that clients value lawyers who demonstrate genuine concern for their wellbeing, not just those who are skilled in legal matters. Developing emotional intelligence in lawyers, particularly in client-facing roles, enhances the firm's reputation for personalized client care.

The Legal Education and Training Review[14] (a joint project between the Solicitors Regulation Authority, the Bar Standards Board, and ILEX Professional Standards) reports that law firms are placing greater emphasis on developing "soft skills" such as communication, emotional intelligence, and relationship management. These skills are now considered just as important as legal knowledge. Stanford Law School's[15] work in this area highlights that lawyers who excel in client relationships are those who actively invest in understanding their clients' businesses and personal circumstances, positioning themselves as trusted advisors rather than just service providers.

By cultivating empathy and communication skills among their fee earners, law firms can differentiate themselves and build deeper connections with clients. A firm that listens and responds empathetically is more likely to earn client loyalty and foster long-term relationships, crucial for retaining business in a competitive marketplace.

This reflects the growing need for businesses to adopt a more personalized approach in skills development focused on individual client care. One effective method is to step into the client's shoes to pinpoint areas where the skills of a fee earner could be enhanced. Many firms in our network use the audio recordings of conversations between customer experience researchers and fee earners to identify skill gaps. This has led to the creation of resources such as crib sheets to support both fee earners and support staff during client interactions, ensuring a consistently high standard of service together with structured learning to develop targeted skills where needed.

Further evidence of the value of building empathetic connections through skills development is reflected in the improvements observed by our network member firms when they focus on enhancing their lawyers' communication skills. Sales is an area where many lawyers feel out of their depth, often unsure how to communicate the value of their firm in terms of expertise and service rather than cost. There can also be reluctance to pursue potential business opportunities, with follow-up consistently the lowest scoring area in client experience reviews. However, when lawyers receive the appropriate training and support in these skills, feedback indicates that potential clients are more confident in making decisions. This not only fosters empathetic engagement but also significantly improves the overall client experience, leading to stronger, more valuable relationships.

Another way to build stronger relationships is to take a more individualized route to matching fee earners with clients, with some firms in the sector using psychometric models and formalized, data-driven approaches. But one of our member firms is conducting an innovative trial that uses a simple, human-based approach for match-making new client instructions with those fee earners deemed the best fit. A central team receives the instruction and builds an understanding of the client's approach and communication preferences, after which they work with the relevant department to agree the best match, bearing in mind both individual styles and availability. This offers a practical and low-investment way to trial the process and identify potential issues. Like psychometric profiling, it aims to give those critical client/lawyer relationships the best chance of success from the outset.

Employees equipped with strong communication skills can become powerful advocates for the firm, delivering a service that exceeds expectations, especially when they are given the autonomy to do so. CEOs from our member firms have shared the importance of empowering staff in this way, granting them the freedom to go above and beyond for clients. The results have ranged from encouraging employees to openly share what they value about working for the firm, to more tangible client outcomes, like a private client lawyer who felt able to head to the supermarket on Christmas Eve after discovering a vulnerable client had no groceries and didn't know how to order online.

Developing such skills can also help foster a healthy working environment in which staff feel comfortable asking questions, learning from mistakes, and building the confidence they need to improve. This sense of psychological safety allows employees to approach client service with creativity and innovation.

Law firms that prioritize the professional growth of their employees, offering mentorship, training, and career development opportunities, are more likely to foster a client-centric culture. This, in turn, strengthens client relationships, leading to higher levels of client satisfaction and retention, according to research by the CIPD.[16]

Building trust through transparent communication and efficient processes

Open, timely, and regular communication is essential for building trust in any professional relationship, particularly in legal services, where clients are often dealing with complex and stressful issues. Clients want clear, honest communication about their case status, legal options, and cost implications.[17] By providing consistent updates and explaining processes in plain language, law firms can alleviate client anxiety and generate confidence in how their case is being handled.

LexisNexis[18] research shows that clients frequently express frustration when they feel kept in the dark about progress on their case. Miscommunication, delayed updates, or lack of communication altogether are some of the top reasons clients switch legal providers. Ensuring transparent, regular, and proactive communication can prevent misunderstandings and set realistic expectations. Clients who feel informed are more likely to trust their legal team and remain loyal, particularly during prolonged or challenging cases.

In today's fast-paced and individualistic environment, clients expect communication and engagement on their own terms, through the channels and locations they prefer. They want businesses to meet them in their chosen spaces, whether virtual or physical. A good example of this is seen in our member firms adopting platforms that would not be traditional marketing avenues or communication routes, such as social media or app-based channels. Clients also want flexibility in timing, and we've observed firms responding by offering services during hours that would previously have been considered outside the norm.

Changing expectations are also driving a shift towards more streamlined, customer-centric onboarding processes within our member firms. At a recent leadership forum we hosted on customer experience, it was the key topic. One managing partner highlighted a major project aimed at automating each step to enhance the client's experience, rather than focusing solely on what was easiest for the firm. The core philosophy was about "putting ourselves in the shoes of our clients".

We have seen this approach across our network, with many adopting technology to improve the client experience. The use of cutting-edge identity verification platforms is having a significant impact on this experience, ensuring a seamless process that can be completed in a matter of a few minutes.

Leveraging technology to enhance client care
We're witnessing the potential of technological advancements to profoundly impact all areas of our lives, including the delivery of legal services, with tools already available to improve efficiency, streamline processes, and enhance communication. Clients expect prompt and professional service when they engage with law firms, making efficient onboarding and ongoing case management processes crucial.

However, law firms must strike a balance between using technology to enhance individual client care and potential overuse in ways that might depersonalize client interactions. Clients still value the human touch in their legal matters, and technology should be used to support this.

A study in the US by the International Legal Technology Association[19] highlights how law firms are increasingly adopting automation for routine tasks like document management, billing, and client onboarding. They found this can enhance client interactions by speeding up processes, reducing human error, and freeing up time for lawyers to focus on strategic client interactions, resulting in higher client satisfaction levels. However, it also found that relying too heavily on automated solutions can risk losing the personal touch that clients expect, such as regular personal updates or nuanced advice tailored to their specific situation.

The use of AI and technology in the law is drawing wide-ranging and occasionally heated debate.[20] Advocates highlight that advanced technology can enhance client service by providing data-driven insights and faster service. Others warn that over-automation could lead to alienating clients who prefer more direct, personal communication. The key is to find a balance where technology brings efficiency but leaves human interaction at the core of the client relationship, ensuring that personalized interaction is preserved even in a tech-driven environment.

The theme for our Excellence Mark program of client experience support to our member firms in the coming year is "Next Generation Excellence". This aligns to the primary focus for many of our firms, which is on the introduction of further digital tools and AI integration, while reinforcing and enhancing personalization of the client experience at every opportunity.

In embracing this approach, firms are encouraged to focus on personalization in client care that extends beyond improving initial interactions and automating efficiency. While technology, such as AI-driven task prioritization or enhanced digital systems, can streamline processes, true personalization requires deeper analysis of the data these systems generate. The real value lies in how this information is used to shape and enhance the next stage of the client journey.

Personalization becomes impactful when firms act on insights gathered not only from automated systems but also from more nuanced feedback like Net Promoter Scores, which indicate whether clients would recommend the firm. Often, clients may rate a firm's legal services highly but still hesitate to refer others due to a lack of personal connection. To bridge this gap, firms must take proactive steps to improve client engagement, reinforcing their commitment to a client-centric culture.

To enhance personalization, the emphasis should be on what happens after the initial interaction – the second step. It's about making follow-up actions intuitive, engaging, and memorable. The real opportunity for personalization comes from building rapport and delivering an experience that goes beyond basic expectations, ensuring clients feel valued and happy to recommend the firm.

The future of personalization in the legal landscape

As law firms continue to adopt new technologies, the future of personalized client care in legal services will be shaped by how firms balance innovation with the human touch. Client expectations are evolving rapidly, and firms that can adapt to these changes while maintaining strong personal relationships will stand out in a competitive market. One of the key challenges lies in using technology as a tool to enhance, rather than undermine, client-focused care.

Reports by PwC[21] forecast that the legal profession will see increasing integration of artificial intelligence, blockchain, and other emerging technologies. These advancements will allow law firms to automate more administrative tasks, provide more data-driven legal insights, and offer faster service. However, the importance of human relationships in law – built on trust, empathy, and understanding – will remain a fundamental aspect of successful legal practice.

Future-proofing client relationships requires law firms to stay adaptable, keeping pace with technological advancements while maintaining the ability to connect with clients on a human level through personalized, attentive service, even as both sides benefit from the efficiencies brought by technology. As the Law Society[22] predicted in a recent report, the firms that succeed will be those that recognize that, despite all technological advances, the legal profession remains a people-centered business.

There is evidence that the sector is aware and adapting to the challenge. A recent report[23] highlights that nearly 80 percent of SME law firms expect to drive revenue growth in 2025 by placing client experience at the forefront of their strategies, on equal standing with digital-first approaches.

The most successful law firms of the future will recognize that personalized client service is crucial and the result of a firm-wide virtuous circle. Investing in people development – by fostering empathy and instilling a client-first mindset – combined with a strategic commitment to creating a client-centric culture, will drive the personalized care that strengthens client loyalty and fuels the firm's success.

This is what will determine which firms thrive in an increasingly competitive landscape.

References

1   Aaker, "Brand personality in a membership-based organisation", 1996.
2   *Harvard Business Review*, "Creating a Customer-Centric Culture", 2020.
3   McKinsey & Company, "Employee Engagement and Client Experience", 2020.
4   Edmondson, A. C. "The fearless organization: Creating psychological safety in the workplace for learning, innovation, and growth", 2018.
5   Gallup, "The Impact of Workplace Culture on Client Satisfaction", 2019.
6   Chartered Institute of Marketing, "Client-Centric Law Firms: Why Culture Matters", 2021.
7   McKinsey & Company, "Employee Engagement and Client Experience", 2020.
8   Chartered Institute of Marketing, "Client-Centric Law Firms: Why Culture Matters", 2021.
9   LawNet, "LawNet Mark of Excellence: Lessons for law firms", 2019.
10 UKCSI, "The state of customer satisfaction in the UK", July 2024.
11 Goleman, Daniel, "Emotional Intelligence: Why It Can Matter More Than IQ," 1995.
12 Society for Human Resource Management, "Why People Development Is Essential for Client Care", 2022.
13 Association of Corporate Counsel (ACC), "Emotional Intelligence: The Key to Building Client Relationships", 2019.
14 LETR, "The Importance of Relationship Skills in Modern Law", 2018.
15 Stanford Law School, "Developing Lawyer-Client Relationships: The Role of Soft Skills", 2020.
16 CIPD, "Building Skills for Client-Focused Law Firms", 2021.
17 Legal Services Consumer Panel, "What Clients Want: Transparency and Communication", 2021.
18 LexisNexis, "The Importance of Transparent Communication in Law Firms", 2022.
19 ILTA, "Improving Client Care Through Efficient Legal Operations", 2023.
20 *Financial Times*, "Tech and Client Care: Can Lawyers Balance Efficiency and Relationships?", 2023.
21 PwC, "Client Experience in the Future of Law", 2022.
22 Law Society of England and Wales, "Adapting to Client Needs in a Tech-Driven Future", 2023.
23 Legal Practice Management / Access Legal, "Frontiers", 2024.

Chapter 14:
Building lasting, positive relationships with clients

By Thomas Santram, senior vice president and general counsel, Cineplex

The trusted advisor

Building a lasting, positive relationship with a client is a marathon, not a sprint. Once you have made the effort to make a connection, wine and dine a prospective client, and build a personal relationship, the hard work really begins. If you are effective, you may well evolve into that mythical creature to which many lawyers aspire – the trusted advisor.

What does it mean to be the trusted advisor? It means that you will be much more than an external hired gun retained to manage a specific, discrete task. It means that your client will seek your guidance and counsel when contemplating choices and making business decisions – such as mergers, acquisitions, divestitures, new business ventures, corporate and regulatory filings, litigation, and press/publicity. It also means that you will be top of mind when the choice of outside counsel is being considered.

It is important to recognize that, once you attain the distinction of being a trusted advisor, your counsel, guidance, and opinion will likely be sought in areas not related to your core practice area. Once a trusted advisor, you will effectively be an extension of the in-house legal department and perhaps even the company's management team.

Although implicit in the phrase, the trusted advisor has earned the trust of the general counsel and key business leaders. Your conduct, demeanor, and professionalism determine whether you achieve this distinction. Although trite and obvious, you must always put your client's interests first – and always above your own. As I've observed over the years, this is often easier said than done.

Why do general counsel retain external counsel?

As you embark on your relationship with general counsel, it's important to understand the circumstances in which a GC may seek the assistance of external counsel. When I was in private practice, I was a subject matter expert and a revenue generator. I practiced in a discrete area of law, and I generated revenue for my firm based on my degree of specialization and my years of experience.

As GC of a public company, I am much more a generalist than a specialist, and my colleagues and I are seen as a cost center rather than as a source of revenue. We add value, understand the business, and support the revenue-generating parts of our company, but we do not directly generate revenue.

When determining whether to manage a matter internally or task external counsel to do so, I take four factors into consideration – some or all of which assist me in deciding whether to retain external counsel.

1. Does the in-house legal team have the expertise necessary to manage this matter from beginning to end?

In my experience, it is easier to stay up-to-date in private practice than it is in-house. I am a generalist, working in the various lines of business in which my company operates. While I am diligent about keeping current on statutory amendments and case law, I am involved in all aspects of the company's business – commercial contracts, labor and employment law, privacy law, corporate governance, securities law, intellectual property law, commercial litigation, commercial real estate law, construction law... the list goes on and on. The benefit of having external counsel is that lawyers in private practice focus on a well-defined and discrete area of law, and they are experts and not generalists.

2. Does my in-house legal team have the time and workload capacity to take on this new matter?

It is important to assess whether I should send a matter to external counsel – even though the requisite experience and expertise exists within my legal team. Expertise and familiarity aside, I have to assess whether my team has the capacity to take on new tasks – this will very much depend on the proposed timeline for completion.

3. Based on corporate goals and objectives, is it more efficient to ask external counsel to manage this matter? Will external counsel be able to provide the speed and focus required to move the transaction along efficiently and expeditiously?

This is the opposite and equal mirror image to the point above. If timeliness and efficiency are key, then it often makes sense to ask external counsel to assist. Law firms have teams of lawyers, at all levels of experience, who can pick up a file and run with it. This is especially the case in M&A or financing-related work. If a deal is complex or time-sensitive, it often makes sense to let a law firm do the heavy lifting while the in-house team manages the process.

4. Is the cost of retaining external counsel justified when considering the company's goals and objectives?

You should assume that law firm invoices are closely reviewed and scrutinized. No matter the size of the company, make no mistake that the GC is keeping a close eye on external legal costs. Even generous legal budgets are finite – particularly when being used to address the needs of a large, multi-jurisdictional public company. I carefully review law firm invoices, assess the resources and the hourly rates of the lawyers and clerks involved, and determine whether the cost was commensurate to the value received. Expertise and industry should be rewarded – lawyers only have their time and knowledge to sell. However, it is my responsibility to ensure that external counsel are working efficiently and cost-effectively, by assigning lawyers, paralegals, and law clerks at the appropriate experience levels to my files.

General counsel hire lawyers – not law firms

General counsel don't hire law firms – they hire lawyers. A firm's reputation is important in terms of its bench strength, resources, and track record, but ultimately, it is the lawyers who determine the success (or failure) of a transaction.

Ask yourself what you should do to be the lawyer who is hired to represent a company on a particular transaction. The answer to your question is that it's a matter of responsiveness, dependability, and consistency.

Providing up-to-date and professional legal services is table-stakes. It is expected – you won't receive credit for doing so, but you will be penalized if you fail to deliver. My experience has been that the quality of legal services is consistent across firms of a similar nature. What is not consistent is the manner in which legal services are provided. Service is really what sets external counsel apart. My "go-to" lawyers make me feel as though I am their only client. They are:

- *Responsive* – they acknowledge my emails or return phone calls promptly;
- *Dependable* – they meet all agreed upon timelines; and

- *Consistent* – they produce high quality work product, no matter how rushed or complex the transaction.

How to develop, grow, and maintain a relationship with a general counsel

At the beginning of this chapter, I noted that building a lasting, positive relationship with a client is a marathon, not a sprint. It takes time to make connections. Be patient.

Recognize that general counsel receive many solicitations from law firms. This is in addition to the many corporate, legal, and business events that they also attend on a weekly basis. If your invitation to drinks, lunch, or dinner is accepted, that's a win.

Don't expect to immediately receive a file – and certainly don't be visibly surly, impatient, or irritated if you're not immediately promised a file (as once happened to me). That will just make you look unsophisticated and unaware as to how to develop professional relationships – and you certainly won't get a second kick at the can.

It takes multiple encounters to build a relationship. You can't force this or speed it up – the relationship must develop naturally and it must be genuine. Your goal is to try and be top of mind when an opportunity arises and a GC needs external assistance.

General counsel have networks of people with whom they have worked or built relationships over many years. So, why would a GC consider working with someone new? Perhaps their preferred counsel of choice has a conflict of interest on a file, or is on vacation or sick leave, or simply too busy to devote the necessary time and attention to a file. No matter how or why you've been given the opportunity to work with an in-house legal team, you must make sure that you value and take advantage of the opportunity. Your conduct and demeanor will determine whether you are going to be a hired gun for a single, specific file, or whether you will be called on again in future.

Despite being open to meeting new external counsel, I'm always mindful of the needs of my internal clients – my business colleagues. No matter how accomplished, engaging, or persistent you are, if my business colleagues have a good working relationship with a particular lawyer who is dependable and whom they trust, I won't choose alternate counsel and retain you just for the sake of retaining you. It is possible to create new relationships with general counsel, but recognize that this requires time, perseverance, and patience.

As you develop a relationship with general counsel, it is alright to ask about their preferences, needs, and choices. Here are some questions that may assist you in engaging with general counsel:

- How large is your in-house legal department?
- What is the composition of your in-house legal department vis-a-vis lawyers, paralegals, law clerks, and assistants?
- How long has the GC been at the company?
- Was the GC recruited from a firm that provides external legal services? If so, there may well be internal corporate inertia to remain with such a firm – by the company's senior management as well as by the GC.
- For which areas of law does the company most often rely on external counsel?
- How do external counsel best add value?
- What factors make external counsel most effective?
- What are the GC's expectations of external counsel?
- How does the GC decide which lawyers/firms to retain?
- Does the GC hire lawyers from firms of all sizes, or are external counsel only selected from among the larger regional or national firms?

You've received your first file – now what?

Decide what you want from the relationship

At the start of your relationship with a new corporate client, you have to decide what you want from the relationship. Is your goal simply to generate large fees on the initial file, hoping to impress your client so much that further work will follow – or is your goal to build a relationship that will be mutually rewarding on a long-term basis?

I recommend that you focus more on quality work and building a long-lasting relationship than on milking the first file solely for fees. Yes, you've spent years in school and lots of money to become a lawyer but – I'll say it again – this is a marathon, not a sprint.

The rewards of a long-term relationship aren't just monetary – there is prestige in representing respected companies, referrals and marketing opportunities are created when satisfied clients are willing to sing your praises, and, of course, as you grow your client base you will be financially rewarded.

Invest in the relationship

You are a subject matter expert in the area of law in which your new client needs your assistance. In order to be truly effective and add value, you must learn about your client's business. Ask questions of the GC and members of the in-house legal team as to how best to support them, and how best to update them on file status. Meet with the members of the business team responsible for the transaction on which you are working to understand their priorities. Ask if you may visit the company's retail facilities, warehouses, or manufacturing plants to understand the business better. Review recent public disclosure and press releases to understand the larger lines of business in which the company may be involved. Most importantly, don't charge a penny for any of this.

Ask questions

- What are the company's short-term and long-term goals and objectives?
- What are the company's current major initiatives?
- What are the boundaries within which you should be working? Is the company conservative or liberal in terms of risk taking? Is the company in a highly regulated industry?
- What is the posture that the GC wants you to assume? Are you being retained to be a pit bull or a persuasive facilitator?
- What are the "must-haves" versus the "nice to haves"?
- Are you working on a one-off transaction, or are you working with an established long-term partner, or with a new partner that the company hopes will become a long-term partner?

The answers to these questions will determine the style that you should adopt for the file. Armed with this information, you will have a good foundation upon which to build. You have now been given the opportunity to build a relationship with a new corporate client. If all goes well, this will become a long-term and rewarding relationship.

When in-house counsel wish to retain external counsel in a new area, we generally turn to our in-house peers for their recommendations and thoughts. Some lawyers may have big reputations but are difficult to work with; others may delegate all the work to their juniors, so that you're not getting the level of expertise upon which you were counting; some may be disorganized or late with their deliverables. It's important for general counsel to try and determine the level and manner of service they will receive with new external counsel.

The key takeaway with which I'll leave you is that, if you are diligent, timely, and efficient, your clients will deliver you a steady flow of work and become a key source of referrals.

Treat every file as your first, and don't over-focus on your relationship with the GC. It is good and well if a friendship develops, but friendship alone won't keep new work and new files heading your way. General counsel, especially in public companies, have the luxury of choice and options. Not only do they have the budget to hire the lawyers with whom they want to work, there are many lawyers who would jump at the chance to work for a respected corporate client. Don't become complacent or take the relationship for granted. Your seat at the table depends on the value you add, whether you've achieved the company's goals, and earned the trust and confidence of the general counsel and the internal business team.

How will your performance be assessed?

When one is juggling files, the needs of a diverse group of clients, and assorted deadlines, it's easy to focus only on the law, rather than one's personal brand. In order to create a positive personal brand, I recommend that you focus on the following as you work with the in-house legal team:

- *Remain up-to-date on the law.* Be aware of proposed legislation, recent statutory amendments, and new case law.
- *Pay attention to detail.* You will be judged not only by the quality of your words, but also by the manner in which your work is presented. Spelling errors are unforgivable – there's simply no excuse for misspelling words. Make sure that your documents are set out in a clear, easy-to-read format. Present your thoughts in a well-organized and logical manner.
- *Be dependable.* Make sure you meet your commitments. It is alright to ask the timeframe in which the client expects your deliverables – but, once you've made the commitment to a particular date and a specific set of deliverables, it's essential that you honor it. If you're going to be late, give the GC as much notice as possible and make sure that they are alright with the delay. Remember that the GC must manage the expectations of a business team. Your job is to make the GC look good – not have to explain a missed deadline or delayed deliverables.
- *Be timely.* The business world moves quickly. Members of a legal team have their own workloads to manage. You were hired to make their day easier – not to complicate things. Unless absolutely unavoidable, don't

send documents or lengthy requests for instructions at the last minute. Sending your deliverables at the last minute and asking for your client's review and sign-off makes you look disorganized. Your client may be in all day meetings, on a business trip, on vacation, or even home sick. Make sure you provide plenty of time for your client's review and input – and recognize that with most companies, your client will engage with the larger internal business team to make sure that the business folks and the lawyers are aligned. If you send documents in a timely manner and provide everyone with reasonable time, you will garner the GC's favor and build a positive, professional, and organized reputation for yourself.

- *Be strategic.* Whether negotiating contracts, conducting transactions, or managing litigation, make sure that your client has a full understanding of all possible outcomes as well as your planned response to each. It's easier to manage a process when you've thought through, and prepared your client for, the various scenarios that might present themselves, and it's important that your client not be surprised by circumstances that may arise.
- *Reporting and billing.* Ask the GC how, and how often, status updates should be provided as well as the format and manner of delivery. Does the GC prefer telephone calls, video calls, or emails? Should updates be provided in person? How much detail is required?

Your role is to make it easy for the in-house legal team to manage the transaction for which you've been retained, and to ensure that choosing you as counsel reflects well on the in-house team. At the conclusion of a transaction, even if the end result was positive, all the lunches, gift baskets, and complimentary tickets to concerts and sports events won't matter if you do not appear to be at the top of your game – or if you are perceived as not being easy to work with.

What does success look like for general counsel?

Success may mean many things. Here are some of the considerations I keep in mind when doing a post-transaction assessment of how external counsel conducted themselves.

- *Relationship of the parties.* At the conclusion of the transaction, did the parties have a good relationship – or did overzealous lawyering harm the business relationship? It's critically important to me that new and existing relationships be preserved – and even improved – as a result of the transaction. If the parties' respective businesspeople are unhappy with each other at the end of the transaction, then it is not a win, even if your client's company achieves its desired business goals. It's important that you pay attention to, and be guided by, the tone that the general counsel wants you to take.

- *Goals*. Did the transaction achieve the company's financial goals and business objectives? Were the "must-haves" obtained? You should be practical, weigh priorities, and be willing to give up on some demands in order to achieve the broader needs of the company. You won't win everything. If both sides are a little unhappy with the final deal, that is generally a sign of a "fair" deal. My concern is that, when looking at the transaction as a whole, I can justify the time and expense that we undertook when I look at the results we achieved.

- *Timeliness*. Did the transaction close on time? Were there specific product-related, seasonal, or tax-related reasons why the transaction had to be concluded by a particular date? If so, did we meet the deadline?

- *Cost*. Was the transaction completed on budget? In-house legal departments are perceived as cost centers rather than as revenue generators. Despite often significant budgets, there are many demands on the legal team's budget. The general counsel must adjust to new market realities, unexpected litigation, or simply ensuring that the company's business operations are in good standing in all the jurisdictions in which it operates. All of this is to say that law firm invoices are carefully reviewed to ensure that the legal services were provided as efficiently as possible, and that the appropriate level of expertise (i.e., lawyer, paralegal, law clerk, etc.) was assigned to the file. Clients will not thank you if multiple lawyers are unnecessarily assigned to a file, or if a senior lawyer is attending to tasks best handled by a junior lawyer.

- *Efficiency*. Was external counsel a seamless extension of the in-house legal and business teams? I'm sensitive to the legal department – and by extension, external counsel – being seen as a hindrance to the efficient progress, and successful conclusion, of a deal. Were deliverables on time, or were they late or provided at the last minute? Were the businesspeople worried about the pace at which the transaction was progressing? It is up to you to make sure that no one questions the GC's decision to hire you.

If this is your first file with a new client, you will not have the goodwill earned through a prior working relationship. If you have worked with the client before, the GC will naturally assess your prior performance when determining whether to send another file to you.

Add value to the working relationship

You can deepen your relationship with the in-house team and add value in the following ways:

- *Refer your client to other lawyers / law firms.* Yes, you read that correctly. If asked whether you or your firm can assist with a file, you should definitely let your client know if your firm is not the best choice for a particular file. Better that the client gets an excellent result elsewhere, than you or your firm handle the file and achieve a substandard result. By being willing to consider what's best for the company rather than what's best for you and your firm, you will earn the trust, respect, and appreciation of the GC. This will cement your position as a key business partner of the GC and of the company. You will recall that your challenge as you were trying to develop the relationship was to be top of mind. By giving honest, selfless advice to your client, you will help cement your position as the first person to call when the GC requires external expertise.

- *Offer complimentary attendance at your firms continuing legal education events.* All members of an in-house legal team should strive to remain up-to-date in their respective areas of responsibility. As you work with various members of the in-house legal team, invite them to your firm's educational events. Continuing legal education is not just for lawyers and it's very often non-lawyers who recommend external lawyers to the GC. Inviting members of the in-house team to your events provides you with the opportunity to generate goodwill, and to introduce them to members of your firm in other practice areas.

- *Offer to conduct Lunch 'n' Learns at your client's offices.* Be proactive. Don't wait to be asked. Members of in-house legal teams were specialists when they worked at law firms. Now in-house, they have a broader, more general mandate, often involving many different areas of law. Since you invested in the relationship by learning about your client's business, you will have a keen and informed sense of changes in the law, which will be of interest to your client. Offering Lunch 'n' Learns that are focused on new statutes, regulations, or case law will assist in-house team members with their roles – and if they have questions on an area of law that you covered, they will likely call you if they need to retain external counsel regarding that area of law. An advantage of conducting events like this at your client's offices is that GC will often invite members of business teams to hear what external counsel have to say. This type of exposure deepens your engagement with the in-house legal and business teams.

- *Speaking invitations.* Invite the GC, lawyers, and other senior members of the in-house team to speak on panels at events that your firm is holding or sponsoring. This not only helps raise the profile of the in-house team members, it also allows you to introduce them as your clients. Having high-profile clients helps raise your and your firm's profile and may help attract other similarly high-profile clients.
- *Social engagement with members of your firm.* Law firms hold various client development social events during the course of the year. These events may include cocktail receptions, legal professional events, lunches with prominent speakers, charity dinners sponsored by your firm, sporting events, and concerts. Inviting the GC and members of the in-house team to these events allows you to socialize for fun rather than engage on a specific file-related task. Events like this – especially sporting events and concerts – are a fun night out.
- *Annual or semi-annual lunches.* These lunches are different from the ones you had when you were trying to begin the relationship with the GC. These are "value-add" meetings, based on your day-to-day engagement with members of the in-house legal and business teams. Some of my company's external counsel use these lunches to provide advice and guidance on best practices, risk mitigation, and proposed legislation that may affect business operations. These lunches should be directed to the appropriate legal team member – and not just to the general counsel – as this helps broaden your relationship within the legal team. This is another way in which you might be able to integrate yourself as a natural, trusted extension of the in-house team.
- *Sponsorships.* Companies often hold charity events throughout the year, and they encourage key business partners to participate. By sponsoring such events and by attending with your colleagues, you will affirm your place as a business partner and engage with the senior-most levels of the company.
- *Gift giving.* Companies have policies against employees accepting gifts,

but they understand that it's traditional for suppliers to send gifts to clients – especially in December. It is quite common for law firms to send gift baskets to the GC – all of which are generous and expensive and very much appreciated. My colleagues are as responsible for the legal department's success as I am, and all such gifts are shared among the entire in-house legal team. The trend now is to send practical gifts, such as law firm-branded travel accessories, backpacks, overnight bags, portfolios, travel mugs, chargers, and clothing. These items are useful and provide a longer-term reminder of your firm's support than a gift basket. It doesn't hurt to have your law firm-branded mugs on someone's desk – or a branded charger in someone's bag.

Final thoughts

It is the legal team's role to explain the law to management and to provide advice and recommendations on the company's next steps. Don't engage with members of the management team without the GC's permission. In your eagerness to build relationships within the company, be careful not to step on the GC's toes or deliver advice in a way that the GC does not approve. Translating and messaging complex legal concepts to management is a task best left to the general counsel and members of the in-house legal team.

Remember that every single member of the in-house team is your client – not just the GC. Members of my team are subject matter experts. They know the company and they've earned my trust and respect. I expect them to be accorded the same respect as I am. They work directly with external counsel, and they regularly advise me as to which external counsel add value and are at the top of their game – they also advise me of external counsel who are difficult to work with, miss deadlines, or are disorganized. Please treat each and every one of them with respect; they are as much your client as the GC.

As you build relationships with the in-house team, remember to engage with younger team members. People move from company to company, older people retire, others are promoted. Within a few years, the junior lawyer on the team may have an expanded area of responsibility and a loftier title. If you have built a strong relationship, you will be rewarded as the junior lawyer is promoted or moves to a higher position at another company. The vice president, legal or the VC whom you are now courting were once junior lawyers.

Your goal is to become a trusted advisor. Take the time and make the effort to build a strong foundation for your relationship. Deliver to the highest standards possible and treat every file as your first (lest it be your last).

Chapter 15:
Reimagining the law firm–client relationship in an age of AI ubiquity and data-centricity

By Robert Dilworth, managing director and associate general counsel, Bank of America

Introduction

Shift happens. In two ways, as Ernest Hemingway wrote of bankruptcy: "Gradually and then suddenly."[1] For the legal profession, "suddenly" will soon be our present.

Our opportunity

Advances in Artificial Intelligence (AI) will likely change our profession more within the next decade than in the past century. The consensus at a July 2024 UK solicitors roundtable was that "the legal sector will be significantly transformed, and at a faster pace than is currently expected" and "will be subject to large-scale disruption which.... would likely be larger than the impact of the internet revolution on English law".[2] This prediction extends beyond England and Wales to comparable developed economies and legal systems.

Today, almost 70 years after the first microchip and 30 years after the democratization of internet access, humanity is poised for another fundamental societal leap. We live at the cusp of the fastest transformation in human history,[3] elements of which have been compared to the steam engine of the mind and a cognitive industrial revolution.[4] Decades of exponentially doubled computational power, decreased storage costs, and compounded network effects have converged. Across society, rapid advances in AI, particularly Generative AI (GenAI), are turbocharging the analogue-to-digital transition that the COVID-19 pandemic catalyzed – in speed, expanded breadth, higher stakes, and urgency.[5] This transformation comes against a backdrop of unabated climate change and seismic generational and demographic shifts in many economies.

These AI advances already have transformative consequences for knowledge workers. Neural networks routinely double in performance within months, enabling users of the latest foundational models to produce university student-level work. Legal domain-specific tools generate draft results matching early-career lawyers. OpenAI's GPT-4 foundational model – with no additional training and only single prompts – can pass the US Uniform Bar Examination in the top 90th percentile.[6] Predictions about artificial general intelligence (AGI) – a human-like performance level in learning, reasoning, and adapting to new situations – seem less like science fiction, and interconnected AI agents may soon assist many of our routine tasks as personal work robots.

This trajectory is clear and accelerating. As Wharton professor Ethan Mollick advises, "Assume this is the worst AI you will ever use", and "There is no reason to suspect the abilities of AI systems are going to stop growing anytime soon".[7] Leading legal futurist Professor Richard Susskind frames it similarly: "We are still at the foothills", "There is no apparent finishing line", "The transformation will result from a combination of innovations across our system", and "We should expect accelerated incremental changes".[8]

Legal professionals who use these tools wisely – matching their strengths to appropriate uses, knowing the limitations, and retaining ownership of the process and work product – have powerful new partners that will improve their and the technology's value propositions.[9] Much higher client-centricity and creative professional service levels are attainable; our failure to achieve this will result from human choice, not unintuitive technology or high switching costs. Few practitioners and law firms have such unique franchises and business models that they can risk not adapting.

Our challenge

This chapter challenges individual lawyers to embrace a transformation credo by expanding their professional self-concept and value proposition for our changing world. It examines the evolution of the law firm–corporate client relationship since the emergence of the modern law firm and invites readers to re-imagine this dynamic for an age of AI ubiquity and data-centricity. Drawing from the author's law firm and in-house experience in global financial services, it reframes the relationship to make it more client- and human-focused, fitter for purpose, and able to deliver more significant, lasting value.

Each member of the legal services industry is a subject of and a participant in these fundamental changes. Daily announcements of innovations or improved capabilities reveal our modernity and mindset gaps. Our profession has resisted the level of digital transformation that has affected other industries and spheres of daily life. Some of us believe that our unique role gives us dispensation. Others comfortably believe that incremental changes in our work methods will suffice, mirroring how changes in the substance of the law usually lag society. The latter aids the law's legitimacy in support of the social contract; the former weakens our professional legitimacy if failure to adapt impairs what clients and society need from us – in their minds, "value". Others let themselves off the hook by accepting with resignation the difficulty of change as if they had no agency or responsibility.

Reality is voraciously consuming the exceptionalists', denialists', and defeatists' remaining oxygen. As commentator and legal industry transformation expert Mark Cohen puts it, "Gen AI has revoked their hall pass".[10] Regardless of whether intended, a profession defined by exceptionalism, incrementalism, and defeatism is shortsightedly extractive in practice and hobbled in its potential value to society. Instead, we must boldly reimagine our role and methods for the balance of a century in which the pace of change will vastly dwarf that of the first quarter.[11] This future holds no referendum; instead, we face an existential challenge to our human adaptability that will be decided with or without our consent. Our sole choice is whether to adapt, shape, and thrive rather than merely survive. This challenge is no spectator sport – there is no attendance award. Agile, engaged individuals and teams are best set to flourish.

If granted a greenfield opportunity to design a client-focused legal services delivery model for an AI-ubiquitous, data-centric world, we would not choose the status quo. Deeply ingrained structural and cultural features make a *tabula rasa* approach unlikely. However, our past need not be prologue – we have agency. Ambitious, blue-sky design thinking can inspire us to overcome incrementalism's allure. Readers who understand and embrace this chapter's themes can catalyze a long-overdue user-centric professional transformation and renewal. This would benefit us individually, collectively, and societally.

Value in tectonic times

Our fundamental value

Our value as legal services professionals – whether in law firms, departments, individual practices, or allied ecosystem functions – derives from our evolving societal role.

Rapid and profound technological advances and the most significant single workplace demographic shift since World War II present unprecedented opportunities and challenges for society. This is in addition to the existential consequences of climate change.

Many individuals and institutions will face a crisis of adaptation as machines become more capable and accelerated multi-dimensional change becomes the norm.[12] This includes the legal profession and services industry, where success will require an agile, dynamic blend of human and machine intelligence. The more closely humans and machines interact, the greater the need for human values and emotional (EQ) and social (SQ) intelligence in designing, using, and governing these tools. This is a socio-technical revolution in which changes in employment, longevity, education, climate, and other fundamental aspects of human sustainability will further test governmental, political, and legal institutions and our citizens' commitment to the rule of law. It suffices to look at the daily news to confirm that we do not start from a position of strength – the rule of law and institutions built over decades and centuries are viewed by too many citizens as tools to perpetuate elitist privilege. Reversing this sad reality should be our lodestar as we upgrade ourselves and our profession for the future.

Legal professionals (including many readers of this chapter) typically enjoy privileged educational and learning opportunities and access to key institutions and societal actors. Working with these institutions and actors across multiple remits and disciplines, we have the opportunity and duty to play a critical role in shaping society's responses to the intractable challenges arising from these rapid and fundamental changes. These challenges include responsible, legal, and ethical development, balancing human capital and machine learning, and using AI and other advanced technologies to affirm and uplift our humanity. Our privileged positions grant us no entitlement to join these conversations and be taken seriously. Only a strong, vibrant legal profession can earn a meaningful voice.

From Gutenberg to the Reformation, Enlightenment, Industrial Revolution, and today's globalized information economy, the democratization of knowledge has consistently triumphed over traditional authority and knowledge transmission structures.[13] However, a quarter of the way into the 21st century, much of our profession and major legal systems remain mired in 20th-century ways. Historically and culturally, we are gatekeepers of esoteric learnings and client guardians. Modern society needs much more from us – proactive engagement, not reactive insularity.

The prevailing legal culture fits many of us comfortably. It informs our individual and collective self-perception. Despite our belief that we are client-focused, our profession is deeply *lawyer-centric*. It is maladapted to fulfilling our societal purpose to deliver value in a user, *human-centric* world of accelerated disintermediation, disaggregation of services and expertise, the democratization of access, and relentless focus on collaboration, sharing, and user/customer empowerment.

To thrive in this new world and unlock our potential value, we must reimagine our role for an age of client-centricity, improved access, and human empowerment – positioning us to help shape the rest of our century.

The current service and lawyer formation model
The technological advances and demographic changes challenging civil society also stress our profession's current legal services delivery and training models. This affects our ability to deliver the value that modern society demands. To the extent the present system evolved from holistic design principles, these reflected bygone economic eras of information scarcity and human capital-intensive, one-on-one manual processes. We must first examine the US origin of the current "big law" external firm model to understand and design where we must head.

The development of the "big law" model
The so-called "Cravath System" with its steep pyramidal partnership and tournament "up or out" advancement system, and the rise of in-house legal departments in the US through four phases,[14] responded to the emergence of the share corporation as the predominant business vehicle, specialization, the growth of the legislative and regulatory state in response to societal complexity, and scale – all as they existed in an early and mid-industrial economy. This labor model originated before the rise of the steel industry, the automobile age, mass production, consumer society, professional business management methods and, of course, the information age. It relied on human capital inputs, generally priced by time, experience level, and salary (if work was internalized). It used minimally data-informed work methods and developed in an era of information scarcity about the law's content, lore, and private precedents. Dependent on manual processes, its scalability in response to economic growth and industrialization consisted of adding new one-one-one human inputs or squeezing more units (hours) out of the existing ones. As corporate legal departments grew in number, size, and stature, departing law firm associates (and sometimes partners) became the

in-house talent pipeline – often joining one of the law firm's clients. Many lawyers, once in-house, still reflect cultural traits tied to their legal educations and law firm provenance.

Young lawyer formation followed a similar human capital-intensive pattern. After completing years of law school, focused mainly on doctrinal law and legal reasoning (which followed an undergraduate degree in many countries), practical training occurred through observation and working with more experienced colleagues in a loose apprentice system. This remains the dominant method. The quality of experience and outcome were (and remain) highly variable depending on the firm, the formality of its system (some countries and firms having well-structured traineeships), and individual junior/senior pairings. An inefficient, piecemeal system perpetuates elitism and inequality.

Some firms (led initially in the US by Cravath and its peers) had excellent comprehensive training programs. Their efficacy depended on aligned economic incentives, limited lateral movement, and strong information asymmetry between law firms and clients. Twenty-first-century features lower the incentives for long-term investment in training and developing young lawyers, including the billable hour model and annual billing quotas, higher associate-to-partner leverage ratios, profitability pressure on young lawyers to specialize sooner, frequent lateral movement of associates before firms recoup their training investment, partner mobility, law firm mergers as a means of growth, and corporate client sophistication, specialization, and focus on controlling external costs.[15] These stressors existed well before GenAI's emergence. As discussed below, although AI ubiquity in our industry presents additional economic challenges, it also brings great opportunities, including improving our professional formation system.

Limitations of the "big law" model in the digital age
This model's limitations – already stressed in the aftermath of the 2008-2009 global financial crisis when a buyer's market decisively emerged – are increasingly apparent. Structurally, it suffers from misaligned incentives for innovation and capital investment.[16] Law firms are relatively capital-light enterprises that sell know-how, services, and reputation – credence goods. Some of the most profitable and influential ones sell Veblen goods – their high cost reinforces their desirability.

Adapting to the digital age requires additional investment and a multi-year cultural change program. In many jurisdictions, non-lawyer ownership or investment in a legal practice is prohibited; capital investment must come from earnings. Partners own these earnings and are notoriously focused on annual distributions and league tables. Influence and decision-making power may over-index members closer to the end of their equity partner status. In such cases, near-term interests can trump the strategic since long-term fundamental investments (and distribution decreases) may mainly benefit successors. Younger partners are not absolved – relentless competition for market share, lateral recruitment wars and mergers as a means of growth, and a focus on ever-increasing profits per equity partner as indicia of personal success and firm health also lead some partners to view as optional the longer-term improvements that share corporations treat as investments.

Marked-up, leveraged input costs, rather than outcomes and results, stubbornly remain the primary measure of value and pricing. This dependence leads some partners to resist innovations that reduce billable hours, as the alternative is less proven. The simplicity of billable hour pricing can be a fair risk allocation for novel, highly complex, or open-ended matters with little price experience data. Corporate clients have long insisted that detailed time-based billing replace cursory invoices "for services rendered".[17]

Despite its enduring role, the billable hour did not descend from Mount Sinai with Moses and the Ten Commandments. Today, quality data increasingly exists or can be derived for many commercial law matters. Too few firms and clients have partnered to harness experience data to improve the time-spent proxy, identify its ideal scope, and better inform the development and use of alternate value and pricing models. Standardization, taxonomy, and ontology efforts such as the SALI Alliance and the Standard for Open Legal Information (SOLI) are critical steps towards comparability, transparency, and greater efficiency in buying, selling, and pricing legal services.

Hints of change

Despite these cultural and structural limitations, even before GenAI entered the popular consciousness in November 2022, some firms anticipated the possibility of a significantly changed model, disruption, or clients' need for parallel service models. A handful of UK-based firms were pioneers within the common law countries, gradually influencing others worldwide.

These foresightful actors provide much of the thought leadership in the sector. They establish and hire professional chief operating officers and directors of innovation, knowledge management, AI, and practice innovation.

They recruit data engineers, scientists, and analysts. They publish and speak to promote mindset growth and change. Not content just to *optimize* existing lawyering and delivery paradigms, they *innovate* by considering new paradigms and proven techniques from the rest of society. They intelligently develop learnings and provide markets for vendor innovation through productization and subscription models, alternate advanced delivery solutions groups, internal labs and incubators, or even "self-disruption" subsidiaries that use new work and pricing methods and have independent clients.

Although their expressed mandate may not be to transform and replace the firms' existing models, these firms recognize the potential for a reckoning or disruption and the need to develop parallel service models.[18] They, and those inspired by their example, will be best poised for an age of AI ubiquity and data-centricity.

The in-house dilemma and problems of scale
Working at the coal face, in-house counsels also have structural and cultural handicaps. Their primary work tool is their annual quota of human capital hours in return for an often static (at best) annual salary. Adding new colleagues is frequently extraordinarily challenging. While in-house counsel may have access to external counsel and contract lawyers, they have tight external cost budgets, savings metrics, and constant pressure to internalize more matters ("provide more for less"). Regular outside counsel rate increases stress the legal department's budget, which answers to corporate imperatives, and creates friction in what could be a highly collaborative relationship.

In-house counsels suffer ever-greater work volumes, increased pace and complexity, and compressed time cycles. More is required than simply wringing out cost efficiencies year after year and automating existing workflows. Too few understand that the nature, volume, and pace of legal work are driven by complexity in society – exponential, self-reinforcing, and non-linear. As Microsoft Legal's Jason Barnwell aptly captured it in 2021, "That's not the tide coming in; the seas are rising".[19] The projected new AI-generated world economic activity, even if only half correct or if it takes more time to materialize, will further accelerate legal demand's complexity, volume, and pace. Linear 1:1 human capital addition (where possible) will only temporarily relieve a non-linear problem.[20] Unprepared in-house legal functions will need to sound a tsunami warning.

It is intuitively mathematical that legal professionals must harness the same types of digitalized forces and tools in response to accelerated demand for legal work as the forces and tools that fuel the acceleration. Those who understand this and call for action often face an uphill cultural and organizational struggle. Corporate legal functions typically represent well under 0.5 percent of the company's workforce; we are frustrated that our companies fail to appreciate our uniqueness as much as we do.

Although corporations have capital and reinvest in the business, legal departments (despite being full of trained advocates) have difficulty owning and broadening their value narrative from "only a cost center" to "also a value enabler". This grossly underestimates the enterprise value of an optimized internal legal function – there is substantial latent value to capture.[21] This results in a soul-sapping catch-22 in which it is hard to prove value in the language of business (empirical data and projected return on investment) if the company does not invest in the requisite tools for the legal department, and if the legal department is not sufficiently data-fluent to use them to advantage. If companies and their legal departments fail to break this cycle, legal professionals may have their first exposure to next-generation tools and methods indirectly through the external providers that they are charged with managing proactively. This is suboptimal since, if deprived of experience, many internal counsels will remain information supplicants of external counsel and more susceptible to innovation theatre by firms that are less committed to transformation.

New model solutions – a virtuous cycle?

An alternate, more hopeful client-driven scenario is possible. The following description is primarily based on an article and accompanying diagram (reproduced overleaf) by Richard Tromans, founder of *Artificial Lawyer* and TromansConsulting.[22]

GenAI is a general-purpose technology that is especially fit for the knowledge work at the heart of many corporations. Internal resources and learnings will develop as capabilities improve, corporations normalize GenAI use, and GenAI becomes the center of operational excellence initiatives.[23] Corporate expectations will rise regarding GenAI use in the legal function. In-house teams will develop proficiency and confidence in appropriate uses. They may start with learnings from private experimentation, the GenAI tools generally available in their enterprise, or use cases in legal operations. They will become more in tune with the modern methods of the wider business.

They will mount more effective internal cases, creating a virtuous circle. At a minimum, they will be forced to demand greater GenAI use by external counsel.

Law firms are reactive creatures – they exist in a buyer's market that will only deepen. As firms adapt and recalibrate in response to client pressure, a positive feedback loop could emerge whereby greater use and investment drive improved and more innovative legal sector LLM products. In-house familiarity and use will increase, driving the expectations and recalibration cycle. Lawyers from these firms who later join in-house teams will bring these skills and approaches. The cycle of innovation, corporate acceptance, and normalization, increased exposure/use by in-house teams, heightened expectations of external providers backed by in-house legal control of external spending, and external provider recalibration (including investment in the sector) will continue. Rinse, repeat.

Figure 1 illustrates this scenario.

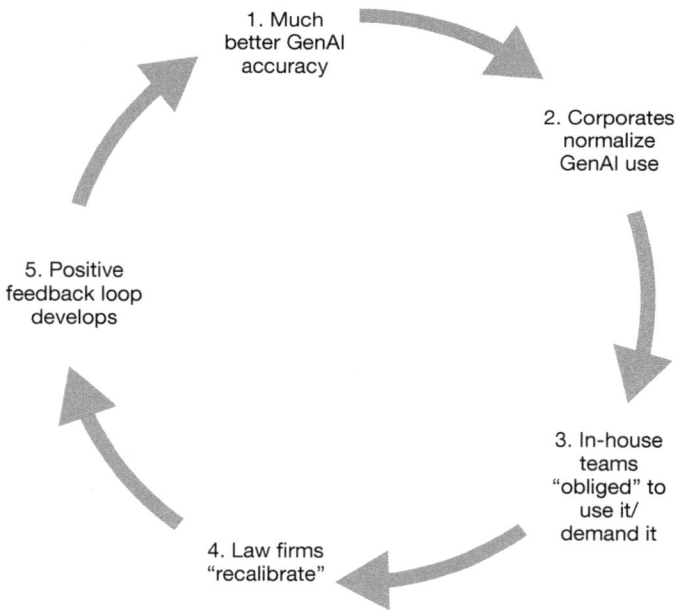

Figure 1: A virtuous cycle of AI innovation. Source: Artificial Lawyer / TromansConsulting.

AI ubiquity, the evolving nature of knowledge work, and the service model challenge

Knowledge work is our stock in trade. The legal order and our mastery are society's operating system (OS),[24] the foundation of which is legal and institutional concepts embedded in language – our coin of the realm. We anticipate outcomes based on obtaining and analysing information. Today, we have an information surfeit, not scarcity. Attention is our scarcest commodity – without it, we cannot offer clients our highest human skills in the needed measure. As a recent *Financial Times* commentary said, "An empty mind may be the devil's workshop, but it is also the birthplace of creativity. The capacity to connect seemingly unconnected facts and have "Aha" moments is unique to humans, and AI will struggle to do the same."[25]

Large Language Models (LLMs) and tools incorporating them excel increasingly in language-based tasks, whether generative, extractive, summary, or otherwise. They read, research, draft, and organize processes with increasing accuracy and agentic autonomy. They provide a powerful lens that enhances our unassisted vision. Unlike humans, they operate at scale. They identify, sift, summarize, and identify patterns. Humans use these outputs as the raw materials for their analysis and judgment.[26]

Appropriately used, these new tools promise to empower, humanize, and elevate our practices by creating space to tap the latent value in us that our current survival struggle against work volumes and information overload traps and obscures. Not only can we do "more for less" – these tools also enable a long overdue boost to our level of client centricity. LLMs' high (and improving) proficiency and semantic awareness enable a material redesign of substantive legal work. The intuitive, natural human-to-computer interactions of GenAI versions erase traditional barriers to tech adoption in our field. We no longer must conform our tasks to fit a rigidly engineered software's view of legal workflows. The pairing of a human expert and a machine working in a fluid conversation mimics how we collaborate with human colleagues. The fact that many of these tools work optimally with a human in the loop to guide inputs and review outputs matches perfectly our high professional standards and ethical obligations.[27]

In a world of AI ubiquity and data-centricity, the above qualities challenge the existing value and pricing paradigms based primarily on reselling human capital – inputs, versus selling outcomes. Legal work has countless language-based process elements that these tools can replace or enhance in outcome or efficiency. Even the most elite "bet or save the company" work may have processes or other elements that can be made more efficient and consistent. Those who delay this realization and the needed adaptation do so at their peril. Followers will not get there first – in the coming era of value differentiation and repositioning, being a fast second may not suffice.

Work resorting and fault lines in the artisanal model

In a foundational 2024 whitepaper, Factor Law states that, "The foreseeable future is a buyer's market, and the GC will flex unprecedented influence in the strategic sorting of legal markets, across service providers and technology vendors".[28] Authors Ed Sohn and Jae Um expect GenAI to reshape legal work comprising 80 percent of corporate legal sending (see Figure 2 overleaf). All commodity work (about five percent of corporate spending) will be affected. The bread and butter "core" work (about 85 percent of corporate legal work) could have an 85 percent GenAI impact since these tools are well-matched against the human factors, organizational complexity, and scale challenges characterizing this segment. Here is the fault line where our profession's artisanal model will most likely crack first and demand alternatives. Even 50 percent of the most elite (or "cream") work (about 15 percent of total spending), presenting the highest novelty and legal complexity, could have a 50 percent GenAI impact as client preferences tilt towards the most innovative and AI-fluent providers.

The lesson is evident – to succeed in an AI-ubiquitous, data-centric world, each legal services supply chain member must offer a compelling value proposition to corporate clients. In the inevitable sorting, each must be ruthlessly honest about its strategic position and differentiating capabilities.[29] This institutional introspection must include a clear-eyed assessment of the provider's culture and willingness to change.

The opportunity for our clients, stakeholders, and profession

Businesses with one or more lawyers drive more than 50 percent of legal services spending globally (with the US share exceeding that of other nations combined),[30] creating the primary market for legal services innovation. Learnings discovered and scale achieved in commercial legal services define the art of the possible and establish the state of the art at any time. Once adopted at scale, innovations in the large enterprise world often diffuse vertically down to smaller businesses and consumers. Successive innovations should ripple down and make providing legal services to historically underserved businesses and individuals financially attractive. Understanding this

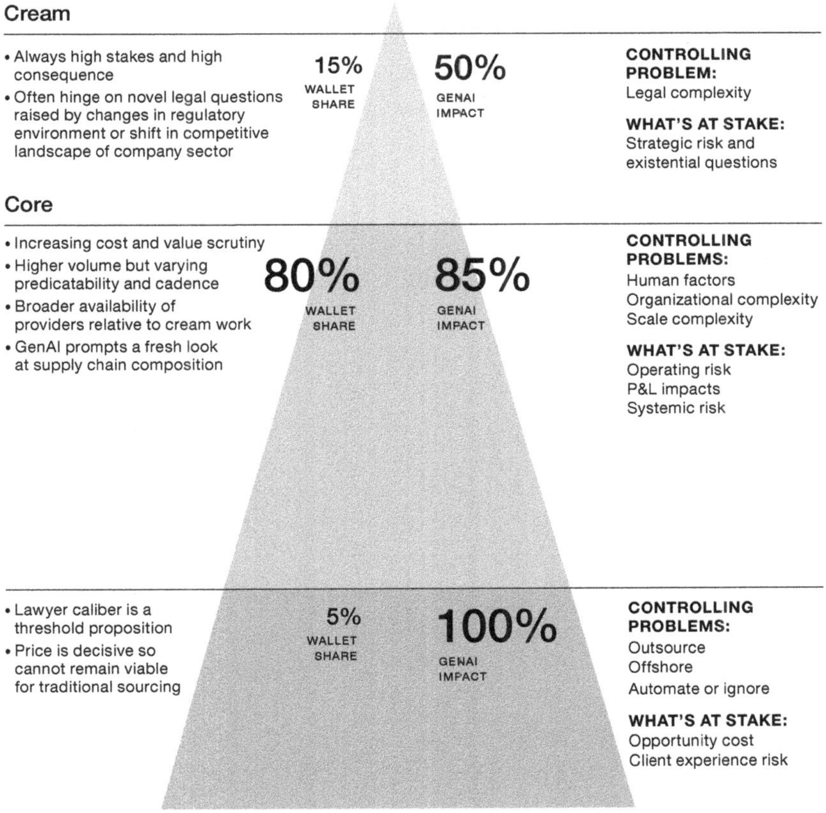

Cream

- Always high stakes and high consequence
- Often hinge on novel legal questions raised by changes in regulatory environment or shift in competitive landscape of company sector

15% WALLET SHARE

50% GENAI IMPACT

CONTROLLING PROBLEM:
Legal complexity

WHAT'S AT STAKE:
Strategic risk and existential questions

Core

- Increasing cost and value scrutiny
- Higher volume but varying predicatability and cadence
- Broader availability of providers relative to cream work
- GenAI prompts a fresh look at supply chain composition

80% WALLET SHARE

85% GENAI IMPACT

CONTROLLING PROBLEMS:
Human factors
Organizational complexity
Scale complexity

WHAT'S AT STAKE:
Operating risk
P&L impacts
Systemic risk

- Lawyer caliber is a threshold proposition
- Price is decisive so cannot remain viable for traditional sourcing

5% WALLET SHARE

100% GENAI IMPACT

CONTROLLING PROBLEMS:
Outsource
Offshore
Automate or ignore

WHAT'S AT STAKE:
Opportunity cost
Client experience risk

Figure 2: Reshaping of the corporate legal wallet. Source: Factor Law and Six Parsecs.

relationship and accelerating this process provide a golden invitation to improve our individual and collective value proposition to meet the needs of our clients and their stakeholders and, by extension, civil society.

Meeting this challenge promises improved professional, client, and stakeholder value. As machines perform or assist with more transactional, procedural, informational, and documentary activities,[31] we can elevate our practices to a higher point on our law licenses, improve our job satisfaction, wellbeing and human sustainability,[32] and create space to be(come) trusted advisors and ethicists at a time of increased need.[33] This future will be empowering and humanizing. We will have time to focus more on the activities that humans do uniquely well and that machines cannot yet replace – personalized, relationship-based, high-value, and strategic advisory and advocacy work.[34]

We can be predictive and preventative, focusing on dispute avoidance, not just its efficient resolution. We can advance new lawyers' training curves to spend less time learning by chance, osmosis, and induction from repetitive tasks. They can deliver client value sooner and contribute to their firms' business. We can attain better service scalability in response to ever-increasing client demand wrought by the same societal forces. This will allow us to offer clients additional services and levels of research, diligence, and advice that require difficult cost-benefit trade-offs under a solely one-on-one human capital model. We can meet the "more for less challenge" by doing more and of greater depth and consistency with the same or fewer resources – this is called *value for money*. Leveraging these tools will empower smaller and minority-owned practices, or even dispersed ad hoc teams,[35] to move up the value chain and compete with larger firms for sophisticated work. Entrepreneurial solo practitioners will have new opportunities to build sophisticated and rewarding practices and retain greater control over their careers.[36]

We should not expect seamless changes. There will be leaders, followers, winners, and losers. As the Shirky Principle affirms, "Institutions will try to preserve the problem to which they are the solution".[37] We must recognize and call out manifestations of this principle in ourselves. This behavior is more prevalent and pernicious in an elitist, exceptionalist culture – a poison that retards innovation through its visceral rejection of successful, but "not invented here, not made by lawyers" solutions.[38]

Our fundamental choice

Rather than clinging to existing service and talent delivery models because they benefit us, and constantly straining to shoehorn a changed world into our construct, being *client-centric* and delivering *value* means we recalibrate these models to the needs of an evolving *world*.[39] Bold thinking and action starting today can transform the law firm–client relationship from a primarily transactional, friction-filled, increasingly zero-sum game to one of intentional (not accidental) design – an essential partnership in a reimagined multi-faceted service delivery ecosystem that is deeply collaborative, strategic, integrated, symbiotic, and rewarding – one fit for purpose in the current age.

We need radical reorientation, focusing *much* less on what the changes discussed in this chapter mean for legal professionals and legal services and much more on what opportunities these changes bring for clients and client service.

Mindset, skills, and formation in a VUCA world

The future belongs to life-long learners – "learn-it-alls", not "know-it-alls". The businesses and legal services providers (individually and collectively) destined to flourish in such a rich, inter-generationally diverse, AI-ubiquitous, data-centric world will possess qualities far beyond those taught to date in law schools and commercial practice. Domain knowledge and technical acumen are table stakes. Our education and training exalt deduction and convergent thinking. We are Olympic medalists in identifying problems – often as solo *problem diagnosticians*.

Our present and foreseeable VUCA (volatile, uncertain, complex, ambiguous) world requires us to be *problem solvers*, often as part of teams that will increasingly be multidisciplinary and seek integrated solutions.[40] Success in this environment requires additional qualities such as a foundational digital literacy and mindset, curiosity, an open inquiry lifelong learning mindset, EQ and SQ, resilience, cross-cultural competency and a global outlook, team mentality, purpose, and outcome orientation.[41] We are called to marshal the full range of convergent, divergent, left-brain (logic, analysis, math, data) and right-brain (creativity, experimentation, empathy, discernment, intuition, visual representation) cognitive approaches to find solutions and relate to people as and where they are. Our teaching, mentoring, and communications must reflect our multigenerational audience's learning and information consumption preferences. We have many of the requisite tools in our factory-installed human kit, just dulled and under-used. We can awaken and sharpen them. We can recruit, attract, and collaborate with people with these skills in greater measure.[42]

Demographics and diversity

Greater human longevity means our workforce now includes five generations or life stages. No part of modern society is untouched. Millennials and Gen Zs are set to take over every major institution of society.[43] This includes law firms, internal legal departments, their respective clients, vendors, customers, opposing parties, and representatives of the institutional and societal actors they work with.

Millennials are already (as of 2022) the most populous group in the US legal profession; Baby Boomers and Gen Xers are shrinking pluralities within law firms and legal departments.[44] Even where older generations (some members described as "pale, male, and stale") still dominate management and strategic decision-making, younger employees and partners have expectations, motivations, and success measures beyond financial security.

Our younger colleagues treasure authenticity and bring their whole selves, including values, to work daily. Skeptical of hierarchy, they value equality and participation in decision-making. They are more apt than their seniors to focus on work–life balance, wellness, sustainability, purpose, and meaning. To many, long hours to the detriment of family or health signal a poor role model, not a badge of honor.[45] As a class, they are set to benefit from the most significant intergenerational wealth transfer in history – some will have the financial cushion to support values-based decisions to improve some of the inherited problems they will live with for decades. They are less likely to aim by default for the safest or most remunerative option or see law firm partnership as the career pinnacle. Mobility in pursuing their career and personal goals is viewed as a virtue, not an indicator of lack of commitment or ambition or a sign of workplace performance or integration issues.[46] They differ in preferred communication and learning means and their need for structure and articulated expectations.[47] In the US, women constitute the majority of law firm associates and the majority of minority associates.[48] This trend is set to continue – in several Western economies, females exceed men in pursuing and completing higher education and attaining higher-income employment or even effective participation in the economy.[49]

We draw our current and future legal services workforce from this demographic well – it is also where we find our clients, customers, future managers, and other stakeholders – in brief, the leaders of tomorrow.

Reimagining the law firm–client relationship in an advanced information economy

The forces discussed above irrevocably alter the workplace's nature, culture, and values – in law firms and the corporations they serve. They beckon us to broaden our notion of value and its quantum. Both firms and in-house departments must accept that we are no longer in an analogue age – the AI advances discussed in this chapter are its overdue death knell. Nor can we alter changing demographics but only adapt and embrace the richer perspectives this brings.

A call to leadership and an expanded concept of value

Law firms, their corporate clients, and ad hoc coalitions must lead with vision and intention to adapt the corporate legal services delivery model to fit an AI-ubiquitous and data-centric future. Organizational and ecosystem change means cultural change by stakeholders. Transformation starts with perceptive, courageous individuals who speak up within their institution, model human adaptation and the behaviors they espouse, and influence others. Providers and clients must join as partners in reimagining their relationships, what success looks like, what they need from each other, what "value" encompasses, and how its various forms can be measured and compensated in such a world.

This cultural conversation must include rigorously identifying the workplace skills needed for success, how both new and experienced legal professionals can develop non-classical skills, and how the practical, early-career technical skills that are currently learned unevenly in the existing in-firm apprentice model can still be mastered earlier in an economic model that is likelier to have smaller entering and supervising classes. Young lawyers will perform fewer manual entry-level tasks, such as first-round document review, in the future. Instead, they will be the humans in the loop, providing quality control for the technology's first pass. They must reach a higher skillset and judgmental level sooner to be value-additive.

Reimagination and adaptation will not occur overnight, and progress will be non-linear. We must resist magical thinking that leads us to expect one giant miracle and tipping point. A series of small wonders over time is more likely, each building on the others and compounding their effects. While we can learn from other industries and providers who were prescient enough to start earlier, there is no roadmap. We must chart the course together. The path will be iterative; dead ends and course corrections are inevitable.

Providers and clients who recognize, understand, and embrace this chapter's themes have a once-in-a-career opportunity to choose, prioritize, and nurture the provider–client relationships that will serve them best strategically. They will identify the ideal cultural partners for this journey.

Lawyers, law firms, and other legal services providers have differentiating, competitive value if they have a coherent plan to address these themes, have embarked on that path, benchmark their progress, and recalibrate the plan iteratively. We do not need more 20th-century legal professionals – only 21st-century ones will have compelling value in this new world. The nature, scope, and pace of such a plan will vary depending on the type and size of the practice, its clients and their expectations, and other factors. However, denial, stasis, and slow-walking change are not strategies for success in the world described in this chapter.

Hallmarks of value in an age of AI ubiquity and data-centricity

How would a 21st-century legal practice look? What might be some of its hallmarks? Below are some non-exclusive, ambitious, aspirational ideas to promote richer ideation and discussion by readers and industry leaders. These are intended as more indicative and principle-based than prescriptive. This blue-sky thinking intentionally does not focus on the practical details or ethical considerations that may affect achievability or the final shape of these suggestions. Motivated parties will find ways to achieve the directional purposes. Law firms and other providers that have embarked on this path or do so now with strategic commitment are the leaders, add value, and are the best cultural partners for corporate clients.

Thought leadership – promoting responsible AI use and best practices

The best way to predict the future is to help shape it by reframing one's purpose and strategy for the digital age. Law firm marketing and recruiting pitches often tout, with gratitude, how the firm has grown in substantive and geographic scope in tandem with client needs. Putting truth to this by *aligning the firm's purpose directly with the in-house clients' purpose* in today's VUCA times will increase the firm's credibility and value proposition. As discussed earlier, corporate counsel are rigorously mandated to maximize value in every choice. They seek outcomes – solutions to the problems at hand, not pricing games. Helping them succeed and accompanying them on their transformative journey is the best way to attract and retain their business in a world of expanding buyer choices.

Providers add more value if they are early adopters and thought leaders, not laggards. They accept that AI will fundamentally change work methods, embrace this inevitability as more of an *opportunity* than a *threat*, build acceptance of our shared future, and educate clients so that their comfort level increases. They are the sherpas of change.

An August 2024 legal pricing and project management survey from the US aptly described the chicken-and-egg problem of stimulating client demand for GenAI use while calibrating how much to invest in front-loaded costs that may not drive revenue and profitability for several years:

"Winning firms may be the ones who proactively frame the implications of GenAI for their clients to help them more fully understand the use cases and the actual risks involved. Educating clients should drive the higher demand and adoption that will justify and monetize these large investments."[50]

These value-adding winners develop policies, governance, and training for responsible AI use in legal practice and iterate based on experience. With peer firms and clients, they promote developing and adopting well-informed ethical principles and guidelines by bar associations, courts, and legal professional regulatory authorities. They share best-practice learnings with clients to promote the transition and deepen client relationships. They help clients develop sensible policies to support AI use in-house and through external firms or other providers. Education and governance breed trust.

An investment approach will benefit the firms, especially with clients whose internal legal functions have thorough, diligence-based vendor management programs. For example, in regulated industries such as financial services, model use (including AI) is subject to rigorous external requirements and corresponding internal policies. Helping clients satisfy these obligations and approve various AI tools and uses will make it easier for them to consent to the firm's use of AI-enhanced tools and services, increasing business and deepening the relationship.

The most foresightful providers will use an iterative process with clients to mutual advantage, crafting the firm's guidelines, governance, and training to address clients' concerns about external providers' AI use in client mandates. While intangible and challenging to price directly, firms must offer these forms of value to become and remain preferred external providers to internal counsel. In a world that will rely less on time-based pricing of services and more on outcomes and value-add, the value forms discussed above should inform clients' perception of overall value and willingness to pay.

Time-based pricing
The billable hour will still have its place for some matters or tasks within a matter. In time, AI ubiquity and data-centricity should narrow this scope. Providers deliver additional client value when they use intelligent, modern work-sourcing techniques. Matters may be disaggregated to identify elements for which time-based pricing would be wholly appropriate – or inappropriate if it would deter the use of more efficient work methods that provide stronger client value.

Within three to five years, providers and clients should have open, clean-slate conversations about the ambit for time-based billing, identifying where it is optimal because it equitably balances the uncertainty risks inherent in some matters and tasks within them. This should be a rigorous data-informed process. Standardization should make pricing more a science than an art. As more quality experience data exists, is harvested and analyzed, and initiatives such as SALI, SOLI, and competitive sourcing and data matching platforms (such as Persuit and Priori, respectively) produce greater transparency, these decisions should become more precise, and the billable hour's scope increasingly targeted. It is foreseeable that this recalibration will result in hourly billing no longer being the default pricing method in large firms within five to ten years.

Redefining value beyond billable hours

Relatedly, an AI-ubiquitous, data-centric world means that humans using machines as co-intelligent partners will perform work more efficiently and with greater accuracy and consistency than through unassisted human-only efforts. Providers focused on delivering client value will propose value metrics incorporating efficiency, innovation, and strategic impact rather than just time spent. Few sellers can risk resisting this shift in a buyer's market that will only deepen.

This requires a paradigm change from a finance-centric approach to an experience-based one; this is a substantial cultural shift since using billing rates as a proxy for value is the path of least resistance and our lowest common denominator of understanding. New metrics and vocabulary will be required.

Providers and clients could inform this conversation and shape this shift by collaboratively developing AI-powered tools to identify, track, and measure new value metrics. These could include dashboards or other jointly agreed-upon tools to track and communicate value. Providers and clients could also hold regular "value review" meetings. These would go beyond traditional billing discussions by highlighting successful value-driven initiatives and assessing strategic impact and innovation opportunities. Firms could harness AI-powered systems for continuous client feedback and service improvement. Retaining the human element, firms could also create client councils or legal quality circles to benchmark progress collaboratively and identify new areas for improvement and innovation. Providers are cautioned against relying solely on transactional feedback. Individual relationships on specific matters between self-interested participants only reflect deal flow, not the digital and transformational vision of the client and its legal department.[51]

Value redefinition should become a virtuous circle. Quality experience data will support greater use of outcome-based pricing models aligning with client goals and objectives. Alternative fee arrangements (AFA) will carry less uncertainty and risk for providers. They will become win–win situations where providers have incentives to maximize efficiency without compromising quality. Better data and transparency will bolster confidence for both sides. Dropping the time-equivalent paradigm for value will eliminate the zero-sum nature of AFA negotiations and the use of shadow billing (still input-focused) to indicate savings.

Providers add value if they proactively lead these conversations; not all clients will know the most informed questions to ask. Ninety percent of corporate clients recently surveyed expect increased use of AFAs or other modified billing for GenAI-augmented work. Yet the surveyed firms reported that many clients need to learn how to evaluate or structure these arrangements effectively. Since firms have the technology and experience data across multiple clients, firms may need to recommend AFA use as a way of monetizing the efficiencies from shifting human labor towards tech-driven productivity.[52]

Providers can develop learnings in preparation for this shift by experimenting with willing clients on agreed matters and tasks. Firms with in-house labs, advanced delivery and solutions divisions, and self-disruption groups have an advantage, but they are not insurmountable. Providers can deliver increased value at scale in advisory areas through productizing knowledge or offering subscription-based services. These scalable models may attract more clients, resulting in more business. Richard Susskind describes this opportunity to providers as "making money while you sleep". This evolution would be consistent with the pattern in other areas of 21st-century life, including in other professional services and consulting fields.

Data-driven insights as value – proactive risk management and legal strategy

Providers possess vast sector- and client-specific data stores. The legal services professionals slated to succeed in the future will be proactive, preventative, and predictive, not reactive. They will no longer talk the talk about "horizon scanning", "seeing around corners", and "skating to where the puck is headed" based on intuition, anecdote, and individual memory. Instead, they will use modern legal and business intelligence tools to provide data-informed, actionable advice about the substance of the law, the market, latent and emerging risks, trend analysis, and their best predictions. They will "walk the walk" by being armed with the requisite kit. They'll be fitted for state-of-the-art skates, learn to use them proficiently, and spend time on the ice under competitive conditions. And only then will they predict the puck's direction.

For example, providers may monetize aggregated, anonymized legal data insights as a new value stream. They could propose joint client–law firm data analytics projects to uncover industry-specific legal trends and risks. They could also develop AI-enhanced collaborative scenario planning exercises to help clients prepare for potential legal challenges or offer ongoing risk monitoring and alerts as a value-added service. Where a client has already paid for the legal work that forms the basis of these data insights, providers may offer these insights as a free additional service or charge clients on a basis that reflects the parties' contributions equitably – the provider having added value through its investment in analytics.

Co-innovation partnerships

In recent decades, the law firm–corporate client relationship is described as more symbiotic than competitive. Buyers have an increasing array of choices. In an AI-ubiquitous era, they will have broader work internalization and smart-sourcing options.

Providers who wish to retain and deepen this symbiosis can distinguish themselves by taking a long-term, ecosystem approach towards clients in which providers and firms collaborate to shape their collective future. As providers mature as innovators, they can provide additional value by helping corporate clients along the same transformational path.

For example, they can partner with significant clients to leverage their combined position as technology purchasers to drive vendor innovation – they can jointly pilot products and give vendors feedback on solutions and features they want to see. They can share learnings about the art of the possible and, anonymized, the trends they see across their client base. They could host innovation labs, create reverse secondments, and invite corporate clients to co-develop AI and data-driven legal solutions or suggest collaborative hackathons or design sprints with corporate clients to solve specific legal challenges ("problem statements") using AI and data.[53]

To build engagement within the firm and clients, they could partner with their pro bono clients or outside groups on AI and AI-based initiatives to improve access to legal services and civil justice by underserved groups – practical, small-scale demonstrations of the potential for commercial practice, all while doing social good. Learnings from these and other collaborations could culminate in shared investment models with clients (or groups of clients) to develop proprietary legal tech tools or new services that benefit both parties. Clients and firms suffer from a common problem – the urgent need for scalable solutions in response to non-linear workload growth. Building solutions should be a shared priority.

A state-of-the-art platform can serve as a client anchor in a world of AI uniquity and data-centricity. As clients increasingly value the platform's advantages, they may be more likely to "hire the firm", not just the lawyer. Likewise, building an advanced platform for 21st-century legal practice may serve as a talent recruitment and retention magnet for associates and partners with whom this chapter's themes resonate.

Enhancing professional formation and upskilling

The traditional lawyer formation model is unfit for an AI-ubiquitous, data-centric world. Success belongs to inquiry and growth-mindset professionals who embrace lifelong learning. They accept that career success and happiness require reinventions in work mentality, methods, and tools. Beyond technical acumen, these professionals will possess or develop many of the qualities discussed earlier, including:

- Digital literacy and mindset;
- Emotional and social intelligence;
- Cross-cultural competency;
- Team collaboration abilities; and
- Design thinking capabilities.

Successful legal teams will include members bringing at least some of these talents and perspectives, whether drawn within providers, clients, or both.

System-wide transformation is needed:

- *Law firms bemoan having to be a "finishing school" for recent law graduates.*[54] In 2017, Harvard Law School professors Scott Westfahl and David Wilkins described the status quo three-way social bargain in which law schools teach how to "think" like a lawyer, law firms teach graduates how to "be" a lawyer, and "corporate clients... foot the bill" as having broken down.[55] The traditional apprenticeship training model in firms based on the Cravath model depended on conditions that no longer prevail.
- *Clients increasingly resist paying directly for junior lawyer development.* Instead, they pay indirectly for the status quo since these costs go into

the rate base for other fee earners. This perpetuates inefficiencies relative to tech-enabled alternatives.

- *Innovative, effective alternative training methods are possible.* Young lawyers need integrated systems that use people and technology (including asynchronous simulations, exercises, and GenAI-based tools) to climb the learning curve sooner and provide more client value. We must prioritize learner-focused approaches employing modern pedagogical means that meet younger generations' expectations of personalized learning.[56] They need to learn from the firm's highest quality work, not its volume, and receive individualized reinforcement feedback that does not depend solely on the supervising professional's availability, temperament, and willingness to review.[57] The demand will be for – and corporate clients will expect – well-trained lawyers supported by modern systems that force-multiply their expertise and deliver value at all experience levels.[58]

- *The in-house hiring pipeline is compromised because it depends mainly on exiting law firm associates.* Corporate legal departments have a vested interest in improvement. In-house counsel must compete for a smaller pool if entering and supervising law firm classes contract in size. If increased use of AI-enabled technology results in less of the traditional young associate training fodder for those whom firms hire, corporate clients can reasonably expect the firms to re-design training to produce higher value, client-focused, strategic thinking lawyers as early as possible – the kind capable of becoming trusted advisors and the partners and in-house counsels of tomorrow.[59]

- *We must act now to develop future-ready professionals.* Waiting for generational change or law school curriculum reform is a fool's errand. With increased life expectancies and five generations in the workplace, passively waiting for "digital natives" to change legal culture is a delusion, not a strategy. Nor can we solely depend on law schools to modernize and produce successive future-fit generations of lawyers to eventually replace retiring, fixed-mindset colleagues and refresh the law firm associate, partner, and in-house hiring pipeline. Legal academic culture has different incentives and timelines. We cannot let the transformation of legal services, as physicist Max Planck described progress among rival schools of scientific thought in gentler days, "advance one funeral at a time".[60]

- *We need to anticipate our profession's future roles and the skills needed, then redesign the system to ensure their development*. The playbook will be in iterative draft for many years. Law schools (if willing), law firms, and corporate legal departments should craft this living playbook together, taking a holistic view. They should focus on solutions and their roles, rather than pointing fingers or expecting others to find magic solutions. By reimagining and assuming an intentional role in the lawyer formation process (including pilot approaches and leveraging GenAI for training), stakeholders can produce practice-ready professionals sooner, improve our profession's diversity, and accelerate the upskilling of professionals already in practice.

The role of the corporate law firm

The next section focuses primarily on the role of corporate law firms and the additional value they can bring through adopting the changes suggested. Recommended intersections with law schools and corporate legal departments are noted.

- **Reimagine training methods**. On-the-job training should:
  - Integrate technology throughout the development process as a pedagogical method and to develop the skills, qualities, and mindsets of the future discussed in this chapter. The development of a digital core or mindset and data-literacy are essential.
  - Leverage learner-focused, asynchronous AI-enabled tools for accelerated learning that supplement and do not depend on the availability and quality of one-on-one human feedback.
  - Create structured skill progression paths.
  - Focus on strategic thinking over process skills. Manual process tasks should be a means to an end, not an end in themselves. They may have an initial training benefit and help young professionals develop rigorous methods and quality control skills. However, once their incremental training benefit has been exhausted, AI-assisted tools should be used to enable earlier substantive work and accelerated professional growth.
  - Incorporate learnings from how industries that are not as insular as the legal profession have adapted to changes in the broader environment in recent decades.[61]

By adopting these and similar measures, more experienced lawyers could spend less time supervising and reviewing process tasks and more time on the substantive skill development of their juniors, as well as practicing law at higher points on their bar licenses. In a world where attention is our scarcest commodity, more efficient use of senior associate and partner time in training would respect their high opportunity cost and existing law firm economics.

- **Broaden the hiring pool.** Value-enhancing steps providers can take include discovering and favoring young graduates who have future-fit training through participation in law and technology programs or may have followed non-traditional paths before their legal education or joining the firm. The most elite schools may not have the leading innovation programs. Mindset and demonstrated excellence in whatever domain are key – firms should look beyond pedigree by broadening the recruitment net. They could make a concerted effort to recruit those with academic or applied backgrounds in management, business, agile work methods, computer science, systems analysis, marketing, data analysis and visualization, design thinking, etc. These young colleagues will likely bring to their workstyles and problem-solving the types of diverse thinking that the future demands. This will make the firm more valuable to its corporate clients, enrich its culture, and improve its social diversity.[62]

- **Build client relationships.** Taking a holistic view, law firms and major corporate clients could collaborate on training design. They could partner on innovation programs and share learnings, especially about effective upskilling techniques for more experienced lawyers. Clients could bring anonymized real-world problems for learning and use in simulations. Tech-enabled teaching tools could include client input, be based on hypothetical matters relevant to external clients, or simulate external firm–client communications and collaboration.

- **Next steps and value proposition.** While there are a few pioneering efforts[63] by providers and significant clients, a broader, holistic, ecosystemic view and strategy are necessary. More firms and, where noted above, clients should adopt the recommended approaches. In hiring and creating approved firm panels, corporate clients should consider whether a provider has a comprehensive, modern approach to training that is regularly reviewed for fitness, considering evolving needs.

Although law schools are the last stakeholder (after general and external counsels) to respond to pressure to change, firms and in-house departments should leverage their reputation, hiring power, and alumni influence to encourage law schools to make lawyer development an existential goal.[64] If AI ubiquity and modernization of law firm training make junior associate roles more lucrative for their firms, law schools must adapt their curricula to attract top students. This could reverse the traditional change dynamic, such that law schools alter their business model to elevate skill development. The more elite schools may not be the first movers for cultural and other reasons.[65] Firms and legal departments could also seed the change by supporting the creation or expansion of law school innovation programs. They could shape future talent through sponsorship of joint activities such as conferences, clinics, and hackathons (all of which could include clients), and financially through scholarships and endowed applied teaching chairs.[66]

These and other forward-thinking lawyer formation steps would increase stakeholder value through:

- Earlier delivery of client value by junior lawyers and earlier firm profitability;
- Improved training without increasing the required level of one-on-one supervision;
- Improved retention through better development, e.g., decreased churn;
- Enhanced ability to serve modern client needs; and
- A more robust pipeline for future legal leaders, be they the partners, in-house counsel, or general counsels of the future.

Success requires a commitment to reimagining professional development as a strategic priority, not just a training function. Those who lead this transformation will gain a competitive advantage while better serving client needs in an AI-enabled future.

From multi- to inter-generational workforces – professional diversity

Law firms and other providers that handle demographic diversity well add direct and indirect value to corporate clients. Those who shape a multi-generational workforce into an integrated, inter-generational one will have competitive strength in obtaining and retaining talent and developing clients – who have and are learning to work with the same diversity.[67] A critical step at the organizational level is to promote inclusiveness within the law firm, weakening the relevance of in-groups and out-groups. Generational councils, up-reviews, and reverse-mentoring pairings can help. Individually, greater empathy, understanding the likely sources of intergenerational conflict, and other emotional intelligence strategies can help older colleagues embrace the changes heralded by the seismic generational shifts.[68]

This is equally true of gender and other diversity in modern workforces. Self-perpetuated homogeneity is a detriment and a value destroyer. We should celebrate our strides but not declare victory. Rather, redouble our efforts. "Value" includes managing workplace diversity (generational and otherwise) well, maximizing its strengths in pursuit of organizational goals, and elevating our EQ, SQ, empathy, and ability to work effectively in a rapidly and fundamentally changing society.

A bold, innovative example already in practice and worthy of study elsewhere is the solicitors' professional apprenticeship program in England and Wales. This alternative to the traditional graduate route to bar or paralegal qualification opens the profession to young people (starting as young as 18) for whom the conventional path's cost is a barrier. These highly structured programs featuring practical and academic rotations over up to six years are sponsored by law firms in partnership with law schools and professional training firms. At least one law firm sponsor laudably takes a systemic view through outreach work with primary and secondary schools to plant the mental seeds about a prospective legal career. The goal is to improve informed choice, social mobility, and our profession's diversity.[69]

Modern communications in a "TL;DR" world

Our currency is words, engrained over centuries in which advanced information was scarce and written language was the most efficient way to transmit learning. Modern technology makes producing and transmitting words easy; anyone can publish (and does – to wit, the world's 1.9 billion websites, 600 million blogs, and 350 billion daily emails). The internet slang term "TL;DR" ("too long; didn't read") captures the Zeitgeist. In a world with no longer a shortage of information but rather a surfeit, our value-add is finding the needle in the haystack, discerning the signal within the surrounding noise, and then amplifying, interpreting, and presenting it in styles and formats the client understands best. A legal services provider adds differentiating value by creatively repackaging advice and communications to deal with scale challenges and information overload.

This requires that providers recognize different personal and generational preferences in information consumption. The more information and AI we have, the more visualization we need. Visualization is an essential superpower that our text-centric profession undervalues and underuses. Law firms and other providers should lead change by hiring more design thinkers and data visualization experts, running clinics with key clients to help develop these skills in-house, and stimulating more demand to elevate the professional norm. GenAI tools already excel in summarization. Marrying these strengths with their rapidly improving visualization, image creation, and audio/video production capabilities offers providers many ways to cheaply and effectively deliver content in formats that are more likely to resonate with current and prospective clients based on their available time and information consumption preferences. User-centricity means meeting people where they are. Providers who do so add value and will find client connections.

Conclusion

The legal profession stands at an inflexion point regarding its ability and willingness to deliver to clients and stakeholders the value they need and rightfully expect. The convergence of AI ubiquity, data-centricity, and seismic demographic shifts presents unprecedented challenges and opportunities. Our response to these forces will determine whether we merely survive or instead thrive in reshaping our profession for the rest of this century.

The traditional law firm–client relationship must evolve from its late 19th and early 20th-century origins to meet the demands of our rapidly changing world. This evolution requires more than incremental adjustments – it demands a fundamental reimagination of delivering value, developing talent, and serving society. Providers who embrace this transformation – viewing it as an opportunity rather than a threat – will help shape the profession's future while deepening their client relationships and expanding their value proposition.

Success in this new era belongs to those who cultivate growth mindsets, embrace continuous learning, and develop the diverse skill sets needed for an AI-ubiquitous world. Law firms and corporate clients must partner in this journey, moving beyond traditional buyer-seller relationships to become strategic allies in navigating change. Together, they can create more efficient, accessible, and human-centric legal services that better serve their stakeholders and society.

The choice is clear – we can actively shape our profession's future or have change thrust upon us. We can create a more collaborative, innovative, and purposeful legal services ecosystem by expanding our professional self-concept, upgrading our skills and methods, and reimagining our client relationships. The path forward requires courage, vision, and resolute commitment from all stakeholders. Those who accept this challenge will not just survive the transformation ahead – they will lead it and prosper.

Author's note: This chapter draws on four decades' experience with leading US- and UK-based law firms and their corporate clients. While focused on "big law", many of these observations may extend to modern corporate legal practices globally, given decades of convergence in business, legal education, and regulation.[70] Readers are invited to consider how these themes resonate with their experience. Views expressed are the author's alone as a member of the New York Bar. The author's sole intent is to promote respectful and robust discussion. He thanks reviewers worldwide (some named, referred to, or cited herein) for their comments, suggestions, and encouragement.

References

1   Hemingway, E., *The Sun Also Rises* (1926).
2   Conway, F. (policy roundtable rapporteur), "Legal Services 2050: the role of AI in a world-leading legal sector" (Reform Research Trust and Solicitors Regulatory Authority), 2 August 2024. See: https://reform.uk/publications/legal-services-2050-the-role-of-ai-in-a-world-leading-legal-sector.
3   Bank of America Institute, "Transformation – Next Gen Tech: Computing" (and sources cited) 07 June 2024. See: https://institute.bankofamerica.com/transformation/next-gen-tech-computing.html; "Accenture Pulse of Change: 2024 Index" ranking six factors of change affecting businesses using a range of key business indicators and surveying more than 3,400 C-suite leaders on how these factors impact their organizations. This indicated the highest change rate on record, with GenAI as the top-cited change agent. See: www.accenture.com/content/dam/accenture/final/accenture-com/document-2/Accenture-Pulse-of-Change-2024-Index-Executive-Summary.pdf.
4   Hoffman, R., "GenAI: Cognitive industrial revolution" in 'At the Edge' (podcast interview, McKinsey & Company), 7 June 2024. See www.mckinsey.com/capabilities/mckinsey-digital/our-insights/gen-ai-a-cognitive-industrial-revolution.
5   Cohen, M., "Creating A Gen AI-Era Legal Function – What It Means, Why It Matters and Where To Start," *Forbes*, 16 July 2024 (available at www.legalmosaic.com/creating-a-gen-ai-era-legal-function-what-it-means-why-it-matters-and-where-to-start).
6   Katz, D., Bommarito, B., Gao, S., Arredondo, P., "GPT-4 Passes the Bar Exam" (15 March 2023, last revised 3 April 2024). The previous version, GPT 3.5, passed only within the lowest tenth percentile. See: https://papers.ssrn.com/sol3/papers.cfm?abstract_id=438923.
7   Mollick, E., *Co-Intelligence: Living and Working with AI* (Penguin, 2024), pp. 60, 62.

8   Susskind, R., "Some thoughts in AI in the law" (email distribution to friends)
    4 Jul 2023; "AI in the Law: Sixth Thoughts", LinkedIn 5 July 2023. See:
    www.linkedin.com/pulse/ai-law-six-thoughts-richard-susskind. Susskind, R. and
    Susskind, D., "Generative AI will upend the professions", *Financial Times* 18 June 2023.
9   Gerstenzang, M. and Logvinova, I., "Best Use of Generative AI in Law Practice Melds
    Human and Machine", *Bloomberg Law*, 1 October 2024. See:
    https://news.bloomberglaw.com/us-law-week/best-use-of-generative-ai-in-law-
    practice-melds-human-and-machine.
10 See Cohen, M., note 5. As to denial: "There are two ways to be fooled. One is to
    believe what isn't true; the other is to refuse to believe what is true." S Kierkegaard
    (1813-1855).
11 See Bank of America Institute, note 3.
12 See Cohen, M., note 5.
13 Barton, T., "Law and Science in the Enlightenment and Beyond", 13 *Social
    Epistemology* 99 (Taylor & Francis, 1999), reproduced in Barton, T., *Preventive Law
    and Problem Solving* (Vandeplas Publishing, 2009), p.161, and Barton, T., "Re-
    designing Law and Lawyering for the Information Age", 30 *Notre Dame Journal of
    Law, Ethics and Public Policy* 1 (2016).
14 Wald, E., "Getting in and out of the House: The Worlds of In-House Counsel, Big Law,
    and Emerging Career Trajectories of In-House Lawyers", 88 *Fordham L Rev* 1,765
    (2020). Wald describes the current state as a symbiotic co-dependency that emerged
    over four phases. (1) Post-US Civil War to 1930s: In-house lawyers were part of the
    legal elite, highly regarded as business and legal advisors. Often from the judiciary,
    they were among the highest-paid executives and sometimes groomed for CEO roles
    due to their practical wisdom. The Gilded Age saw the emergence of large,
    entrepreneurial law firms to meet growing in-house needs. (2) 1940s-1970s: In-house
    counsel lost ground to large law firms as corporate management professionalized.
    Perceived as "also-rans" who could not become partner, they lost stature. Law firms
    marketed themselves as offering superior, independent judgment unclouded by
    insider status. This shift paralleled the growth of elite US law schools, which became
    talent pipelines for firms, reinforcing each other's status and matching the pedigree
    of the new professional management class. (3) 1970s-2000s: In-house counsel
    resurged, reclaiming the general counsel role from elite firms. Drivers included
    increased regulation, more frequent business litigation, high costs of external
    counsel for routine matters, and corporate internalization of other specialized
    functions. In-house lawyers, often bred in law firms, shared their ethos and viewed
    themselves as peers, fostering a more symbiotic than competitive relationship. (4)
    2000s-present: Chief legal officers join the c-suite as departments increase in size
    and sophistication. In-house roles become more attractive career options, offering
    diverse paths such as movement between in-house roles, emerging deputy general
    counsel positions, business roles, lateral moves to other companies, or return to law
    firms.
15 Leonard, J., "Generation AI – reimagining BigLaw lawyer formation in an era of
    unprecedented disruption", *AI and the Legal Profession: Transforming the Future of*

Law (Globe Law and Business, 2023) pp.50-52 and Westfahl, S. and Wilkins, D., "The Leadership Imperative: A Collaborative Approach to Professional Development in the Global Age of More for Less", 69 *Stanford Law Review* 1667 (June 2017).

16 For a masterful treatment, see Parker, I., *Successful Digital Transformation in Law Firms – A Question of Culture* (Globe Law and Business, 2021).

17 For a historical overview of the US experience of the billable hour, see Pardau, S., "Bill, Baby, Bill: How the Billable Hour Emerged as the Primary Method of Attorney Fee Generation and Why Early Reports of Its Demise May Be Greatly Exaggerated", 50 *Idaho L. Rev.* 1 (2014). See: https://digitalcommons.law.uidaho.edu/idaho-law-review/vol50/iss1/1.

18 Cohen, M., "The Enigma Of Big Law Innovation", *Forbes* 1 Nov 2024. See: www.forbes.com/sites/markcohen1/2024/11/01/the-enigma-of-big-law-innovation.

19 Barnwell, J., "Legal evolution is industrial evolution", *Legal Evolution* 28 Nov. 2021. See: www.legalevolution.org/2021/11/legal-evolution-is-industrial-evolution-277.

20 See discussion and sources cited in Dilworth, R., "The (re)making of a modern lawyer – an in-house counsel's reinvention journey" in forthcoming book, *Sustaining the Rule of Law: Artificial Intelligence, E-Justice, and the Cloud* (Axel Springer, 2024 expected).

21 Cohen, M., "What Is the Legal Function's True Enterprise Value?", *Forbes* 3 Sept 2024. See: www.forbes.com/sites/markcohen1/2024/09/03/what-is-the-legal-functions-true-enterprise-value.

22 Tromans, R., "GenAI Triggers The Long Journey To Business Model Change", *Artificial Lawyer*, 24 Sept 2024. See: www.artificiallawyer.com/2024/09/24/genai-triggers-the-long-journey-to-business-model-change.

23 Bank of America Institute, *The AI evolution: Reality justifies the hype* 03 Nov 2023, *Next Gen Tech: Breakthroughs that will transform the world*, 23 April 2024 (both drawing from BofA Global Research, *AI Evolution: Reality Justifies the Hype* 11 October 2023; updated in *AI Revolution: A Polymath in Every Pocket*, 5 August 2024).

24 Santa Fe Institute, "lawOS: Regulations as society's operating system", 9 November 2016. See: www.santafe.edu/news-center/news/lawos-regulations-societys-operating-system; Logvinova, I., *Pioneers and Pathfinders* (podcast interview with Stephen Poor), 28 February 2024. See: www.seyfarth.com/news-insights/pioneers-and-pathfinders-ilona-logvinova.html.

25 Damodaran, A., "Strategies to beat the AI bots", *Financial Times*, 28 September 2024.

26 See Gerstenzang, M. and Logvinova, I., note 9.

27 Sohn, E. and Um, J., "Sense and Sensibility, Part 1 – General Counsels have the power to make good sense of generative AI", Factor Law (whitepaper), September 2023, pp.5-7. See: www.factor.law/white-paper/sense-and-sensibility-part-1. Casado, M. and Wang, S. "The Economic Case for Generative AI and Foundation Models", Andreesen Horowitz (3 August 2023) (discussing when perfection matters and how it is overrated where the operating norm is to keep a skilled human in the loop). See: https://a16z.com/the-economic-case-for-generative-ai-and-foundation-models.

28 Sohn, E. and Um, J., "Sense and Sensibility, Part 2: The challenge for General Counsel to influence and lead", Factor Law (whitepaper), April 2024, p.16. See: www.factor.law/white-paper/sense-and-sensibility-part-2.

29 Ibid., pp.12-16.

30 "UK and US Firms in Merger Talks as Demand for Scale Grows", *American Lawyer / ALM.com*, 17 September 2024. See: www.law.com/americanlawyer/2024/09/17/uk-and-us-law-firms-in-merger-talks-as-demand-for-scale-grows.

31 Furlong, J., "AI and the rise of the Niche Lawyer", 10 October 2024 (Substack blog). See: https://jordanfurlong.substack.com/p/ai-and-the-rise-of-the-niche-lawyer.

32 Saintot, V., "AI and sustainability for legal professionals", *AI and the Legal Profession: Transforming the Future of Law* (Globe Law and Business, 2023) pp.131-145.

33 "[G]eneral counsels are the most important players in the corporate legal system, and are increasingly important in the word of business, and all complex business that business touches." They increasing are engaged earlier alongside colleagues in compliance, government affairs, public relations, strategy and information systems and other functions to develop integrated solutions to today's complex multi-dimensional problems. "The Legal Profession in 2024: The wider view (part II)", *Harvard Law Today*, 21 February 2024 (interview with Prof David Wilkins (part II)). See: https://hls.harvard.edu/today/the-legal-profession-in-2024-democracy-salary-and-hiring-general-counsels-and-legal-education.

34 See Furlong, J., note 31.

35 See Prof David Wilkins interview, part II, note 34.

36 See Furlong, J., note 31.

37 Shirky, C., "The Collapse of Complex Business Models" (blog, 1 April 2010); See: https://web.archive.org/web/20100404013927/http:/www.shirky.com/weblog/2010/04/the-collapse-of-complex-business-models/. *Cognitive Surplus* (Penguin, 2010); "Here Comes Clay Shirky" (interview), *Publisher's Weekly*, 21 June 2010. See https://www.publishersweekly.com/pw/by-topic/authors/interviews/article/43565-here-comes-clay-shirky.html.

38 Kennedy, D., *Successful Innovation Outcomes in Law* (2019, Kindle edition), ch. 2-4.

39 See Gerstenzang, M. and Logvinova, I., note 9. "Lawyers and law firms benefit from a focus on client service and an adaptation of their business model to serve that priority, adjusting the model as needed, rather than attempting to preserve a more traditional and familiar way of working at the expense of progress."

40 Prof David Wilkins interview, part II, note 33.

41 Cohen, M., note 5; Westfahl, S. and Wilkins, D, note 15, p.1,702 ("the lawyers of the future will need to be technically capable, professionally nimble [using skills that are adaptable to any professional context] and able to use broad, interdisciplinary networks to solve problems.").

42 See Leonardi, P. and Neeley, T., *The Digital Mindset: What It Really Takes to Thrive in the Age of Data, Algorithms, and AI* (Harvard Business Review Press, 2022), Waisberg, N. and Hudek, A., *AI For Lawyers: How Artificial Intelligence is Adding Value, Amplifying Expertise, and Transforming Careers* (Wiley, 2021), Siebel, T., *Digital Transformation: Survive and Thrive in an Era of Mass Extinction* (Rosetta Books, 2019).

43 Prof David Wilkins interview, part II, note 33.

44 Furlong, J., "Building a generationally integrated law firm", 19 September 2024
    (Substack blog). See: https://jordanfurlong.substack.com/p/building-a-
    generationally-integrated. "Boomers (re)made law firms according to their values;
    now, they're barely a quarter of the population in their own firms."

45 Ziercke, E. and Hartung, "Ok, Boomer! Intergenerational Conflict in Law Firms",
    Legal Business World, 27 May 2021. See: www.legalbizworld.com/post/ok-boomer-
    intergenerational-conflict-in-law-firms.

46 Prof David Wilkins interview, part II, note 33.

47 See Furlong, J., note 44; Ziercke, E. and Hartung, note 45.

48 "The Legal Profession in 2024", *Harvard Law Today*, 14 February 2024 (interview with
    Prof David Wilkins). See: https://hls.harvard.edu/today/harvard-law-expert-explains-
    how-ai-may-transform-the-legal-profession-in-2024.

49 Burn-Murdoch, J., "Young women are starting to leave men behind", *Financial Times*,
    19 September 2019; Wolfe, R., "America's Young Men Are Falling Even Further Behind",
    Wall Street Journal, 28 September 2024.

50 Legal Value Network and Blickstein Group, *Fourth Annual Legal Pricing & Project
    Management Survey Report (including parallel data from the 16th Annual Law
    Department Operations Survey*, August 2024 p.7. See:
    https://mailchi.mp/2d3abb2266e9/2sqdhw6ct8.

51 "In conversation with Thomas Barothy", *Modern Lawyer* (Globe Law and Business,
    April 2022), p.5.

52 Legal Value Network and Blickstein Group, note 50, p.11.

53 Notable examples include Law x LLM hackathons at Kings College Cambridge
    (June 2024) and Kings College London (September 2024) in which major law
    firms contributed prize money, problem statements, and speakers for a parallel
    educational track.

54 Furlong, J., "Forget law school recruitment. Build your own lawyers", 3 September
    2024 (Substack blog). See https://jordanfurlong.substack.com/p/forget-law-school-
    recruitment-build.

55 Westfahl, S. and Wilkins, D., note 15, pp.1,667, 1,688.

56 Furlong, J., "New ways to develop new lawyers", 21 May 2024 (Substack blog). See:
    https://jordanfurlong.substack.com/p/new-ways-to-develop-new-lawyers.

57 Flaherty, D. Casey, "Education in the Age of Gen AI: The Old way of Training Law Firm
    Associates 'Just Doesn't Work'", *Legal Tech News*, 28 March 2024 (including comments
    of Caitlin Vaughn, MD of Learning and Practice Development at Goodwin Procter
    LLP). See: www.lexfusion.com/post/education-in-the-age-of-gen-ai-the-old-way-of-
    training-law-firm-associates-just-doesnt-work.

58 Flaherty, D. Casey, note 57, citing legal services pricing strategist Jae Um.

59 Furlong, J., n.54. See Tromans, R., "How Do We Train Lawyers In The Age of AI",
    Artificial Lawyer, 28 October 2024. See: www.artificiallawyer.com/2024/10/28/how-
    do-we-train-junior-lawyers-in-the-age-of-ai.

60 Literally, "Science advances one funeral after another". (Translated from the paraphrase "Ein Begräbnis nach dem anderen bring die Wissenschaft voran.")

61 Leonard, J., note 15, p59.

62 The benefits of social and cognitive diversity on teamwork and decision-making are well established. As well as the preventive contributions that cognitively diverse, growth mindset lawyers and compliance professionals bring to corporate decisions. DeStefano, M., Parker, I. and Vulcano, G., "The Unconscious conscience of digital transformation: The Chief Compliance Officer?" in *Compliance Elliance Journal*, Vol. 9, No. 3 (2023). DeStefano posits convincingly that lagging law firm progress in diversity and innovation initiatives are inextricably related – more innovative, growth mindsets with firms would foster a deeper understanding of the causes of, and more creative solutions to address, poor sustained diversity improvement. Moreover, a more diverse composition within law firms would foster cognitive diversity and increased service innovation. DeStefano, M., "Chicken or Egg: Diversity and Innovation in the Corporate Legal Marketplace", *Fordham Law Review*, Vol. 91 (2023), pp. 1,209-48.

63 Westfahl, S. and Wilkins, D., note 15, pp.1,686, 1,699-1,700, noting a co-author's earlier efforts at Goodwin Procter LLP and Milbank@Harvard, a decade-old first-in-kind program between the Milbank firm and Harvard Law School Executive Education Program. See: www.milbank.com/en/careers/milbank-harvard/index.html.

64 Ibid. note 15, p.1,705.

65 Leonard, J., note 15, pp.54-55.

66 See note 53.

67 Furlong, J., note 44.

68 Ziercke, E., "Can Intergenerational Conflict In Law Firms Be Attributed To Lawyer Identity Threat?", 20 January 2021. See: www.law-school.de/news-artikel/can-intergenerational-conflict-in-law-firms-be-attributed-to-lawyer-identity-threat. The author notes a study and her own work (see note 45) suggesting that older generations of lawyers develop negative perceptions of younger generations of lawyers because they perceive that latter's values as a threat to the former's identity based on factors such as hierarchy (in which they have top position), long hours, and ever-expanding firm profitability.

69 Goodman, E., "Earning and learning", *The Law Society Gazette,* 5 August 2024. See: www.lawgazette.co.uk/features/earning-and-learning/5120560.article.

70 Wilkins, D. and Papa, M., "The Rise of the Corporate Legal Elite in the BRICS: Implications for Global Governance", 2013 *Boston College Law Review* p.1,149.

About Globe Law and Business

Globe Law and Business was established in 2005. From the very beginning, we set out to create legal books that are sufficiently high level to be of real use to the experienced professional, yet still accessible and easy to navigate. Most of our authors are drawn from Magic Circle and other top commercial firms, both in the United Kingdom and internationally.

Our titles are carefully produced, with the utmost attention paid to editorial, design and production processes. We hope this results in high-quality publications that are easy to read and a pleasure to own.

In 2021, we were very pleased to announce the start of a new chapter for Globe Law and Business following the acquisition of law books under the imprint Ark Publishing. Our law firm management list is now significantly expanded with many well-known and loved Ark Publishing titles.

We are also pleased to announce the launch of our online content platform, Globe Law Online, which allows for easy access across firms. Details of all titles included can be found at www.globelawonline.com. Email glo@globelawandbusiness.com for further details and to arrange a free trial for you or your firm.

We'd very much like to hear from you with your thoughts and ideas for improving what we offer. Please do feel free to email me on sian@globelawandbusiness.com. Happy reading and thank you for your time.

Sian O'Neill
Managing director
Globe Law and Business
www.globelawandbusiness.com

www.ingramcontent.com/pod-product-compliance
Ingram Content Group UK Ltd.
Pitfield, Milton Keynes, MK11 3LW, UK
UKHW051106060125
453116UK00002B/2

9 781837 230617